FocusPrep™

FOCUS FOUNDATION PRACTICE

PSAT 8/9

MATH WORKBOOK

for students in Grades 8 and 9

Vivek Raghuram

1st EDITION

Published by:

Gift Of Logic, Inc
http://www.GiftOfLogic.com

FocusPrep™ is an imprint of Gift Of Logic, Inc.

ISBN-13: 978-1512373776
ISBN-10: 151237377X

7 15

TABLE OF CONTENTS

ORIENTATION & FOCUS

PSAT 8/9 for Grades 8 and 9

The College Board is introducing the PSAT 8/9 starting October 2015. You need to **orient** yourself correctly so that you know what content areas are tested, and the details of the format and duration of this test. Once you have oriented yourself, you need to **focus** on the lessons to stay on track and prepare comprehensively. Please read the following questions and answers to learn more about PSAT 8/9.

Q1 How do I **orient** myself to face the PSAT 8/9?

A1 Begin your **orientation** by familiarizing yourself with the SAT suite of assessments shown below. Then, read the questions and answers that follows to get the details of PSAT 8/9. The College Board is introducing PSAT 8/9 for students in grades 8 and 9 to help them track their progress for college readiness. PSAT 8/9 is aligned with PSAT 10, PSAT/NMSQT, and SAT.

Contact your school counselor for test availability in your school. Visit the College Board website for up to date information. The table below shows the entire suite of PSAT and SAT assessments and the corresponding grades when you take these tests.

SAT SUITE OF ASSESSMENTS				
Grade	**When**	**Tests**	**Registration**	**Purpose**
NEW PSAT 8/9				
8	Fall or Spring	PSAT 8/9	contact counselor	to track college readiness
9	Fall or Spring	PSAT 8/9	contact counselor	to track college readiness
REDESIGNED PSAT/NMSQT and PSAT 10				
10	Fall	PSAT/NMSQT	contact counselor	check college readiness; National Merit Qualifier
10	Spring	PSAT 10	contact counselor	check college readiness
11	Fall	PSAT/NMSQT	contact counselor	check college readiness; National Merit Qualifier
REDESIGNED SAT				
11	Spring	SAT	register online	college admission
12	Fall	SAT	register online	college Admission

Q2 How many sections and questions are there in the PSAT 8/9?

A2 The breakup of the PSAT 8/9 is shown below.

PSAT 8/9		
Section	**Questions and Duration**	**Score Range**
Reading	42 questions 55 minutes	120-720
Writing	40 questions 30 minutes	
Math	38 questions 60 minutes 2 sections(calculator and no-calculator)	120-720
Total	120 questions 145 minutes (2 hours 25 minutes)	240-1440

Q3 What is the syllabus for the PSAT 8/9 Math section?

A3 PSAT 8/9 Math problems are drawn from three content areas: Problem Solving and Data Analysis, Heart of Algebra, and Passport to Advanced Math. There will be two math sections – a CALCULATOR section and a NO CALCULATOR section. Each of these sections has problems in specific areas of Math as shown below.

PSAT 8/9 -- MATH SECTION		
Section	**Time**	**Questions**
CALCULATOR SECTION	40 minutes	25 questions 21 Multiple Choice + 4 GRID IN 16 Problem Solving and Data Analysis 8 Heart of Algebra 1 Passport to Advanced Math
NO CALCULATOR SECTION	20 minutes	13 questions 10 Multiple Choice + 3 GRID IN 8 Heart Of Algebra 5 Passport to Advanced Math
Total	**60 minutes**	**38 questions**

Q4 How do I **focus** and prepare with a strong **foundation** for the PSAT 8/9?

A4 This math workbook has **24 lessons** to give you **focus and foundation** on the three content areas of PSAT 8/9 : **Problem Solving and Data Analysis, Heart of Algebra, and Passport to Advanced Math.** Within each of these four areas, there are several lessons. These lessons and their content broadly mirror the details outlined in the blueprint for the redesigned test specifications published by the College Board. Each lesson has practice problems that are classified as **CALCULATOR and NO CALCULATOR**. Each lesson contains multiple choice questions and student produced response questions (GRID IN). The following table shows the FocusPrep lessons in each content area.

Content Area	FocusPrep Lessons	
Problem Solving and Data Analysis	Lesson 1	Numbers and Operations
	Lesson 2	Factors and Multiples
	Lesson 3	Word problems
	Lesson 4	Ratio, Rate, and Variation
	Lesson 5	Percentages
	Lesson 6	Unit Conversions
	Lesson 7	Scatterplots
	Lesson 8	Graphs and Tables
	Lesson 9	Growth and Decay
	Lesson 10	Statistics
	Lesson 11	Population and Sample
	Lesson 12	Counting
	Lesson 13	Probability
Heart of Algebra	Lesson 14	Linear Equations
	Lesson 15	System of Linear Equations
	Lesson 16	Linear Inequalities
	Lesson 17	System of Linear Inequalities
	Lesson 18	Linear Models and Graphs
	Lesson 19	Absolute Equalities and Inequalities
Passport to Advanced Math	Lesson 20	Polynomials and Quadratic Equations
	Lesson 21	Linear- Quadratic Systems
	Lesson 22	Functions and Transformations
	Lesson 23	Radicals and Fractional Exponents
Appendix	Lesson 24	Calculator

Q5 How long will it take for me to complete all the lessons?

A5 FocusPrep recommends a **6-week plan** to complete the lessons as shown in the table below. You need to focus on developing a strong foundation in these lessons. You can complete the lessons sooner if you are able to, but don't rush - progress with confidence.

Week 1 Problem Solving and Data Analysis	Lesson 1	Numbers and Operations
	Lesson 2	Factors and Multiples
	Lesson 3	Word problems
	Lesson 4	Ratio, Rate, and Variation
	Lesson 5	Percentages
Week 2 Problem Solving and Data Analysis	Lesson 6	Unit Conversions
	Lesson 7	Scatterplots
	Lesson 8	Graphs and Tables
	Lesson 9	Growth and Decay
	Lesson 10	Statistics
Week 3 Problem Solving and Data Analysis	Lesson 11	Population and Sample
	Lesson 12	Counting
	Lesson 13	Probability

Week 4 Heart of Algebra	Lesson 14 Lesson 15 Lesson 16 Lesson 17	Linear Equations System of Linear Equations Linear Inequalities System of Linear Inequalities
Week 5 Passport to Advanced Math	Lesson 18 Lesson 19 Lesson 20 Lesson 21	Linear Models and Graphs Absolute Equalities and Inequalities Polynomials and Quadratic Equations Linear- Quadratic Systems
Week 6 Passport to Advanced Math	Lesson 22 Lesson 23 Lesson 24	Functions and Transformations Radicals and Fractional Exponents Calculator

Q6 How are the lessons structured?

A6 Each lesson has a Review, Practice, and Answer section.

- The **Review section** begins with a checklist of key questions for the lesson in a box titled FocusPrep CheckList. This is followed by topic material presented in an easy-to-digest **QuickReview™ format**. This question and answer format will help you review the math concepts and formulas quickly and remember them for a long time. After reviewing the questions and answers, proceed to the Practice section.

- The **Practice section** has several questions that are marked as either CALCULATOR SECTION or NO CALCULATOR SECTION. If the problem is a Multiple Choice type, circle the answer. If it is a GRID IN type question, write the answer below the question. Proceed to check your answers from the Answer section that immediately follows.

- The **Answer section** shows the answer key and detailed explanation along with tips and alerts relevant to the problem.

CHAPTER 1 PROBLEM SOLVING AND DATA ANALYSIS	
Lesson	**Title**
Lesson 1	Numbers and Operations
Lesson 2	Factors and Multiples
Lesson 3	Word problems
Lesson 4	Ratio, Rate, and Variation
Lesson 5	Percentages
Lesson 6	Unit Conversions
Lesson 7	Scatterplots
Lesson 8	Graphs and Tables
Lesson 9	Growth and Decay
Lesson 10	Statistics
Lesson 11	Population and Sample
Lesson 12	Counting
Lesson 13	Probability

PROBLEM SOLVING AND DATA ANALYSIS		
Lesson 1	Numbers and Operations	Review

FOCUSPREP CHECKLIST

- What are the different types of numbers?
- What are the properties of Real numbers?
- What are the operations involving exponential numbers?
- What are special operators?
- Workout practice problems in Numbers and Operations

Q1 How are numbers classified?

A1 Numbers are classified as Real Numbers or Complex Numbers. Real numbers are in turn classified as rational and irrational numbers.

Real numbers:

Rational Numbers: Numbers that can be expressed in the form of $\frac{a}{b}$, $b \neq 0$

Natural Numbers (also called Counting numbers) : 1,2,3,4,5...

Whole Numbers: 0, 1, 2,... Even numbers: 0,2,4,... Odd numbers 1,3,5,...

Integers: ..., -5, -4, -3, -2, -1, 0, 1, 2, 3, 4, 5 ...

Fractions: $\frac{2}{3}$, $\frac{5}{9}$

Decimals $0.58, 0.374,\ 204.56\ , 0.6\overline{6}$ (repeating decimal)

Irrational Numbers: Numbers that **cannot** be expressed in the form of $\frac{a}{b}, b \neq 0$

Example: $\sqrt{2},\ \pi$ are irrational numbers.

Q2 What is a number line? Why is it important?

A2 All real numbers can be placed on the number line, shown below.

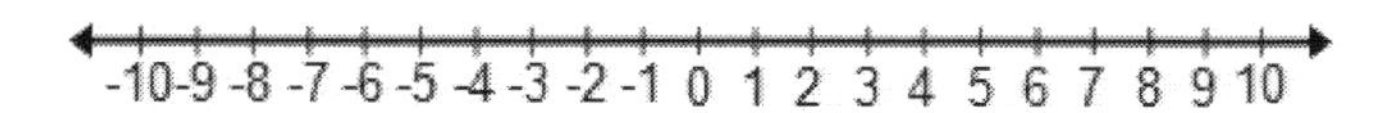

relative size of numbers, and their signs. The negative numbers are on the left of 0, and the positive numbers are on the right of 0. The numbers increase going from left to right. For example, -4 is greater than -5, -3 is greater than -4, and 0 is greater than -3. Similarly, 4 is greater than 3 and 10 is greater than 4. When numbers are added, subtracted, multiplied, or divided, the resulting numbers fall on the number line. Think of two positive numbers a and b such that $a < b$ and place them on the number line. Now place $-a$ and $-b$ on the number line and verify if $-a < -b$ or $-a > -b$. Verify whether $-2a > -2b$. Number lines help to verify answers to these questions.

Q3 What are the operation rules regarding positive and negative Real numbers?

A3 When you operate on numbers that have positive and negative signs, certain rules must be followed.

Adding numbers	When adding two negative numbers, add the numbers and place a negative sign.	$3+4=7$ $-3+(-4)=-(3+4)=-7$
Subtracting numbers	When subtracting two numbers, subtract the small number from the large number and place the sign of the large number.	$4-3=1$ $3-4=-1$
Multiplying numbers	The following sign rules apply for multiplying real numbers. $(+)\cdot(+)=+$ $(+)\cdot(-)=-$ $(-)\cdot(+)=-$ $(-)\cdot(-)=+$	$3\cdot 4=12$ $3\cdot(-4)=-12$ $-3\cdot 4=-12$ $-3\cdot(-4)=+12$
Dividing numbers	The following sign rules apply for dividing real numbers. $\frac{(+)}{(+)}=+$ $\frac{(+)}{(-)}=-$ $\frac{(-)}{(+)}=-$ $\frac{(-)}{(-)}=+$	$\frac{12}{4}=3$ $\frac{12}{-4}=-3$ $\frac{-12}{4}=-3$ $\frac{-12}{-4}=+3$
Comparing numbers	if $a<b$ *and* $c>0$ then $ac<bc$ if $a<b$ and $c<0$ then $ac>bc$ Note that the inequality has changed from < to > when you multiply by the same negative number c on both sides. If $c=-1$, then you have the following rule: if $a<b$ then $-a>-b$	$2<5$; so $2\cdot 3<5\cdot 3$ $-4<-2$; so $-4\cdot 3<-2\cdot 3$ $2<5$; so $2\cdot(-1)>5\cdot(-1)$ i.e $-2>-5$

Q4 What are the arithmetic properties of Real numbers?

A4 Commutative, Associative , and Distributive properties are described in the table below.

Property	Meaning	Example
Commutative	$a + b = b + a$ $a \cdot b = b \cdot a$ Two numbers can be added or multiplied in any order; this law does not apply to subtraction and division. $a - b \neq b - a; \frac{a}{b} \neq \frac{b}{a}$	$2 + 3 = 3 + 2$ $3 \cdot 5 = 5 \cdot 3$ $2 - 3 \neq 3 - 2$ $\frac{2}{3} \neq \frac{3}{2}$
Associative	$a + (b + c) = (a + b) + c$ $a \cdot (b \cdot c) = (a \cdot b) \cdot c$ Three numbers can be added or multiplied in any order; this law does not apply to subtraction and division. $a - (b - c) \neq (a - b) - c$ $\frac{a}{b - c} \neq \left(\frac{a}{b}\right) - c$	$7 + (8 + 9) = (7 + 8) + 9$ $7 \cdot (8 \cdot 9) = (7 \cdot 8) \cdot 9$ $7 - (8 - 9) \neq (7 - 8) - 9$ $\frac{7}{8 - 9} \neq \frac{7}{8} - 9$
Distributive	$a \cdot (b + c) = (a \cdot b) + (a \cdot c)$ $a \cdot (b - c) = (a \cdot b) - (a \cdot c)$ Multiplication is distributive over addition and subtraction.	$7 \cdot (8 + 9) = 7 \cdot 8 + 7 \cdot 9$ $7 \cdot (8 - 9) = (7 \cdot 8) - (7 \cdot 9)$

Q5 What comparison operations can be performed on Real numbers?

A5 Real numbers can be compared as follows using symbols:

Comparison symbol	Meaning	Example
$>$	Greater than	$n > 4$
$<$	Less than	$n < 6$
$=$	Equal to	$n = 6$
$\geq$	Greater than or equal to	$n \geq 89$
$\leq$	Less than or equal to	$n \leq 77$
$\neq$	Not equal to	$n \neq 5$

Q6 What is PEMDAS?

A6 When you perform arithmetic operations on a series of numbers, use the PEMDAS rule from left to right to decide which operation to perform first. PEMDAS stands for Parenthesis, Exponents, Multiplication, Division, Addition, and Subtraction.

Example: $6-(4 \div 2) \cdot 3^2 = 6 - 2 \cdot 3^2 = 6 - 2 \cdot 9 = 6 - 18 = -12$; parenthesis first and then exponent, and then multiplication, and then subtraction.

Example: $2 - (4 \div 2) + 6 \cdot 3 = 2 - 2 + 6 \cdot 3 = 2 - 2 + 18 = 18$; parenthesis first and then multiplication.

Q7 What are fractions? What are the operations regarding fractions?

A7 Fractions are real numbers that represent parts of a whole. They are of the form $\frac{a}{b}, b \neq 0$, typically with $b > a$. For example, if you ate 3 slices out of 8 slices of pizza, you ate $\frac{3}{8}$ of the pizza. Fractions with $b < a$, such as $\frac{9}{5}$ are called improper fractions. Operations involving fractions are shown in the table below.

Adding fractions	$\frac{a}{b}+\frac{c}{b}=\frac{a+c}{b}$ $\frac{a}{b}+\frac{c}{d}=\frac{ad+bc}{bd}$	$\frac{3}{7}+\frac{2}{7}=\frac{3+2}{7}=\frac{5}{7}$ $\frac{3}{7}+\frac{2}{5}=\frac{3\cdot 5+2\cdot 7}{7\cdot 5}=\frac{29}{35}$
Subtracting fractions	$\frac{a}{b}-\frac{c}{b}=\frac{a-c}{b}$ $\frac{a}{b}-\frac{c}{d}=\frac{ad-bc}{bd}$	$\frac{3}{7}-\frac{2}{7}=\frac{3-2}{7}=\frac{1}{7}$ $\frac{3}{7}-\frac{2}{5}=\frac{3\cdot 5-2\cdot 7}{7\cdot 5}=\frac{1}{35}$
Multiplying fractions Follow the multiplication sign rules for real numbers.	$\frac{a}{b}\cdot\frac{c}{d}=\frac{ac}{bd}$ $(+)\cdot(+)=+$ $(+)\cdot(-)=-$ $(-)\cdot(+)=-$ $(-)\cdot(-)=+$	$\frac{3}{7}\cdot\frac{2}{5}=\frac{3\cdot 2}{7\cdot 5}=\frac{6}{35}$ $\frac{3}{8}\cdot -\frac{4}{5}= -\frac{3}{10}$ $-\frac{1}{2}\cdot -\frac{1}{3}= +\frac{1}{6}$
Reciprocal of a fraction.	$\frac{1}{\frac{a}{b}}=\frac{b}{a}$	$\frac{1}{\frac{5}{6}}=\frac{6}{5}$

Dividing fractions Follow the division sign rules for real numbers	$\frac{a}{b} \div \frac{c}{d} = \frac{a}{b} \cdot \frac{d}{c}$ $(+)/(+) = +$ $(+)/(-) = -$ $(-)/(+) = -$ $(-)/(-) = +$	$\frac{\frac{3}{7}}{\frac{2}{5}} = \frac{3}{7} \cdot \frac{5}{2} = \frac{15}{14}$ $-\frac{\frac{2}{5}}{\frac{3}{5}} = -\frac{2}{5} \cdot \frac{5}{3} = -\frac{2}{3}$
Comparing fractions	If $a > b, then \frac{a}{d} > \frac{b}{d}$ provided $d > 0$ To compare $\frac{a}{b}$ and $\frac{c}{d}$, convert both fractions to the same denominator and then compare.	$\frac{4}{5} > \frac{2}{5}$; because denominator is same and not negative and $4 > 2$, larger the numerator, larger the fraction $\frac{4}{8} > \frac{4}{9}$; numerator is same, and $8 < 9$; larger the denominator, smaller the fraction
Reducing fractions	Factorize the numerator and denominator and cancel the common factors.	$\frac{8}{24} = \frac{2 \cdot 4}{6 \cdot 4} = \frac{2}{6} = \frac{2}{2 \cdot 3} = \frac{1}{3}$ OR $\frac{8}{24} = \frac{8}{8 \cdot 3} = \frac{1}{3}$

Q8 What are Decimals? What are the operations regarding decimals?

A8 Decimals are obtained by dividing the numerator of a fraction by its denominator. For example, the fraction of $\frac{1}{2}$ is written as 0.5. The fraction $\frac{10}{30}$ can be converted to decimal form as 0.333. Use your calculator whenever possible to convert difficult fractions to decimals. For example, the fraction $\frac{2}{7}$ can be converted to the decimal 0.286 by using a calculator. Operations on decimals are similar to operations on real numbers.

Adding decimals	When adding two negative decimals, add the numbers and place a negative sign.	$22.45 + 45.20 = 67.65$ $-22.45 - 45.20 = -67.65$
Subtracting decimals	Line up the decimals and subtract. Apply the appropriate signs.	$4.6 - 2.5 = 2.1$ $2.5 - 4.6 = -(4.6 - 2.5) = -2.1$
Multiplying decimals	Multiply the numbers without considering the decimals and then	$-2.2 \cdot 1.1 = -2.42$

	account for the decimal places. Apply the multiplication sign rules for real numbers. $(+)\cdot(+)=+$ $(+)\cdot(-)=-$ $(-)\cdot(+)=-$ $(-)\cdot(-)=+$	$-1.2\cdot -2.3 - +2.76$
Dividing decimals	If possible, multiply the numerator and denominator by a multiple of 10 and then simplify. Apply the division sign rules for real numbers. $(+)/(+)=+$ $(+)/(-)=-$ $(-)/(+)=-$ $(-)/(-)=+$	$\frac{2.2}{1.1}=\frac{2.2\cdot 10}{1.1\cdot 10}=\frac{22}{11}=2$

Q9 What is an exponential number?

A9 Numbers written in the form b^x are called exponential numbers. b is called the base and x is called the exponent. b and x can be any real number(integers, fractions, decimals, and they can be positive or negative). b^x is read as b raised to the power of x. For example, 10^3 is read as 10 raised to the power of 3.

<u>**Examples**</u>: 5^4; 3^{-5}, $7^{\frac{2}{3}}$; $3^{4.2}, 15.6^4, 27^{\frac{1}{3}}, (-3)^2$, $8^{\frac{1}{2}}$.

Q10 What are the mathematical rules regarding exponential numbers?

A10 Rules regarding exponential numbers are summarized in the following table. Radicals such as the square root, cube root, etc. are covered in a separate lesson.

Rule	Meaning	Example
$b^0=1$	Any non-zero number raised to the power of 0 is defined as 1 , 0^0 is undefined.	$100^0=1$; $87^0=1$
$a^m\cdot a^n=a^{m+n}$	The product of two exponential numbers with the <u>same base</u> is equal to the base raised to the sum of the exponents.	$6^3\cdot 6^4=6^{3+4}=6^7$ $6^3\cdot 6^{-4}=6^{3+(-4)}=6^{-1}$ This is true only if the base is the same.
$\frac{a^m}{a^n}=a^{m-n}$	The quotient of two exponential numbers with the <u>same base</u> is equal to the base raised to the difference of the exponents.	$\frac{6^5}{6^4}=6^{5-4}=6^1$ This is true only if the base is the same.
$(a^m)^n=a^{mn}$	When an exponential number is raised to another exponent, multiply the exponents	$(6^3)^2=6^{3\cdot 2}=6^6$ $(6^8)^{\frac{1}{2}}=6^{8\cdot\frac{1}{2}}=6^4$
$(ab)^m=a^m b^m$	Two numbers multiplied and raised to a power is the same as the two	$(8\cdot 7)^4=8^4\cdot 7^4$ conversely $8^4\cdot 7^4=(8\cdot 7)^4$

	numbers raised separately to the same power and then multiplied.	
$a^{-m} = \frac{1}{a^m}$ when $m = 1$, $a^{-1} = \frac{1}{a}$	A number raised to a negative power equal to -1 is the same as its reciprocal.	$6^{-1} = \frac{1}{6}$ $6^{-4} = \frac{1}{6^4}$
Fractional Exponents	Numbers can be raised to fractional powers such as $\frac{1}{2}, \frac{2}{3} etc$	$5^{\frac{1}{2}}, 6^{\frac{2}{3}}$
Square root	A positive number raised to a power of $\frac{1}{2}$ is called its square root, represented by the radical $\sqrt{}$ symbol.	$9^{\frac{1}{2}} = \sqrt{9} = +3$ $7^{\frac{1}{2}} = \sqrt{7}$
Multiplying and dividing square roots.	$\sqrt{a}\,\sqrt{b} = \sqrt{ab}$ $\frac{\sqrt{a}}{\sqrt{b}} = \sqrt{\frac{a}{b}}$	$\sqrt{8} \cdot \sqrt{3} = \sqrt{24}$ $\frac{\sqrt{9}}{\sqrt{3}} = \sqrt{\frac{9}{3}} = \sqrt{3}$
Cube root	A positive number raised to a power of $\frac{1}{3}$ is called its cube root , represented by $\sqrt[3]{}$ symbol.	$8^{\frac{1}{3}} = \sqrt[3]{8}, \quad 45^{\frac{1}{3}} = \sqrt[3]{45}$

Q11 What are special operators?

A11 Special operators are operators that are defined in the problem itself. They use special symbols.

Example: If $a♣b = \frac{a+b}{a-b}$, what is $3♣4$?

Solution:

Use the definition of the operator ♣. $3♣4 = \frac{3+4}{3-4} = -7$

Example: If $a♣b = \frac{a+b}{b-a}$, what is $3♣(4♣5)$?

Solution:

Evaluate the value of the expression in the parenthesis by using the definition of the operator ♣.

$$4♣5 = \frac{4+5}{5-4} = 9$$

$$3♣(4♣5) = 3♣9 = \frac{3+9}{9-3} = \frac{12}{6} = 2$$

PROBLEM SOLVING AND DATA ANALYSIS		
Lesson 1	Numbers and Operations	Practice

NO CALCULATOR SECTION

1. 2^{16} is equal to

(A) 4^4
(B) 4^8
(C) 8^4
(D) 8^3

2. $(3^4)^6 =$
(A) 3^{10}
(B) 3^{24}
(C) 3^2
(D) 3^{-2}

3. $\frac{1}{(3^4)^6} =$
(A) 3^{-10}
(B) 3^{24}
(C) 3^{-24}
(D) 3^{-2}

4. If $3^{p-2} = 81,\ p^2 =$
GRID IN

NO CALCULATOR SECTION

5. If $a^m\ b^m = 16^m,\ \frac{4}{ab} =$
(A) 4
(B) $\frac{1}{4}$
(C) $\frac{1}{2}$
(D) 16

6. If $x^m = 16^m$ and $2^8 = 16^y, xy =$
(A) 8
(B) 16
(C) 32
(D) 64

7. If $x^m = 16$ then $16^3 =$
(A) x^{2m}
(B) x^{3m}
(C) $x^{\frac{m}{3}}$
(D) x^{m-3}

8. If $\frac{x^m}{x^n} = x^2$ and $x^m x^n = x^4$ then $\mathrm{m} \cdot \mathrm{n} =$
(A) 1
(B) 2
(C) 3
(D) 4

NO CALCULATOR SECTION

9. $\sqrt{4}\sqrt{64} =$

(A) $\frac{1}{4}$

(B) 4

(C) 16

(D) 32

10. If $A = x \cdot y,\ 3x \cdot 4y =$

(A) $2A$

(B) $3A$

(C) $4A$

(D) $12A$

11. $18^m 9^n =$

(A) $9^m 2^{m+n}$

(B) $9^m 2^n$

(C) $9^{m-n} 2^n$

(D) $9^{m+n} 2^m$

12. If $\frac{1}{a^n} \div \frac{1}{b^n} = 15^n$, then $b =$

(A) a

(B) $3a$

(C) $12a$

(D) $15a$

NO CALCULATOR SECTION

13. $\frac{\sqrt[3]{8}}{\sqrt{8}} =$

(A) $\frac{1}{\sqrt{2}}$

(B) $\frac{2}{\sqrt{2}}$

(C) $\frac{\sqrt{2}}{2}$

(D) $\frac{1}{2\sqrt{2}}$

14. $\frac{8^{\frac{2}{3}}}{27^{\frac{4}{3}}} =$

(A) $\frac{2}{81}$

(B) $\frac{4}{81}$

(C) $\frac{2}{27}$

(D) $\frac{4}{27}$

15. How many positive integer values of x satisfy the inequality $\sqrt{x} < 8$?

(A) 7

(B) 8

(C) 63

(D) 64

16. If x is a positive integer and $1 < \sqrt{x} < 3$, the minimum value of $10 - x$ is

GRID IN

NO CALCULATOR SECTION

17. If $\frac{1}{2} \cdot x = \frac{1}{3} \cdot y$, then $\frac{x}{y} =$
(A) $0.2\overline{2}$
(B) $0.3\overline{3}$
(C) $0.5\overline{5}$
(D) $0.6\overline{6}$

18. John shared a 12-slice pizza equally with two of his friends. After his friends ate their share, he ate two thirds of his share. What fraction of the pizza is still left?
(A) $\frac{1}{9}$

(B) $\frac{2}{9}$

(C) $\frac{5}{9}$

(D) $\frac{7}{9}$

19. One third of the cars available for sale in a dealership are used cars. If there are 20 new cars, how many cars are there in the dealership?
(A) 5
(B) 10
(C) 15
(D) 30

NO CALCULATOR SECTION

20. A recipe for one full cake calls for one fourth cup of sugar. If three eights cup of sugar is used, how many cakes were made?
(A) $\frac{3}{2}$

(B) $\frac{5}{2}$

(C) $\frac{7}{2}$

(D) $\frac{1}{3}$

21. One half of a container is filled with water and one eighth of it is filled with milk. If the remaining space can hold 12 gallons of oil, what is the size of the container in gallons?
(A) 8
(B) 16
(C) 32
(D) 64

22. When 4 gallons of gasoline are pumped into a tank that is half full, the tank becomes three fourths full. How many gallons of gasoline does the tank have now?
(A) 4
(B) 8
(C) 12
(D) 16

NO CALCULATOR SECTION

23. A cylindrical bucket has water up to half its height. One fourth of this water was used to water a tree. If 5 gallons of water were used to water the tree, then how much water is left in the bucket?
(A) 10
(B) 15
(C) 40
(D) 80

24. In a pet care facility, two thirds of the animals are dogs and one sixth are cats. If there are 20 animals that are neither dogs nor cats, how many cats are there in the facility?
(A) 20
(B) 80
(C) 100
(D) 120

25. When Jenny finished reading one third of one half of a novel, there were still 40 pages unread. How many pages are there in the novel?
(A) 40
(B) 48
(C) 58
(D) 60

26. After reading one half of a novel and ten percent more, there are still 40 more pages to read. How many pages does the novel have?
(A) 40
(B) 80
(C) 100
(D) 120

NO CALCULATOR SECTION

27. A school that originally had 12 teachers now has only 10. Due to this change, the student to teacher ratio has increased by 5. How many students are there in the school?
(A) 100
(B) 200
(C) 300
(D) 350

28. If a positive integer n is odd, then all of the following are odd EXCEPT
(A) $n(n+2)$
(B) $n(n+1)$
(C) n^2
(D) n^2+2

29. In the rational number $\frac{2x-1}{2x+1}$, x can take any value EXCEPT
(A) - 0.5
(B) 0.5
(C) 0
(D) 1

30. $\frac{9}{8}\cdot\frac{8}{7}\cdot\frac{7}{6}\cdot\frac{6}{5}\cdot\frac{5}{4}\cdot\frac{4}{3}\cdot\frac{3}{2}\cdot\frac{2}{1}=$
(A) 0
(B) 1
(C) 8
(D) 9

31. If $a♣b = \frac{a+b}{a-b}$, and $c♠d = -\frac{c}{d}$ what is the value of $(3♣4)♠11$?
GRID IN

#	Explanation	Comments
1 B	Notice that the answers have different bases, 4, and 8. This gives you a clue to simplify this exponential number to a number with base of 4 or 8. $2^{16} = 2^{2\cdot 8} = (2^2)^8 = 4^8$	Use $a^{mn} = (a^m)^n$
2 B	$(3^4)^6 = 3^{4\cdot 6} = 3^{24}$	Use $(a^m)^n = a^{mn}$
3 C	$\frac{1}{(3^4)^6} = \frac{1}{3^{24}} = 3^{-24}$	Use $\frac{1}{(a^m)^n} = \frac{1}{a^{mn}} = a^{-mn}$
4 36	$3^{p-2} = 81 = 9^2 = 3^4$ $p - 2 = 4; so\ p = 4 + 2 = 6$ $p^2 = 6^2 = 36$	
5 B	$a^m\ b^m = 16^m$ $(ab)^m = 16^m$ $ab = 16$ $\frac{4}{ab} = \frac{4}{16} = \frac{1}{4}$	Use $a^m\ b^m = (ab)^m$
6 C	$x^m = 16^m\ and\ 2^8 = 16^y$ $x^m = 16^m$; so $x = 16$ $2^8 = (2^4)^y = 2^{4y}$ $so\ 4y = 8; y = 2$ $xy = 16 \cdot 2 = 32$	Pause for a second to observe the given facts and the question; question asks for the product of x and y, and you have two equations-one for x and one for y; so, proceed to find x and y and then xy.
7 B	$x^m = 16$ $16 = x^m$ $16^3 = (x^m)^3 = x^{3m}$	
8 C	$\frac{x^m}{x^n} = x^2$ $x^{m-n} = x^2; so\ m - n = 2$ $x^m x^n = x^{m+n} = x^4$; so $m + n = 4$ $m - n = 2;$ $m + n = 4;$ adding these equations, you get $2m = 6;$ $m = 3;$ $n = m - 2 = 3 - 2 = 1$ So, $m \cdot n = 3 \cdot 1 = 3$	Get the m and n from the two equations and find the product.
9 C	$\sqrt{4}\sqrt{64} = 2 \cdot 8 = 16$	
10 D	$A = x \cdot y,$	The question may look confusing but pause

	$3x \cdot 4y = 12\,xy = 12A$	for a few seconds to observe the question to get a clue.
11 D	$18^m 9^n = (2 \cdot 9)^m 9^n = 2^m 9^m 9^n = 2^m 9^{m+n}$	
12 D	$\frac{\frac{1}{a^n}}{\frac{1}{b^n}} = 15^n \quad \frac{b^n}{a^n} = 15^n;$ $\left(\frac{b}{a}\right)^n = 15^n;\ \frac{b}{a} = 15; b = 15a$	
13 A	$\frac{\sqrt[3]{8}}{\sqrt{8}} = \frac{(2^3)^{\frac{1}{3}}}{\sqrt{2 \cdot 4}} = \frac{2^1}{2\sqrt{2}} = \frac{1}{\sqrt{2}}$	
14 B	$\frac{8^{\frac{2}{3}}}{27^{\frac{4}{3}}} = (2^3)^{\frac{2}{3}} \frac{1}{(3^3)^{\frac{4}{3}}} = \frac{2^2}{3^4} = \frac{4}{81}$	
15 C	$\sqrt{x} < 8$ squaring both sides; $x < 64$ there are 63 positive integers less than 64 (1 to 63)	
16 2	$1 < \sqrt{x} < 3,$ Squaring all sides, $1 < x < 9$ So the minimum values of $10 - x$ is when x is maximum; maximum x value is 8. So $10 - 8 = 2$ is the minimum value of $10 - x$.	Note that $1 < x < 9$; so the maximum integer value of x is 8.
17 D	$\frac{1}{2} \cdot x = \frac{1}{3} \cdot y$ $\frac{x}{y} = \frac{1}{3} \cdot 2 = \frac{2}{3} = \ 0.6\overline{6}$	$0.6\overline{6}$ is a repeating decimal.
18 A	John shared the pizza with two of his friends – that make it 3 – so his share is $\frac{1}{3}$ of the whole. He ate $\frac{2}{3}$ of his share – so, what is remaining is $\frac{1}{3}$ of his share of the whole pizza=$\frac{1}{3} \cdot \frac{1}{3} = \frac{1}{9}$.	Note that the number of slices of pizza does not matter. It has been given to confuse you. You need to calculate the fraction of the total pizza left – not the fraction of his share- that will be $1 - \frac{2}{9} = \frac{7}{9}$.
19 D	The total number of cars = used cars + new cars $u = \frac{1}{3}(u + 20)$ $3\,u = u + 20;\ \ 2u = 20; u = 10; n = 20$; total number of cars = used + new = $10 + 20 = 30$	This is a tricky question; information about used cars is given in fractions and info about new cars is given as an integer. Set up the equation carefully and solve.
20 A	$\frac{1}{4}$ cup of sugar gets you 1 cake $\frac{3}{8}$ cup of sugar = $\frac{1}{\frac{1}{4}} \cdot \frac{3}{8} = \frac{3}{2}$ cakes	See the lesson on Ratio, Rate, and Variation to learn how to setup a direct proportion.
21 C	Let the container hold c gallons $\frac{1}{2}$ is water; $\frac{1}{8}$ is milk. Remaining is $1 - (\frac{1}{2} + \frac{1}{8}) = 1 - \frac{5}{8} = \frac{3}{8}$ of the containter. $\frac{3}{8}$c = 12 gallons; so c= $12 \cdot \frac{8}{3} = \ 32$ gallons	Get the clue from the statement "if the remaining space can hold 12 gallons".
22 C	Let the tank capacity be t gallons.	Note the tank levels carefully; the information is given in fractions; set up the

	$\frac{3}{4}t - \frac{1}{2}t = 4$ $\frac{1}{4t} = 4$ $t = 16$ When the tank is $\frac{3}{4}$ full, it has $\frac{3}{4} \cdot 16 = 12$ gallons	equation and know that you still have to calculate how much gasoline is there in the tank when it is $\frac{3}{4}$ full.
23 B	Let b be the capacity of the bucket; water is filled to $\frac{1}{2}$ b. $\frac{1}{4}$ of this water is used for the tree; so $\frac{1}{4} \cdot \frac{1}{2}$ b $= \frac{1}{8}$ b $= 5$; so, b $= 40$ gallons; originally the bucket had $\frac{1}{2}$ b $= \frac{1}{2} \cdot 40 = 20$ gallons; Now it has $20 - 5 = 15$ gallons.	Pay attention to fractions.
24 A	$\frac{2}{3}$ are dog, $\frac{1}{6}$ are cats, 20 are neither; So $1 - (\frac{2}{3} + \frac{1}{6}) = 1 - \frac{5}{6} = \frac{1}{6}$. So, $\frac{1}{6}$ ·total animals $= 20$. So, total animals $= 6 \cdot 20 = 120$; cats$= \frac{1}{6} \cdot 120 = 20\ cats$	Note that the remaining fraction has to be found and equated to 20.
25 B	Let n be the number of pages in the novel $\frac{1}{3} \cdot \frac{1}{2} \cdot n = \frac{1}{6}\ n$; remaining is $1 - \frac{1}{6} = \frac{5}{6} \cdot n = 40$; $n = 6 \cdot \frac{40}{5} = 48$ pages	Pages that have been read is given in fraction; pages yet to be read is given; find the remaining fraction and equate to 40.
26 C	Let p be the number of pages in a novel After reading 0.5p+0.1p=0.6p, 40 more page are yet to be read – so the remaining pages are 1-0.6 p=0.4p=40; p=40/0.4=400/4=100	Calculate the remaining number of pages in decimals.
27 C	Let s be the number of students. When there were 12 teachers, ratio is $\frac{s}{12}$. When there are 10 teachers, ratio is $\frac{s}{10}$. so $\frac{s}{10} - \frac{s}{12} = 5$ $\frac{(12s - 10s)}{120} = 5$ $\frac{2s}{120} = 5$; $s = 5 \cdot \frac{120}{2} = 300$ students	
28 B	Eliminate each answer choice by plugging in an odd number; only $n(n + 1)$ will be an even number.	Pay attention to problems that have EXCEPT in them. The answer choice that does not obey the facts in the question is the correct answer.
29 A	The definition of rational number is $\frac{a}{b}$ where $b \neq 0;\ so\ 2x + 1 \neq 0\ or\ x \neq -1/2$	
30 D	$\frac{9}{\cancel{8}} \cdot \frac{\cancel{8}}{\cancel{7}} \cdot \frac{\cancel{7}}{\cancel{6}} \cdot \frac{\cancel{6}}{\cancel{5}} \cdot \frac{\cancel{5}}{4} \cdot \frac{4}{\cancel{3}} \cdot \frac{\cancel{3}}{\cancel{2}} \cdot \frac{\cancel{2}}{1}$ Except 9 and 1, all numbers cancel out Answer is 9/1	Pause and observe the pattern.
31 $\frac{7}{11}$	$a♣b = \frac{a+b}{a-b}$, and $c♠d = \frac{-c}{d}$; (3♣4)♠11=? (3♣4) $= \frac{3+4}{3-4} = -7$. Continuing on, $-7♠11 = -\frac{-7}{11} = \frac{7}{11}$	Pay attention to the definition of the special operation and the symbol of the special operators. There are two different special operators.

FOCUSPREP CHECKLIST

- What are the divisibility rules for 2,3,4,5,6,9, and 10?
- What is the difference between a Factor and a Multiple?
- What are Prime numbers and Composite numbers?
- What are Prime factors? How do I Prime factorize?
- How do I calculate the LCM and GCF?
- Workout practice problems in Factors and Multiples, LCM and GCF

Q1 How do I find out if a number is divisible by 2 ,3, 4, 5, etc.

A1 Divisibility rules are shown in the table below.

Divisibility rule for	Rule	Example
2	If the number is even, then it is divisible by 2; A number is even if it ends with either 0,2,4,6 or 8.	1216 is even since it ends with a 6. So it is divisible by 2. 1315 is not divisible by 2.
3	If the sum of the digits of a number is divisible by 3, then it is divisible by 3	453 is divisible by 3 since 4+5+3=12 is divisible by 3.
4	If the last 2 digits of a number are divisible by 4, then it is divisible by 4	552 is divisible by 4 since 52 (last 2 digits) is divisible by 4.
5	If the last digit of a number is 0 or 5, then it is divisible by 5	5095 is divisible by 5 since the last digit is a 5.
6	If a number is divisible by 2 and 3, then it is divisible by 6	1236 is divisible by 2 and 3, so it is divisible by 6.
9	If the sum of the digits of a number is divisible by 9, then it is divisible by 9	189 is divisible by 9 since 1+8+9=18 is divisible by 9.
10	If the last digit of a number is 0, then it is divisible by 10	1010 is divisible by 10, 1005 is not divisible by 10.

Q2 What is the difference between a factor and a multiple?

A2 Factor: A number n is a factor of number x, if the number n divides x without leaving a remainder.
<u>**Example:**</u> 1,3, and 5 are factors of 15.Each of these factors will divide 15 without leaving a remainder.

Multiple: The multiples of a number x are $x, 2x, 3x, \ldots$.
<u>**Example:**</u> The multiples of 6 are 6,12,18, etc.

Q3 What are Prime numbers and Composite numbers?

A3 A prime number is a number that has only two factors, 1 and itself. For example, the factors of 11 are 1 and 11, the factors of 13 are 1 and 13, and the factors of 97 are 1 and 97. 11,13, and 97 are examples of prime numbers. By convention, 1 is neither a prime number nor a composite number.

A composite number is a number that has more than two factors. For example, the factors of 12 are 1,2,3,4,6 and 12. There are more than two factors, so it is composite. Note that some of the factors are prime and some are not.

Q4 What is LCM? How do I find it?

A4 LCM is acronym for Least Common Multiple. You can find the LCM of two (or more) numbers by writing the multiples of the two numbers and finding the least multiple that is common to all numbers.

Example: Find the LCM of 12 and 18.
Multiples of 12 are 12, 24, **36**,...
Multiples of 18 are 18, **36**, ..
The first common multiple is 36 and since this is the least common multiple of 12 and 18, the LCM of 12 and 18 is 36.

Q5 What is GCF? How do I find it?

A5 GCF is acronym for Greatest Common Factor. You can find the GCF of two numbers by writing the factors of the two numbers and finding the greatest factor that is common to both numbers.

Example: Find the GCF of 12 and 18.
Factors of 12 are 1,2,3,4,**6**,12
Factors of 18 are 1,2,3,**6**,9

The last common factor is 6 and since this is the greatest common factor of 12 and 18, the GCF of 12 and 18 is 6.

Q6 What does Prime Factorization mean?

A6 Prime factorization is the process of converting a number to a product of prime numbers. Keep breaking the number down to its factors until you cannot anymore.

Example: Prime factorize 28:
Solution: $28 = 2 \cdot 14 = 2 \cdot 7 \cdot 2$. So, $2 \cdot 2 \cdot 7$ is the prime factorization of 28.

Example: Prime factorize 35:
Solution: $35 = 5 \cdot 7$

Example: Prime factorize 156:
Solution: $156 = 2 \cdot 78 = 2 \cdot 3 \cdot 26 = 2 \cdot 3 \cdot 2 \cdot 13$

PROBLEM SOLVING AND DATA ANALYSIS		
Lesson 2	Factors and Multiples	Practice

NO CALCULATOR SECTION

1. When a number n is divided by 7, the quotient is 2 and the remainder is x. In terms of n, x is =
(A) $n-7$
(B) $n-14$
(C) $n+7$
(D) $n+14$

2. The prime factorization of 36 is
(A) $4 \cdot 3^2$
(B) $2^2 \cdot 3^2$
(C) $2^3 \cdot 3^2$
(D) $2^2 \cdot 3^3$

3. Which of the following is true?

I. All even numbers are divisible by 3
II. Some even numbers are divisible by 3
III. No even number is divisible by 3

(A) I only
(B) II only
(C) III only
(D) I and II only

NO CALCULATOR SECTION

4. Maria wants to cut a rope that is 20 feet long into several equal pieces with no rope left over. How many pieces will she have if the length of each piece is the greatest integer possible?
(A) 2
(B) 4
(C) 5
(D) 10

5. Scott has two ropes of length 20 feet and 36 feet respectively. He wants to cut the ropes into several pieces of equal length with no rope left over. What is the most number of pieces he can have if the length of each piece is the greatest integer possible?
(A) 3
(B) 4
(C) 14
(D) 18

6. Stephanie wants to cut two ribbons of length 18 feet and 24 feet respectively into several strings of equal length with no ribbon left over. What is the total number of strings she will have if the strings need to be of maximum length?
(A) 3
(B) 6
(C) 7
(D) 12

7. The fifth graders at Stinson Elementary are going to the Zoo. The boys have to be in a group of 7 and the girls have to be in a group of 5. If the same number of boys and girls went to the Zoo, what is the least number of students that went to the zoo?
GRID IN

8. The sixth graders at Otto Middle School are going to the Museum. The boys have to be in a group of 11 and the girls have to be in a group of 22. If the same number of boys and girls went to the Museum, what is the least number of boys that went to the Museum?
GRID IN

NO CALCULATOR SECTION

9. The PE teacher at Mockingbird High School needs to split 15 boys and 20 girls into groups such that there are the same number of boys and girls in each group. A group can have boys or girls but not both. If the greatest number of students are there in each group, how many groups are possible?
GRID IN

10. If p is an even integer, then the remainder when $2p + 1$ is divided by 2 is
GRID IN

PROBLEM SOLVING AND DATA ANALYSIS

Lesson 2	Factors and Multiples	Answers

#	Explanation	Comments
1 B	when a number n is divided by 7, the quotient is 2 and the remainder is x. So, $n = 7 \cdot 2 + x;\ \ x = n - 14$	
2 B	When a number has been prime factorized, it has to be represented with a prime base. Choice A is not correct since it has 4 in its prime factorization and 4 is not prime. Test the other choices to see if they multiply to 36. $2^2 3^2 = 36$	
3 B	All even numbers are NOT divisible by 3; 4 is not divisible by 3. No even number is divisible by 3 is false; 12 is an even number that is divisible by 3. So, choice B is the correct answer – some even numbers are divisible by 3.	
4 A	A 20 feet long rope needs to be cut equally with the condition that each piece is the greatest length possible. The factors of 20 are 1,2,4,5,10,20. If the length is 20 feet, then there is no cut required but the question states that she wants to cut the rope into several pieces. If she cuts the rope such that each length is 10 feet, then there will be $\frac{20}{10} = 2$ pieces of rope.	After listing the factors, apply the constraints – in this problem, there should be several pieces left after the cut – so 20 is not a valid choice for the length.
5 C	Factors of 20 are 1,2,4,5,10,20 Factors of 36 are 1,2,3,4,6,9,18,36 GCF of 20 and 36 is 4. He should cut the 20 feet and 36 feet ropes into pieces that are 4 units long. So, he will have $\frac{20}{4} = 5$ pieces and $\frac{36}{4} = 9$ pieces, a total of $5 + 9 = 14$ pieces.	
6 C	The two ribbons are 18 feet and 24 feet long. If the cut strings need to be maximum length, then the GCF of 18 and 24 will yield that length. Note that the string must be of equal length. Factors of 18 are 1,2,3,6,18 Factors of 24 are 1,2,3,4,6,12,24 GCF of 18 and 24 is 6. So, each ribbon must be cut such that the length of the strings are 6 feet each. The question asks for the total number of strings - she will have 3 strings after cutting the 18 feet string ($\frac{18}{6} = 3$), and 4 more strings after cutting the 24 feet string ($\frac{24}{6} = 4$) – so a total of 3+4=7strings	Don't just calculate the GCF and think you got the answer. Make sure you understand what the question is – it may require you to use the GCF.
7 70	Boys have to be in group of 7; girls in group of 5 Same number of boys and girls went to the zoo Multiples of 7 are 7,14,21,28,35,..	Know when to use LCM and when to use GCF.

	Multiples of 5 are 5,10,15,20,25,30,35,... LCM of 7 and 5 is 35. So, 35 boys and 35 girls went to the zoo; boys in group of 7 and girls in groups of 5. Totally 35+35=70 students went to the zoo	
8 22	This is a LCM question; Multiples of 11 are 11,22,33,... Multiples of 22 are 22,44,66, LCM= 22 22 boys and 22 girls went to the zoo.	This question forces you to use the LCM.
9 7	This is a GCF question; Factors of 15 are 1,3,5,15 Factors of 20 are 1,2,4,5,20 GCF is 5. Each group has 5 boys or 5 girls. So, the total number of groups = $\frac{15}{5} + \frac{20}{5} = 3 + 4 = 7$	This question forces you to use the GCF.
10 1	p is an even integer when $p = 0,2,4,6..$ etc, $2p + 1$ is $1,5,9,13,..$etc so, when $2p + 1$ is divided by 2, the remainder is always 1.	

PROBLEM SOLVING AND DATA ANALYSIS		
Lesson 3	Word Problems	Review

FOCUSPREP CHECKLIST

- How do I translate word problems from English to Math?
- Workout practice Word problems

Q1 What are Word problems?

A1 Word problems are problems that describe real life situations verbally. You have to convert them to mathematical form using variables, constants, etc. and then apply mathematical principles to solve the problem.

Q2 What should I know before doing Word problems?

A2 The following table shows statements and their equivalent mathematical expressions. When you solve a word problem, you can use the first letter of the person or thing to write the math expression. For example, if the phrase is "John is eight years older than Mary", use J for John and M for Mary. Naming variables like this will help you to avoid confusion when dealing with them.

Topic	Word problem	Math expression
Addition	John is eight years older than Mary	J=M+8
	John ate three more apples than Mary	J=M+3
	John has four more dollars than Brandi	J=B+4
	When 3 is added to a number you get 9	X+3=9
	The sum of two numbers is 19	X+Y=19
	A number increased by 10 is equal to 50	X+10=50
Subtraction	John is six years younger than Mary	J=M-6
	John's age is six years less than Mary's	J=M-6
	John's age is 6 less 4	J=6-4=2
	John ate three apples less than Mary	J=M-3
	John has 7 dollars less than Linda	J=L-7
	100 less than the weight of the box is 20	w-100=20
	The difference of two numbers is 250	X-Y=250
	55 subtracted from a number yields 22	X-55=22
	A number when decreased by 40 gives 80	X-40=80
	John's salary was reduced by 100	S=J-100
Multiplication	Area of a carpet is 3 by 4.	$A = 3 \cdot 4 = 12$
	The product of 6 and a number is 24	$6 \cdot n = 24$
	The cost of a red shirt is twice the cost of a blue shirt	$r = 2 \cdot b$
Division	8 people shared the cost of a cake equally	$\frac{c}{8}$
	A number, when divided by 6, yields 3 without a remainder	$\frac{x}{6} = 3$
	A number, when divided by 6, yields 3 with a remainder of 1	$x = 6 \cdot 3 + 1$

	A number m multiplied by 5 is the same the number n divided by 6	$m \cdot 5 = \frac{n}{6}$
	The quotient is 7 when a number is divided by 8	$\frac{n}{8} = 7$
Fraction	One half of all the money was spent on movies	$\mathrm{M} = \frac{1}{2} \cdot \mathrm{T}$; where T=Total, M=movies
	One half of one third of 24 is your share	$\frac{1}{2} \cdot \frac{1}{3} \cdot 24$
	Two thirds of this 24 gallon tank is empty	$\frac{2}{3} \cdot 24 = 16$
Percentage	The shirt is discounted by 20% off the price.	$\mathrm{D} = \frac{20}{100} \cdot \mathrm{P} = 0.2\ \mathrm{P}$ D = Discount P=Price
	X is 22 percent of Y	$\mathrm{X} = \frac{22}{100} \cdot \mathrm{Y} = 0.22\mathrm{Y}$
	Four percent of a number is 10	$0.04 \cdot x = 10$
	The price (p) of the sweater was increased by 12%	$p + \frac{12}{100} p = 1.12p$
	The price (p) of the sweater was decreased by 12%	$p - \frac{12}{100} p = 0.88p$
Limits	The new car will cost at least $20,000	$c \geq 20000$
	The new car will cost at most $20,000	$c \leq 20{,}000$
	The red watch costs more than the blue watch	$r > b$
	The red watch costs less than the blue watch	$r < b$
Combination	20 plus a number equals 13 minus the number.	$20 + x = 13 - x$
	20 plus a number equals the number less 13.	$20 + x = x - 13$
	x is twice as much as y	$x = 2y$
	20 percent of a number is greater than 100	$0.2\,x > 100$
	Six times a number increased by two is 15	$6x + 2 = 15$
	The difference of three times and two times a number is 99	$3x - 2x = 99$
	One fourth of the difference between x and 2 is 9	$\frac{1}{4} \cdot (x - 2) = 9$
	The square of a number is 121	$x^2 = 121$
	The square of 2 more than a number is 9	$(x + 2)^2 = 9$
	Price of the watch plus 10 is hundred dollars or less	$p + 10 \leq 100$

PROBLEM SOLVING AND DATA ANALYSIS		
Lesson 3	Word Problems	Practice

NO CALCULATOR SECTION

1. If the ratio of 7 less than a number and 7 more than the number is 2, what is the number?
(A) -21
(B) -7
(C) 7
(D) 14

2. The sum of two numbers x and y is at least 10 and at most 50. This fact can be expressed as
(A) $10 < x + y < 50$
(B) $10 \leq x + y < 50$
(C) $10 < x + y \leq 50$
(D) $10 \leq x + y \leq 50$

3. If 12 times a number is 40 more than 2 times the number, the number is
(A) 1
(B) 2
(C) 3
(D) 4

4. In a game, Mark scored 3 more than twice what Nancy scored. Nancy scored 2 less than 4 times what Olivia scored. If Olivia scored 2 points, what did Mark score?
(A) 10
(B) 12
(C) 15
(D) 18

NO CALCULATOR SECTION

5. Andy is as old today as John was 10 years ago. Which one of the following choices is true?
I Andy is older than John
II John is older than Andy
III John is 20 years old
(A) I only
(B) II only
(C) III only
(D) II and III only

6. If one fourth of the difference between a number and 2 is 9, the number is
(A) 36
(B) 37
(C) 38
(D) 40

7. Paula and Olivia have a total of $60. Olivia has three times as much as Paula. How much does Paula have?
(A) 5
(B) 10
(C) 15
(D) 20

8. If 0.05 percent of a number is 1, then 2 percent of the number is
(A) 10
(B) 20
(C) 30
(D) 40

NO CALCULATOR SECTION

9. If the square of 2 more than a number is 9, the number could be
(A) -5
(B) -4
(C) -3
(D) -1

10. Tim had $100 in his bank account at the beginning of the month. During the month, he withdrew w dollars and deposited d dollars. If the deposit was twice as much as the withdrawal, then how much did he deposit if he had a balance of $150 at the end of the month?
GRID IN

11. If the square of the sum of two numbers is the same as the square of the difference of the two numbers, then one of the numbers must be
GRID IN

12. If the radius of a circle is doubled, by what factor will the area increase by?
GRID IN

CALCULATOR SECTION

13. The length of a rectangle is increased by 10 percent. By how much percent should the width be decreased if the area is to be kept the same?
(A) 0.91
(B) 1.1
(C) 9
(D) 11

14. A cab driver charges $5 for the first 0.75 miles, $8 for the subsequent 0.25 miles and $2 for each additional mile. How many miles can you travel in the cab if you paid $50?
GRID IN

15. Playing golf costs a one-time $50.25 deposit and an additional 25.75 dollars per game. How many full games can be played for $1500?
GRID IN

PROBLEM SOLVING AND DATA ANALYSIS		
Lesson 3	Word Problems	Answers

#	Explanation	Comments
1 A	Let x be the number; $\frac{x-7}{x+7}=2$ $x-7=2(x+7)=2x+14$ $x=-21$	Set the ratio carefully; note the phrases " 7 less than" and "7 more than".
2 D	"Sum of x and y is at least 10" is expressed as $10 \leq x+y$; Sum of x and y is at most 50 is expressed as $x+y \leq 50$; combining them, you get $10 \leq x+y \leq 50$	Note the difference between $<$ and $\leq, >$ and $\geq$ signs.
3 D	The word problem can be translated to math as $12\,x = \; 2x+40$ $10x=40; x=4$	
4 C	Let m be the score for Mark and n be the score for Nancy and o be the score for Olivia. "Mark scored 3 more than twice what Nancy scored" can be translated to math as $m=3+2n$. "Nancy scored 2 less than 4 times what Olivia scored" can be translated as $n=4o-2$; "Olivia scored 2 points" can be translated to $o=2$. Put all these equations together and solve. $m=2n+3$ $n=4o-2$ $o=2$ $m=2n+3=2(4o-2)+3=8o-4+3$ $=8\cdot 2-4+3=15$	Using variables like m, n, and o to correspond to the Mark, Nancy , and Olivia will help you to stay focused on the problem. If you use variables like x, y, and z then you will waste time trying to figure out what each variable represents.
5 B	Note that the problem talks about their ages today and 10 years ago. Let a be Andy's age today and j be John's age today. "Andy is as old today as John was 10 years ago" can be translated to $a=j-10$, since John was $j-10$ years old 10 years ago. So, John is older than Andy. Choice B is true. In problems of the Roman Numeral type, you must also evaluate other choices. Choice A is false. Choice C is false since you cannot infer that John was 20 years old. Only choice B is correct.	In problems with choices given in Roman Numerals, evaluate all the choices and then select your answer choice.
6 C	"one fourth of the difference between a number and 2 is 9" can be translated to $\frac{1}{4}\cdot(x-2)=9$. $x-2=9\cdot 4=36;\; x=38$	You could argue that this equation could be set up as $\frac{1}{4}\cdot(2-x)=9$; when in doubt, go with the most straight forward math translation. The problem says "difference between a number and 2", with "number" mentioned first and then "2" mentioned after that. So go with $x-2$.

7 C	"Paula and Olivia have a total of $60" can be translated to $p + o = 60$; "Olivia has three times as much as Paula" can be translated to $o = 3p$ Solve by substitution; $p + o = p + 3p = 60$ $4p = 60$ $p = 15$	
8 D	0.05 percent of a number is 1 $\frac{0.05}{100}x = 1$ $x = \frac{100}{0.05}$ 2 percent of the number = $\frac{2}{100} \cdot \frac{100}{0.05} = \frac{2}{0.05} = \frac{200}{5} = 40$	x percent of y is translated as $\frac{x}{100} \cdot y$
9 A	square of 2 more than a number is 9 can be translated as $(x + 2)^2 = 9$ $x + 2 = \pm 3$ $x = -2 + 3 = 1 \text{ or} - 2 - 3 = -5$ Choice A is -5 and is the correct answer.	If you arrive at two solutions, and only one solution is in the answer choice, pick that choice.
10 100	Initial amount = 100, withdraw w and deposit d Balance = 150, $\mathrm{d} = 2\mathrm{w}$ $100 - \mathrm{w} + \mathrm{d} = 150$ $100 - \mathrm{w} + 2\mathrm{w} = 150$ $100 + \mathrm{w} = 150$ $\mathrm{w} = 50;\ \text{so } \mathrm{d} = 2\mathrm{w} = 100$	
11 0	$(x + y)^2 = (x - y)^2$ $x^2 + 2xy + y^2 = x^2 - 2xy + y^2$ $4xy = 0; xy = 0$ Since $xy = 0$, either x or y or both must be 0.	
12 4	$A = \pi\, r^2$ After the radius is doubled, $A = \pi\, (2r)^2 = 4\, \pi r^2$ The question asks by what factor does the area increase- this is the same as asking "how many times" – new area/ old area= factor = $\frac{4\pi r^2}{\pi r^2} = 4$.	By what "factor" something has increased or decreased – is the same as finding the ratio of the new quantity and the old quantity. For example if the price of bread increased from $4 to $5, it increased by a factor of $\frac{5}{4} =\ 1.25$. Note that this is NOT the same as calculating the percentage increase or decrease.
13 C	Old area $A = l \cdot w$ New area $\acute{A} = 1.1l \cdot \acute{w}$ Old area= new Area $lw = 1.1l\, \acute{w}$	Note that the question asks "by how much percent should the width be decreased" . This is different from asking "by what factor should the width be decreased ".

	$w = 1.1\,\acute{w}$ $\acute{w} = \frac{1}{1.1}w = 0.91\,w$; use calculator So, the old width w has to be reduced to 0.91 w This is a percentage decrease of $\frac{0.91w - 1w}{w} \cdot 100 = 9\%$	
14 19.5	\$5 for the first 0.75 miles; \$8 for the next 0.25 miles, \$2 each additional mile. How many miles can you travel for \$50? Let m me the miles traveled for \$50; m miles can be broken down, based on each fare segment ; this must to add up to m miles; $m = 0.75 + 0.25 + (m-1)$; The first mile is included in the m. now apply the fares to each segment $5 + 8 + (m-1) \cdot 2 = 50$ $13 + 2m - 2 = 50$ $2m = 39$ $m = 19.5\ miles$	In these "cab driver " type of problems, first break down the total miles that you are calculating based on the fare segments and then apply the fares to each segment; this will help you avoid making mistakes; review the answer to this question to see how this is done.
15 56	Let n be the number of games that you can play for \$1500; the total cost of playing n games must be less than or equal to 1500. $50.25 + 25.75n <= 1500$ $25.75n <= 1500 - 50.25 = 1449.75$ $n = 56.30$ Since the question asks "how many full games" can be played, the answer is 56.	Note that the dollars are not whole dollars; so use your calculator correctly.

FOCUSPREP CHECKLIST

- What is a Ratio? Is it the same as a proportion?
- What is a Rate?
- What are Direct and Inverse variations?
- How do I solve problems with direct and inverse variations?
- Workout practice problems in Ratio, Rate, and Variation

Q1 What is a Ratio? What is a proportion?

A1 Ratio of two quantities a and b is defined as the quotient of $\frac{a}{b}$ where $b \neq 0$. Proportion is the fraction of one quantity with respect to the whole. From this fraction, you can calculate the percentage.

Example: There are 50 boys and 20 girls in a class. So, the ratio of boys to girls is $\frac{50}{20}$ which can be simplified as $\frac{5}{2}$. The proportion of boys in the class is $\frac{5}{7} \cdot 100$ and the percentage of boys in the class is $\frac{5}{7} \cdot 100$=71.43%.

Example: There are 700 students in a school. The ratio of boys to girls is $5:2$. How many boys are there?
Solution: The proportion of boys with respect to the whole is $\frac{5}{5+2} = \frac{5}{7}$. So the number of boys = $\frac{5}{7} \cdot 700 = 500$.

Q2 Can ratios be reduced like fractions?

A2 Since ratios are fractions, you can reduce them: $\frac{A}{B} = \frac{2}{6}$ can be reduced to $\frac{A}{B} = \frac{1}{3}$. For example, if the ratio of boys to girls is $50:20$, you can reduce it to $5:2$ without loss of meaning.

Q3 How do I specify ratios between three quantities?

A3 If you have two ratios P:Q and Q:R involving three quantities P,Q, and R, then the ratio of the three quantities is P:Q:R. Note that Q must be the same number in both ratios.
Example: P:Q = 1:3 Q:R=3:4, since Q=3 in both ratios, the ratio P:Q:R=1:3:4

Example: P:Q = 1:4 Q:R=8:16 What is P:Q:R ? What percentage of the whole is R?
Solution: Since Q is not the same in both ratios, you make it the same by reducing Q:R from 8:16 to 4:8. Now P:Q=1:4 and Q:R=4:8. So P:Q:R = 1:4:8. R is $\frac{8}{1+4+8} = \frac{8}{13}$ of the whole or $\frac{8}{13} \cdot 100$=61.5% of the whole.

Q4 In what context can I expect to see problems on ratios?

A4 You will encounter ratios in problems typically in Social and Scientific contexts.
Examples : in Physics- Velocity = distance/ time; Current = Voltage/ Resistance; in Economics - Per capita income=Total Income / population ; in Business: P/E ratio= Stock Price/ Earnings ratio.

Q5 What is a Rate?

A5 Rate is the change of one quantity with respect to unit-change of another and is expressed in the form of a ratio.
Examples: speed= 20 miles/hour; snow accumulation = 3 inches/hour; Taxi rate= $10/mile; Phone call charge= $0.20/minute; mowing rate=1/3 lawn/hr.

Examples:
If a man can paint 8 houses in 2 days – his rate of work is 8 houses/2 days = 4 houses/day.
If Tom takes 5 hours to mow a lawn, his rate of work is $\frac{1}{5}$ lawn/hr
If a car travels 100 miles in 2 hours, its rate of distance covered (speed) is 100/20=50 miles/hr
If a contractor charges $800 for 8 hours of work, his rate of pay is 800/8=$100/hr

You can see the different units of measure in the numerator and denominator. Problems involving Rate appear in distance problems, machine capacity problems, work rate problems, and direct and inverse relation problems.

Q6 What does a typical distance problem look like?

A6 **Example**: Tim drives from home to work at the rate of 20 miles/hour and drives back to home at the rate of 30 miles/hour. If he drives for 3 hours in total, how much distance does he travel?
Solution: Speed=s=$\frac{distance}{time}$ =$\frac{d}{t}$; $t = \frac{d}{s}$, where d is the one-way distance from home to work. You know the speed and time; you know that total time $t = 3$ hrs= time to work+ time to home. So $3 = \frac{d}{20} + \frac{d}{30}$; $3 = \frac{50d}{600} = \frac{d}{12}$; $d = 36$; but this is one way distance; so the total distance = $2d = 2 \cdot 36 = 72$ miles.

Q7 When are variables said to be in <u>DIRECT</u> relationship (or direct variation)?

A7 Two variables are in direct relationship(variation) when one increases as the other increases, maintaining a constant ratio at all times. For example, when P is in DIRECT variation with Q, $\frac{P}{Q} = k$, where k is the constant of proportionality. For example, the more hours a contractor works, the more money he makes – so the money he makes is in DIRECT variation with the hours that he works.

If four numbers a, b, c, d are in DIRECT proportion, then $\frac{a}{b} = \frac{c}{d}$.

Q8 When are variables in an <u>INVERSE</u> relationship (or inverse variation)?

A8 Two variables are in inverse variation when one increases as the other decreases. For example, when P is in INVERSE variation with Q, then $P = \frac{k}{Q}$ $or\ PQ = k$, where k is the constant of proportionality. For example, if more men are available to do a job, then it will take less time to finish the job - so the number of men available and the time taken to finish the job are in INVERSE variation.

Q9 What is the procedure for solving DIRECT and INVERSE variation problems?

A9 DIRECT and INVERSE variation problems can appear in work rate problems, capacity problems, labor problems etc. Follow these steps to solve the problem.

Step 1: Identify the variables involved and their relationship (DIRECT or INVERSE)

Step 2: Write the information with the unknown quantity x that you are trying to find at the bottom right as shown below.

a c

b x

Step 3: Setup the ratio for DIRECT or INVERSE variation and solve for the unknown variable.

DIRECT variation: $\frac{a}{b} = \frac{c}{x}$ or $\frac{b}{a} = \frac{x}{c}$

INVERSE variation: **<u>Flip only one</u>** of the ratios: $\frac{a}{b} = \frac{x}{c}$ or $\frac{b}{a} = \frac{c}{x}$

Step 4: Cross multiply and solve for x.

Q10 What does a typical labor problem look like?

A10 **<u>Example</u>**: Tim will take 3 hours to paint one room. How long will he take to paint 2 rooms?

<u>Solution</u>: step 1: identify the variables and their relation- time to paint and number of rooms. Clearly, if he takes 2 hours to paint 1 room, he is going to take more time to paint 2 rooms. So, the time and number of rooms are in DIRECT variation.

step 2: Write the given information so that the quantity you are trying to find is at the bottom right.

1 room 3 hours

2 rooms x hours

step 3: setup the ratio for DIRECT variation

$\frac{1}{2} = \frac{3}{x}$. Cross multiply to get $x = 3 \cdot 2 = 6$

<u>Example</u>: 20 men can do a job in 3 hours. How many men are needed to do the same job in 2 hours?

<u>Solution</u>: step 1: Identify variables and relation: number of men and time to do the job. Less time to do the job means more men are needed –so, they are in inverse relationship. step 2: write the information such that the quantity that you are trying to find is on the bottom right.

3 hours 20 men

2 hours x men

step 3: setup the ratio for INVERSE variation, remember to <u>flip</u> one of the ratios.

$\frac{3}{2} = \frac{x}{20}$

$x = \frac{3}{2} \cdot 20 = 30$

$x =$ 30; so 30 men are required to do the job in 2 hours.

Q11 What does a typical capacity problem look like?

A11 Capacity Problems involve rate at which machines output certain products. Pay attention to unit of time in the question (seconds,minutes,hours). Also verify whether the problem is a direct or inverse relation/variation problem.

Example: A machine has a capacity to make 300 buttons/hour. How many buttons can it make in 45 minutes?

Solution step 1: identify variables and relation - number of buttons and time; more time, more buttons – DIRECT variation step 2: write the info in correct format so that the quantity you are trying to find is at bottom right; all quantities of the same type should be in the same units; for example time should be in minutes.

60 minutes 300 buttons
45 minutes x buttons

step 3: setup the ratio for direct relation

$\frac{60}{45} = \frac{300}{x}$; cross multiply

$x = \frac{45}{60} \cdot 300 = 225$

Q12 Can rate problems have 3 variables? How do I solve them?

A12 Rate problems can have 3 variables – for example, number of men, number of jobs, and time. You need to know how to calculate the work rate per hour and how to set up direct and inverse relations. Remember that for inverse relationships, flip the numbers in only one ratio and then cross multiply.

Example: 4 men can do 1 job in 3 hours. What fraction of a job can be completed by 1 man in 8 hours?
Solution:

4 men – 1 job – 3 hrs;
1 man- x job – 8 hrs;

The work rate of 4 men is $\frac{1}{3}$ job/hr; so work rate of 1 man is $\frac{\frac{1}{3}}{4} = \frac{1}{12}$job/hr; The question is what portion of the job can 1 man do in 8 hours? You know 1 man can do $\frac{1}{12}$ job/hr.

1 hour $\frac{1}{12}$job
8 hours x job

Set up the direct relation ratio

$$\frac{1}{8}=\frac{\frac{1}{12}}{x}=\frac{1}{12x}$$

$12x = 8;\ x = \frac{8}{12} = \frac{2}{3}$

So, in 8 hours, he will do $\frac{2}{3}$ job.

Example: 4 men can do 1 job in 3 hours. How long will it take 1 man to finish 2 jobs?

4 men – 1 job - 3 hrs

1 man- 2 jobs – x hrs

The work rate of 4 men is $\frac{1}{3}$ job/hr; work rate of 1 man is $\frac{\frac{1}{3}}{4} = \frac{1}{12}$ job/hr;

$\frac{1}{12}$ job 1 hour

2 jobs x hours

Set up a DIRECT variation equation:

$$\frac{\frac{1}{12}}{2}=\frac{1}{x}$$

$$\frac{1}{24}=\frac{1}{x}$$

$x = 24$

So, 1 man will take 24 hours for 2 jobs;

Example: 4 men can do 1 job in 3 hours. How many men will it take to do 2 jobs in 4 hours?

4 men – 1 job – 3 hrs

x men - 2 jobs – 4 hrs;

4 men-1 job- 3 hrs;

so 4 men – 2 jobs – 6 hours, since they are doing double the work

But, you need to find how many men can do 2 jobs in 4 hours. Since the 2 jobs needs to be done in less time – 4 hours instead of 6, more men will be needed. This is INVERSE variation. Setup the ratio as follows. Remember to flip one ratio, since this is an INVERSE relation.

6 hrs 4 men

4 hrs x men

$\frac{6}{4} = \frac{x}{4}$; so $x =$ 6 men

PROBLEM SOLVING AND DATA ANALYSIS		
Lesson 4	Ratio, Rate, and Variation	Practice

NO CALCULATOR SECTION

1. If, the four numbers $\frac{1}{40}, \frac{1}{80}, \frac{1}{70}, \frac{1}{x}$ form a proportion, what is the value of x?
(A) 6
(B) 7
(C) 14
(D) 140

2. If 20 men can build a home in 360 days, how many men are needed to build the home in 150 days?
(A) 6
(B) 12
(C) 24
(D) 48

NO CALCULATOR SECTION

3. George takes 3 hours to mow a lawn. Jacob takes 6 hours to mow the same lawn. How long will it take if both of them mow 3 lawns together?
(A) 3
(B) 6
(C) 9
(D) 12

4. A piece of ribbon is cut into three pieces that have lengths in the ratio 7:8:9. The length of the ribbon is 96 centimeters. Each centimeter is worth 75 cents. How much does the smallest piece of ribbon cost in dollars?
(A)2.10
(B)19.00
(C)21.00
(D)27.00

NO CALCULATOR SECTION

5. If x is an integer such that $-3 \leq x \leq 0$ and k is an integer such that $-8 \leq k \leq 17$. What is the largest possible value of $\frac{x}{k}$?

(A) $-\frac{3}{8}$

(B) 0

(C) $\frac{3}{17}$

(D) $\frac{3}{8}$

6. Machine A can make 8 toys in one hour. Machine B can make 9 toys in 30 minutes. If each machine works simultaneously, how many toys will be made after 90 minutes?

(A) 26
(B) 29
(C) 36
(D) 39

NO CALCULATOR SECTION

7. Bob drives from home to a shopping center at 30 miles/hr and returns back at 20 miles/hr. If he takes 60 minutes for the round trip, how much distance in miles did he drive in total?

(A) 12
(B) 24
(C) 600
(D) 720

8. If $\frac{x}{z} = \frac{3}{4}$, then what is $\frac{100x}{32z}$?

(A) $\frac{32}{75}$

(B) $\frac{3}{4}$

(C) $\frac{25}{32}$

(D) $\frac{75}{32}$

NO CALCULATOR SECTION

9. The number of pencils that Pam has is inversely proportional to the number of erasers that she has. When she has 120 pencils, she has 2 erasers. How many erasers will she have when she has 80 pencils?
(A) 1
(B) 2
(C) 3
(D) 4

Gums	Mint
1000	50
1250	40

10 The number of Bubble Gum and Mint candies sold are related as shown in the table. If 2500 Bubble gums are sold, how many Mint candies will be sold?
(A) 10
(B) 20
(C) 25
(D) 40

NO CALCULATOR SECTION

11. The length of a rectangle of x units is increased by 10% and its width of y units is increased by 15%. What is the ratio of the area of the old rectangle to the area of the new rectangle?
(A) 1:1.0265
(B) 1:1.265
(C) 1:1.562
(D) 1.625:1

12 A farmer loads bags of rice, wheat, and corn into his truck. The ratio of the weight of rice to that of wheat is 2 to 3.1. The ratio of the weight of wheat to that of corn is 6.2 to 1. Which of the following loadings, in pounds, is possible?
(A) Rice 200, Wheat 410, Corn 620
(B) Rice 400, Wheat 310, Corn 100
(C) Rice 200, Wheat 310, Corn 620
(D) Rice 400, Wheat 620, Corn 100

CALCULATOR SECTION

13. Rachel invested $100 at a bank that gives a simple interest of 3% per year. She invested another $100 at a Credit Union that gives her a simple interest of 5% per year. After one year, what is the ratio of her balance at the bank to that of her balance at the credit union?
(A) 0.6
(B) 0.66
(C) 0.89
(D) 0.98

14 The ratio of poor people to rich people in a town in the year 1990 was 6 to 1. The same ratio in the year 2000 was 10 to 3. What is the percent increase of rich people in the town from 1990 to 2000?
(A) 2.67
(B) 6.69
(C) 8.79
(D) 9.23

CALCULATOR SECTION

15. A box contains two red balls, five green balls, and eight blue balls. The number of red balls is directly proportional to the number of green balls. The number of green balls is inversely proportional to the number of blue balls. If the number of green balls is increased to twenty, then what is the ratio of red balls to blue balls?
GRID IN

PROBLEM SOLVING AND DATA ANALYSIS		
Lesson 4	Ratio, Rate, and Variation	Answers

#	Explanation	Comments
1 D	If four numbers, A, B, C and D form a proportion, then $\frac{A}{B}=\frac{C}{D}$. In this question, the numbers are fractions. $\frac{\frac{1}{40}}{\frac{1}{80}}=\frac{\frac{1}{70}}{\frac{1}{x}}$ $\frac{80}{40}=\frac{x}{70}$; $x=140$	4 numbers a,b,c,d are in direct proportion if $\frac{a}{b}=\frac{c}{d}$.
2 D	20 men – 360 days 150 days – how many men; step1: days and men – less days will require more men – inverse variation; step 2: write the facts down with unknown quantity at bottom right 360 days 20 men 150 days x men Step3: setup the equation for inverse relation; flip one of the ratios. $\frac{x}{20}=\frac{360}{150}$ $x=\frac{360}{150}\cdot 20=48$ men	While setting up the equation for INVERSE variation, remember to flip one of the ratios. See review section for solved examples.
3 B	George takes 3 hrs/lawn; his rate of work is $\frac{1}{3}$ lawn/hr Jacob takes 6 hrs/lawn; his rate of work is $\frac{1}{6}$ lawn/hr If they work together, they will mow $\frac{1}{3}+\frac{1}{6}=\frac{1}{2}$ lawn/hr $\frac{1}{2}$ lawn – 1 hr 3 lawns – x hrs DIRECT relation $\frac{\frac{1}{2}}{3}=\frac{1}{x}$ $\frac{x}{2}=3$ $x=6$ hrs	Calculating the rate of work is important to solve this problem.
4 C	You have to find the cost of $\frac{7}{24}$ of the 96 centimeter ribbon. $\frac{7}{24}\cdot 96=28$ centimeters. $28\cdot 75=2100$ cents. Converting this to dollars gives $21.00.	The smallest portion of a ribbon that is cut in the ratio of 7:8:9 is $\frac{7}{7+8+9}=\frac{7}{24}$.
5 D	The largest possible value of $\frac{x}{k}$ is obtained if $x=-3$ and $k=-8$. This makes the fraction equal to $\frac{3}{8}$.	

6 D	Machine A: 8 toys in 60 minutes Machine B: 9 toys in 30 minutes, meaning 18 toys in 60 minutes. Totally 8+18=26 toys in 60 minutes. The question is how many toys in 90 minutes. 60 minutes 26 toys 90 minutes x toys More time, more toys ; so DIRECT variation $\frac{60}{90} = \frac{26}{x}$ $60x = 26 \cdot 90$ $x = 26 \cdot \frac{90}{60} = 26 \cdot \frac{3}{2} = 39$	
7 B	Speed=distance/time; so time=distance/speed; you know the speed for the two segments ; let d be the distance from home to shopping center. Total time t= 1 hr = time to shopping + time to home; $1 = \frac{d}{30} + \frac{d}{20} = \frac{50}{600}d;$ so $d = 12$ miles. Remember that this is just one-way; so the total distance= $2 \cdot 12 =$ 24 miles.	Remember to keep the unit of time as hours – the equation must have 1 hour – not 60 minutes – since the speed is in miles/hour.
8 D	Take a few seconds to just "look" at the problem to see if there is any pattern or trick that you can identify. If $\frac{x}{z} = \frac{3}{4}$, then $\frac{100x}{32z} = \frac{100}{32} \cdot \frac{x}{z} = \frac{100}{32} \cdot \frac{3}{4} = \frac{75}{32}$	Always pause for a few seconds to observe anything tricky or spot a pattern; this will help you move forward with the correct strategy.
9 C	Since the number of pencils is inversely proportional to the number of erasers, you can write pencils · erasers = k; so pencils · erasers = k =120 · 2 = 240. Now, when she has 80 pencils, 80 · erasers = $k = 240$; so the number of erasers that she will have is $\frac{240}{80} = 3$.	If p is in inverse variation with q, then $pq = k$. That is, if p increases, then q will decrease so that the product of p and q is still equal to k.
10 B	Note that the problem says that the sales of gums and mint are related – but you need to find out if they are in direct or inverse relation. Observe that as gums increase, mints decrease. Now check if their product is a constant; 1000 · 50=50000=1250 · 40=50000. So, the constant of proportionality is k=50000. So, when 2500 bubble gums are sold, 2500 · mints = 50000; or mint=$\frac{50,000}{2500} = 20$.	If the data is in a table, visually observe if the two quantities are in direct or inverse relation. If they are in inverse relation, their product will be constant; if they are in direct relation, then their ratio will be constant.
11 B	x increased by 10% is 1.1 x; y increased by 15% is 1.15 y. So, the new area is 1.1 $\cdot$ 1.15 y = $1.265\,xy$. The ratio is $\frac{xy}{1.265\,xy} = 1{:}1.265$	x increased by 10% is $x + \frac{10}{100} \cdot x = x + 0.1x = 1.1x$
12 D	Note that there are three quantities- rice, wheat, and corn $\frac{rice}{wheat} = \frac{2}{3.1}$ and $\frac{wheat}{corn} = \frac{6.2}{1}$	Review how to compare three quantities. Though the problem looks complex, once you simplify

	To be able to compare, bring the wheat portion to 6.2 in the rice/wheat ratio. $\frac{rice}{wheat} = \frac{4}{6.2}$ and $\frac{wheat}{corn} = \frac{6.2}{1}$; therefore, rice:wheat:corn = 4:6.2:1 Now, a possible loading of the truck in pounds will have to satisfy this ratio - be 400, 620 and 100 (multiply all the items by 100)	the ratios, the problem is solved easily.
13 D	Use the calculator. Balance after one year at the bank =100 + 0.03 ·100 = \$103 Balance after one year at the credit union =100 + 0.05 ·100 = \$105 The ratio = $\frac{103}{105}$=0.98.	
14 C	In 1990 $\frac{poor}{rich} = \frac{6}{1}$; so the percentage of rich people=$\frac{1}{7} \cdot 100 = 14.29\%$ In 2000, $\frac{poor}{rich} = \frac{10}{3}$; so the percentage of rich people= $\frac{3}{13} \cdot$ 100= 23.08% So, the percentage increase is 23.08-14.29=8.79%	Starting with a ratio, learn to calculate proportion of one part with respect to the whole and then its percentage of the whole.
15 4	Initially red 2 green 5 blue 8; note that red and green are directly proportional- so $\frac{red}{green} = \frac{2}{5}$ and green and blue are inversely proportional – so, initially, green · blue =5 ·8=40 and this inverse relationship must be maintained. Now, the number of green balls is 20; so the number of red and blue balls must be different in order to maintain the direct and inverse relationship; So, $\frac{new\ red}{20} = \frac{2}{5}$; so $new\ red = 8$ new green · new blue=40 20·new blue=40 new blue=2 So $\frac{new\ red}{new\ blue} = \frac{8}{2} = 4$	Review the direct and inverse relationship fundamentals.

PROBLEM SOLVING AND DATA ANALYSIS		
Lesson 5	Percentages	Review

FOCUSPREP CHECKLIST

- How do I calculate a percentage increase or decrease?
- How do I convert a fraction, or a decimal to a percentage?
- How do I convert a ratio to a percentage?
- Workout practice problems in Percentages

Q1 What is a Percentage?

A1 Percent means "for every 100". "cent" means centum, which is Latin for 100.

Q2 How do I convert a fraction or a decimal to a percentage?

A2 Fraction to percentage: Multiply by 100. $\frac{2}{3}$ converted to percentage is $\frac{2}{3} \cdot 100 = 66.67\%$

Decimal to percentage: Multiply by 100. 0.25 converted to percentage is $0.25 \cdot 100 = 25\%$

Q3 How do I convert a percentage to a fraction or a decimal?

A3 Percentage to fraction: Divide by 100. $25\% = \frac{25}{100} = \frac{1}{4}$

Percentage to decimal: Divide by 100. $25\% = \frac{25}{100} = 0.25$

Q4 How do I convert a ratio to a percentage?

A4 If the ratio of boys to girls is $\frac{2}{5}$, then the percentage of boys= $\frac{2}{2+5} = \frac{2}{7} \cdot 100 = 28.57\%$. The percentage of boys is NOT $\frac{2}{5} \cdot 100 = 40\%$. The percentage of girls=$\frac{5}{2+5} = \frac{5}{7} \cdot 100 = 71.43\%$.

Q5 How do I calculate the percentage increase or percentage decrease?

A5 If a quantity a becomes quantity b, then the percentage increase or decrease is given by the formula $\frac{(b-a)}{a} \cdot 100$. If $b > a$, then the percentage is positive and indicates an increase; If $b < a$, then the percentage is negative and indicates a decrease.

Example: Sales of an automobile was 2000 last year and 3000 this year. What is the percentage change?

Solution: $\frac{3000-2000}{2000} \cdot 100 = 50\%$. Since the percentage change is positive, it indicates an increase in sales.

Example: Sales of an automobile was 3000 last year and 2000 this year. What is the percentage change?

Solution: $\frac{2000-3000}{3000} \cdot 100 = -33.33\%$. Since the percentage change is negative, it indicates a decrease in sales.

Q6 What kind of problems can I encounter with percentages?

A6 Problems regarding percentages can appear in algebra, geometry, banking, taxes, science, census, etc. – wherever there are two numbers and you want to figure out how much increase or decrease there has been relative to the first number as a percentage. You can expect to encounter percentage problems in data analysis involving tables and graphs.

Q7 How do percentages relate to sale price, cost price, profits, and discounts?

A7 Get familiar with these terms as you will encounter them frequently. Suppose a product costs c dollars to make and the product is sold for s dollars. The profit is $s - c$ dollars and profit as a percentage is $\frac{s-c}{c} \cdot 100.$

Example: Suppose a product that is sold for $20 is discounted by 20%. What is the discount and the new sales price?

Solution: The discount is $20\% = \frac{20}{100} \cdot 20 = 4.$ The new sales price is old sales price-discount = 20-4= $16;$ Another way to quickly arrive at the answer is to figure out that if the discount is 20%, then the remaining 80% is the new sales price $- so \frac{80}{100} \cdot 20 = 16.$

Example: A toy costs $50. The tax is 8.25%. What is the sale price of the toy?

Solution: The sale price is cost + tax = $50 + \frac{8.25}{100} \cdot 50 = 50 + 0.0825 \cdot 50 = 50 + 4.13 = 54.13$

Q8 A shopkeeper increases the price of a shirt by 10% and then increases it again by 10% of the new price. Should he instead be increasing the price once by 20% if he wants more profit?

A8 **Solution**: Assume that the shirt is originally sold at $ s. He increases by 10% - so the price now is 1.1s. He increased it again by 10% of this new price – so the price now is 1.1s · 1.1 = 1.21s. If he increased it just once by 20%, he would be selling the shirt for 1.2s, which is less than 1.21s. So he should not be increasing it by 20% if he wants to have more profit.

Q9 What should I be aware of with regard to word problems involving percentages?

A9 Watch out for phrases such as "what is the percentage increase", "what is the percentage decrease", "what is the change in percentage", "what percentage of", etc.

Example: What percentage of 20 is 10? $\frac{x}{100} \cdot 20 = 10;\ x = 50\%$

What percentage is 3 of 20? $3 = \frac{x}{100} \cdot 20;\ x = 15\%$

CALCULATOR SECTION

1. A small zoo has lions, tigers, and cheetahs only. The ratio of lions to tigers is 1:2 and the ratio of tigers to cheetahs is 3:7. What percentage of the zoo population is made of lions?
(A) 12.04%
(B) 13.04%
(C) 15.38%
(D) 20%

2. If the length and width of a rectangle are doubled, the area will increase by what percentage?
(A) 4%
(B) 20%
(C) 300%
(D) 400%

CALCULATOR SECTION

3. If the radius of a circle is halved, then by what percentage does the area decrease by?
(A) 25%
(B) 50%
(C) 75%
(D) 100%

4. If $x = 4y$, where x and y are positive integers, then what percent of x is y?
(A) 15
(B) 25
(C) 40
(D) 100

CALCULATOR SECTION

5. Lisa donated $1600 for charity in 2014. If there are 52 paychecks in one year, and she gets $1200 in each of her paychecks, what percentage of her salary does Lisa donate?
(A) 2.56
(B) 2.65
(C) 6.5
(D) 7.5

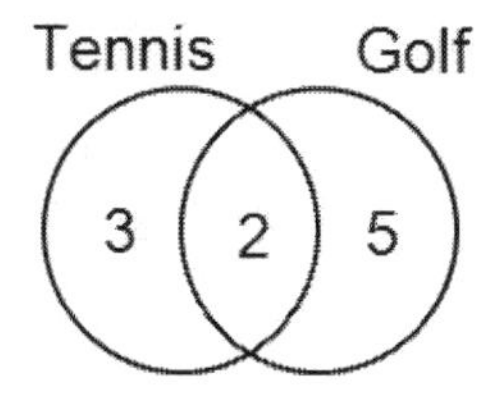

6. The Venn diagram above shows students who play tennis and golf. What percentage of tennis players play golf as well?
(A) 40.00
(B) 42.86
(C) 71.42
(D) 100

CALCULATOR SECTION

7. At a car dealership, sales of model-A were 100 cars in 2010 and it increased at the same percentage for the next two years. The sales of model-B were 1600 in 2010 but the sales decreased by the same percentage for the next two years. If the percentage increase in sales of model-A cars is the same as the percentage decrease in sales of model-B cars, and the total number of model-A cars sold in 2012 is the same as model-B cars, what is the percentage increase or decrease?
GRID IN

8. A sculpture worth $5000 loses 5% of its value for 2 years and then loses 6% of its value for two more years. Another sculpture loses its value by 7% for two years and then by 9% for two more years. If the value of the two sculptures is the same after the four years of losses, what is the value of the second sculpture?
GRID IN

PROBLEM SOLVING AND DATA ANALYSIS		
Lesson 5	Percentages	Answers

#	Explanation	Comments
1 B	You have three animals and the ratios linking them; $\frac{lions}{tigers}=\frac{1}{2}; \frac{tigers}{cheetahs}=\frac{3}{7}$ To find the percentage of lions, you need to represent the ratios in lions:tigers:cheetahs format. Since the tigers are not in the same quantity in the two ratios (2 and 3), you need to make them the same. The least common multiple of 2 and 3 is 6. So, make lions/tigers as $\frac{3}{6}$ and tigers/cheetahs=$\frac{6}{14}$. This gives us lions:tigers:cheetahs=3:6:14. So, the percentage of lions is $\frac{3}{3+6+14}\cdot 100 \cong 13.04\%$	Review the lesson on ratios to learn how to work with ratios involving three quantities and how to bring them into the a:b:c format. Doing this is critical to answer a problem of this type. Be prepared to encounter problems that have a mix of ratios, variations, and percentages.
2 C	Let length = l and width= w, Area= $l\cdot w$ New length = $2l$ New width=$2w$, New Area = $2l\cdot 2w = 4\,lw$. The percentage increase = $\frac{4lw-lw}{lw}\cdot 100 = 300\%$	Note that percentage increases can be more than 100. Review the percentage increase and decrease formula.
3 C	Area = $\pi\cdot r^2$ New area = $\pi\cdot\left(\frac{r}{2}\right)^2 = \pi\cdot\frac{r^2}{4}$ The percentage decrease is $\frac{\frac{\pi r^2}{4}-\pi r^2}{\pi r^2}\cdot 100 = \frac{\frac{1}{4}-1}{1}\cdot 100 = -75\%$	When you apply the percentage formula, if you get a negative percentage, don't be alarmed - negative percentage indicates that there is a decrease in quantity.
4 B	$x = 4y$; what percentage of x is y? $so\ y = \frac{1}{4}x = 0.25\,x = \frac{25}{100}x = 25\%$ of x	This problem highlights conversion from fraction to decimal to percentage.
5 A	percentage donation = donation/salary · 100 Lisa's salary = 52 · 1200= 62400 Her donation = 1600; In percentage, $\frac{1600}{62400}\cdot 100 = 2.56\%$	Be careful while entering large numbers like 62400. Don't miss any zeros!
6 A	Total # of tennis players = 3+2 = 5 Total Number of players who play both golf and tennis=2 Percentage = $\frac{2}{5}\cdot 100 = 40\%$	
7 60%	Let the increase in percentage of model-A cars and decrease in percentage of model-B cars=$x\%$. Make a table to show the sales of the two models.	This is a harder problem; setup the equation carefully.

<table>
<tr>
<td></td>
<td>
<table>
<tr><td>Year</td><td>Model-A</td><td>Model-B</td></tr>
<tr><td>2010</td><td>100</td><td>1600</td></tr>
<tr><td>2011</td><td>$100\,(1+x)$</td><td>$1600(1-x)$</td></tr>
<tr><td>2012</td><td>$100(1+x)(1+x)$</td><td>$1600(1-x)(1-x)$</td></tr>
</table>
You know that in 2012 the sales is the same for the two models. So
$100(1+x)^2 \ = \ 1600(1-x)^2$

$\frac{(1+x)^2}{(1-x)^2} \ = \frac{1600}{100} \ = \ 16$
$\left[\frac{1+x}{1-x}\right]^2 \ = \ 16$
$\left[\frac{1+x}{1-x}\right] = \ \pm 4$
If $x = +4, 1+x \ = \ 4 - 4x$
$5x = 3$
$x = \frac{3}{5} \ = \ 0.6 \ = \frac{60}{100} = \ 60\%$
So the percentage increase of model-A and percentage decrease of model-B=60%.
Verify your answer: for model-A, starting with 10 in 2010, the sales in 2012 is $100(1.6)^2$. For model-B, starting from 1600 in 2010, the sales in 2012 is $1600(1-0.6)^2 \ = \ 256.$
If $x = -4, 1+x \ = \ -4 + \ 4x, x = -\frac{5}{3} = -166.67\%$. This cannot be a solution since the sales of model-A increased and so x must be positive.
</td>
<td></td>
</tr>
<tr>
<td>8
5538</td>
<td>5% decrease in value for two years = 95% of value. 6% decrease in value for two years = 94% of value. 7% decrease in value for two years = 93% of value. 9% decrease in value for two years = 91% of value.

Value of the first sculpture after 4 years = 5000 · 0.95 · 0.95 · 0.94 · 0.94 = $3987.
Let x be the value of the second sculpture.
Value of the second sculpture after 4 years =
$x \cdot \ 0.93 \cdot 0.93 \cdot 0.91 \cdot 0.91 \ = \ 0.72x$
You know that the value of the two sculptures are the same after 4 years; So, $0.72x = 3987; \ x = \ \$5538$</td>
<td>Be careful with decreasing percentages and discounts – if the value of a sculpture x decreases by 7%, then its new value is 100-7=93% of the old value=$0.93x$. If this new value again decreases by 7%., then the new value will again be multiplied by 93%= $0.93x \cdot 0.93 =$ $x \cdot 0.93 \cdot 0.93$</td>
</tr>
</table>

PROBLEM SOLVING AND DATA ANALYSIS		
Lesson 6	Unit Conversions	Review

FOCUSPREP CHECKLIST

- What is Unit of Measurement?
- How do I convert one unit to another?
- Workout practice problems in Unit Conversions

Q1 What is an Unit Of Measurement?

A1 Unit of Measurement refers to the unit that is used to measure length, weight, speed etc. For example, the unit of measurement of length is feet, miles, kilometers, etc.; the unit of measurement of weight is pound, kilogram, ton, etc.; and the unit of measurement of time is seconds, minutes, month, week, etc.

Q2 What is unit conversion?

A2 Unit conversion is the process of converting measurements from one unit to another. For example, you convert feet to inches by using the fact that $1\, feet = 12\, inches$. So, $3\, feet = 3\, \cancel{feet} \cdot 12 \frac{inches}{\cancel{feet}} = 36\, inches$. Notice that you started with feet and ended with inches.

Q3 Do I need to remember unit conversion tables for PSAT 8/9?

A3 You need to know the basic conversion data regarding measurements of lengths, weight, and time in order to answer questions quickly. However, any required conversion information will be given in the problem itself. Browse through the table below to familiarize yourself with some common conversions.

Length	1 feet = 12 inches 1 mile = 1760 yards 1 yard = 3 feet
Volume	1 gallon= 4 quarts 1 quart= 2 pints 1 pint = 2 cups 1 cup = 8 fluid ounces
Time	1 year = 12 months 1 year = 52 weeks 1 week = 7 days 1 day = 24 hours 1 hour = 60 minutes 1 minute= 60 seconds
Mass	1 ton = 2000 pounds 1 pound = 16 ounces
Density	Pounds per cubic feet $\frac{lbs}{ft^3}$
Pressure	Pounds per square inch $\frac{lbs}{in^2}$
Money	1 US Dollar = 100 cents

Q4 When will I need to convert units?

A4 You need to convert units when information is provided in one unit and a question is asked where the answer will be in another unit.

Example: John spent 2 hours and 30 minutes studying for an exam. How many seconds did he study?

Solution: Convert 2 hours to minutes => $2\ \cancel{hrs} \cdot 60\frac{minutes}{\cancel{hr}} = 120$ minutes

Add 30 minutes => 120+30=150 minutes . Convert to seconds = $150\ \cancel{minutes} \cdot 60\frac{seconds}{\cancel{minute}} =$ 9000 seconds.

Example: Sometimes, you may be introduced to a new item and its unit of measurement that you may not have come across in your life. For example, a Watt-Hour is how the electricity consumed is measured. A 40 Watt appliance that is operated for 25 hours consumes 40 · 25=1000 Watt Hours of electricity.

Q5 What is Kilo, Mega, etc.?

A5 When the magnitude of the item being measured is very high, it is customary to represent these numbers in terms of Mega, Kilo etc.

Tera = 10^{12} ; example: 3 Tera Bytes = $3 \cdot 10^{12}$ Bytes
Giga = 10^{9} ; example: 1 Giga Byte = 10^{9} Bytes
Mega = 10^{6} ; example: 2 Mega Bytes = $2 \cdot 10^{6}$ Bytes
Kilo = 10^{3}; example: 1 Kilo Byte = 10^{3} Bytes; 3 Kilo Meters= $3 \cdot 10^{3} = 3000\ m$

Q6 Where am I most likely to make mistakes during unit conversion?

A6 You are most likely to make a mistake when you are converting a unit two or more times to get to your final unit and did not properly cancel out the units.

Example: How many hours are there in 3 weeks?

Solution: If you are not careful, you might calculate it as 3 · 24 and end up with a wrong answer. A week does not have 24 hours. Carefully write out the units from beginning to end.

$3\ \cancel{weeks} \cdot 7\frac{\cancel{days}}{\cancel{week}} \cdot 24\frac{hours}{\cancel{day}} = 504\ hours.$ Note that after cancelling the units in the numerator and denominator, you are left with hours only in the numerator. This is the unit of measure you want in your answer.

Q7 What are some examples of unit conversion problems?

A7

Example

A carpenter earns $20/day. If he works for 3 days/week for 3 weeks in a month, how much does he earn in one month? $\frac{\$20}{\cancel{day}} \cdot \frac{3\ \cancel{days}}{\cancel{week}} \cdot \frac{3\ \cancel{weeks}}{month} = \frac{\$180}{month}$

Example

There are 5 cities in a state, 9 schools in each city, 200 students in each school. How many students are there in the state?

$$\frac{5\ \cancel{cities}}{state} \cdot \frac{9\ \cancel{schools}}{\cancel{city}} \cdot \frac{200\ students}{\cancel{school}} = \frac{9000\ students}{state}$$

PROBLEM SOLVING AND DATA ANALYSIS		
Lesson 6	Unit Conversions	Practice

CALCULATOR SECTION

1. There are 14 books in Sonia's shelf. There are 20 chapters in each book, 6 lessons in each chapter, and 5 pages in each lesson. Sonia has so far read 10 books fully, and 3 lessons each from 4 other books. How many pages are yet to be read?
(A) 1170
(B) 2340
(C) 2430
(D) 4680

2. A 20 Watt bulb burning for 50 hours consumes $20 \cdot 50 = 1000$ Watt-Hours or 1 Kilowatt-Hour(KWh). If the Simpson household consumes 200 KWh in January, this consumption is equivalent to how many 20 Watt bulbs burning for 8 hours?
(A) 650
(B) 1050
(C) 1250
(D) 2500

CALCULATOR SECTION

3. 50 painters can paint 3 buildings in 6 days. Painters are paid $20/hour each day and they work for 8 hours per day. If more painters are hired to paint 2 buildings in 1 day, how much money will be needed to pay them?
(A) 12,000
(B) 14,000
(C) 16,000
(D) 32,000

4. 100 people planned to run to raise funds for a charity. Twenty percent of them ran 3 miles, two fifth ran 6 miles, and the rest ran 9 miles. For every mile run, they raised $20. What was the total amount raised for the charity?
(A) 3600
(B) 7200
(C) 13,200
(D) 24,600

CALCULATOR SECTION

5. A cable company provides Internet data transmission speeds of 1.5 MBPS, where 1 MBPS=1 Million Bits Per Second. If a file is 100 Mega Bytes and 1 Byte=8 Bits, how many minutes will it take to download half the file? (Mega= 10^6)
(A) 4.44
(B) 5.44
(C) 6.44
(D) 6.68

6. A city that is facing a water shortage developed a plan to restrict water usage as follows:

Family size	**Permitted Usage**
Less than 3	20 gallons/day/family
3 to 5	25 gallons/day/family
More than 5	28 gallons/day/family

In the city, there are 700 families of 2 people each, 800 families of 4 people each, and 1000 families of 6 people each. If a TGAL represents thousand gallons, how many TGALs of water can be used by the residents of this city in one day?
GRID IN

CALCULATOR SECTION

7. After an empty rectangular wooden crate was filled with some material that has a density of $8\ \text{lb}/\text{ft}^3$, the mass increased by 2400 lbs. If this material is replaced by another material that has a density of $17\ \text{lb}/\text{ft}^3$, what will the mass of the crate increase by? $\text{Density} = \frac{mass}{volume}$
GRID IN

8. Water is pumped from three lakes to an empty water tank every day according to the following information.

Lake	Pumping rate	Pumping Hours
Lake 1	20 gallons/hr	2 hrs
Lake 2	30 gallons/hr	3 hrs
Lake 3	40 gallons/hr	5 hrs

Water is drained from the tank every day at the rate of 40 gallons/hr for 5 hours. How much water will be in the tank after 15 days?
GRID IN

#	Explanation	Comments
1 B	Note that the question asks- how many pages are yet to be read?. Sonia has read 10 books = $10\ \cancel{books} \cdot \frac{20\ \cancel{chapters}}{\cancel{book}} \cdot \frac{6\ \cancel{lessons}}{\cancel{chapter}} \cdot \frac{5\ pages}{\cancel{lesson}} = 6000$ pages. 3 lessons each from 4 books = $12\ \cancel{lessons} \cdot \frac{5\ pages}{\cancel{lesson}} =$ 60 pages So, totally, Sonia has read 6000+60= 6060 pages. Total number of pages in all the books = 14 books $\cdot$ $600 \frac{pages}{book} = 8400$ pages. So the pages that she is yet to read is $8400 - 6060 = 2340$.	Verify that the units cancel out and pay attention to what units you are left with at the end.
2 C	One 20 Watt bulb burning for 8 hrs = $20 \cdot 8 = 160$ Watt-Hrs. Let b be the number of 20 Watt bulbs that will burn for 8 hrs that will be equivalent to 200KWh. $b \cdot 160$ Watt − Hrs $= 160b$ Watt − Hrs $= 200{,}000$ Watt − Hrs $b = \frac{200{,}000}{160} = 1250$ bulbs.	Make sure you are comparing the same units on both sides – convert Kilo Watt-Hours to Watt Hours. 1 Kilo=1000.
3 D	50 painters can paint 3 buildings in 6 days. Painters are paid $20/hour each day and they work for 8 hours per day. If more painters are hired to paint 2 buildings in 1 day, how much money will be needed to pay them? 1 painter is paid $20/hr · 8 hrs/day = $160/day Now you need to find how many painters are needed to paint 2 buildings in 1 day. 50 painters – 3 bldgs – 6 days So 50 painters – 1 bldg = $\frac{6\ days}{3\ bldgs} \cdot 1\ bldg = 2\ days$ This means 50 painters – 2 bldgs = $2 \cdot 2 = 4\ days$ So if 50 painters – 2 bldgs – 4 days how many painters- 2 bldgs – 1 day ? since you want to paint the 2 bldgs in less time(1 day instead of 4 days), you will need more painters; the number of painters is inversely proportional to the number of days; 4 days 50 painters 1 day x painters So setup INVERSE relation; flip one of the ratios; $\frac{x}{50} = \frac{4}{1}$ $x = 50 \cdot 4 = 200$ painters. So, now each painter needs to be paid $160/day; therefore total to be paid = $160/day/painter . 200 painters = $32000/day.	This problem combines unit conversion with a labor rate problem. Review the lesson on ratios and variation to get familiar with rate problems.

4 C	20% of 100=20 persons $20\ \cancel{persons} \cdot \frac{3\ miles}{\cancel{person}} = 60\ miles$ $\frac{2}{5} \cdot 100 = 40,\ 40\ \cancel{persons} \cdot \frac{6\ miles}{\cancel{person}} = 240\ miles$ The rest = $100 - (20 + 40)$= 40 persons; $40\ \cancel{persons} \cdot 9 \frac{miles}{\cancel{person}} = 360$ miles Total miles = $60 + 240 + 360 = 660$ miles. Total fund raised=$\frac{\$20}{\cancel{mile}}\ 660\ \cancel{miles} = \$13{,}200$	
5 A	Note carefully that the speed is in MegaBits per second but the file size is in MegaBytes. data speed=1.5 M Bits/s Half the file size = $\frac{100}{2}$ M Bytes = 50 M Bytes = $=50\ M\ \cancel{Bytes} \cdot 8 \frac{Bits}{\cancel{byte}} = 400$ M Bits Let T be the time in seconds that it takes to download half the file. 1.5 M Bits – 1 secs 400 M Bits – $\frac{400}{1.5} \cdot 1$ sec $= 266.66$ secs = $\frac{266.66\ secs}{60\ \text{secs/minute}}$ = 4.44 minutes	Use M for mega to simplify the calculation. Be careful, Bytes and Bits sound similar but are different – 1 Byte=8 Bits.
6 62	Correlate the text with the information in the table. 700 families of 2 consume 700 ~~families~~ $\cdot\ 20 \frac{gallons}{day - \cancel{family}} =$ 14000 gallons/day 800 families of 4 consume $800 \cdot 25 = 20000$ gallons/day 1000 families of 6 consume $1000 \cdot 28 = 28000$ gallons/day Total consumption=14000+20000+28000=62000 gallons/day 1000 gallons = 1 TGAL, so 62000 gallons = 62000 ~~gallons~~/1000 ~~gallons~~ · 1 TGAL = 62 TGALs.	20 gallons/day/family must be written as $20 \frac{gallons}{day - \cancel{family}}$ in order to cancel the units correctly. Practice how to cancel the units.
7 2700	When the density of the filled material is $8\ \text{lb/ft}^3$ the mass is 2400 lbs. Density $= \frac{mass}{volume}$ $8 \frac{lb}{ft^3} = \frac{2400\ lb}{volume}$ volume=$\frac{2400\ \cancel{lb}}{8\ \cancel{lb}/ft^3} = 300\ \text{ft}^3$ Now the density of the new material is 16 So, $17 = mass/300$ Mass= $17 \frac{lb}{ft^3} \cdot 300 ft^3 = 5100$ lbs The mass will increase by $5100 - 2400 = 2700$ lbs.	
8 1950	The daily influx to the tank from the 3 lakes= 20 ·2+ 30 ·3 + 40·5 =330 gallons/day; The drainage from the tank = 40 gallons/hr · 5 hrs = 200 gallons - this is the drainage per day as well – so 200 gallons/day. So, the net addition to the tank = 330-200=130 gallons/day. The amount of water in the tank after 15 days = $130 \frac{\text{gallons}}{day} \cdot 15\ days = 1950$ gallons	

PROBLEM SOLVING AND DATA ANALYSIS		
Lesson 7	Scatterplots	Review

FOCUSPREP CHECKLIST

- What is a scatterplot?
- How do I fit a curve in a scatterplot?
- What is a positive and a negative correlation?
- Workout practice problems in Scatterplots

Q1 What is a Scatterplot?

A1 A scatterplot is a type of graph that is used to verify if there is a correlation between two sets of data. The correlation can be a positive correlation, a negative correlation, or there may not be any correlation at all between the two sets.

Q2 How do scatterplots look?

A2 Scatterplots with positive correlation, negative correlation, and no correlation are shown below.

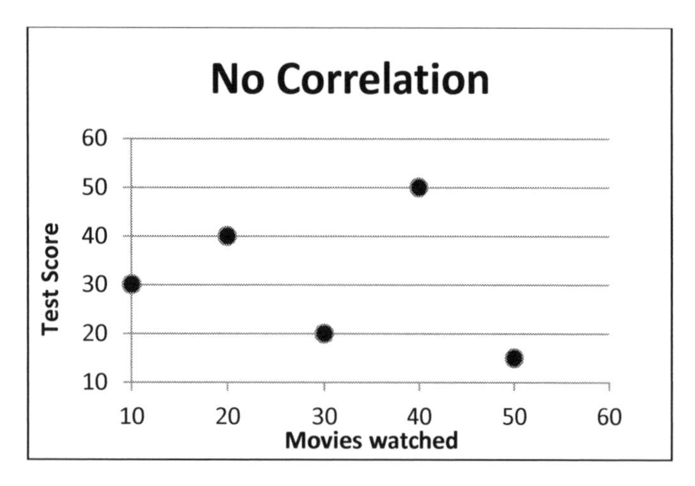

This scatterplot shows that test scores do not depend on the number of movies watched.

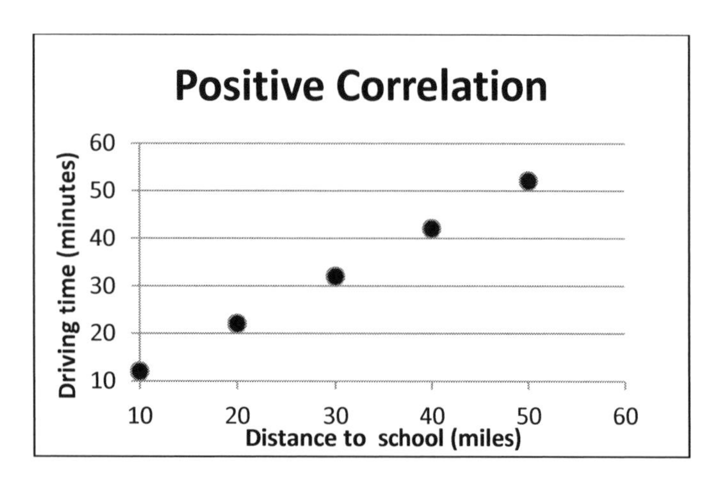

This scatter plot shows a positive correlation between the distance to school and the driving time. As the distance to school increases, the driving time increases.

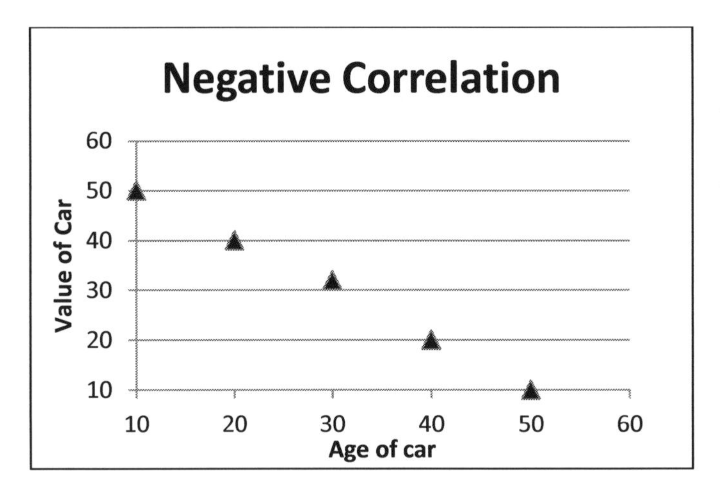

This scatterplot shows a negative correlation between the age of a car and its value. As the car gets older, its value decreases.

Q3 Can scatterplots be used to compare values of two sets of data of the same type?

A3 Scatterplots can also be used to plot data with the same units (scores, dollar value, etc.)

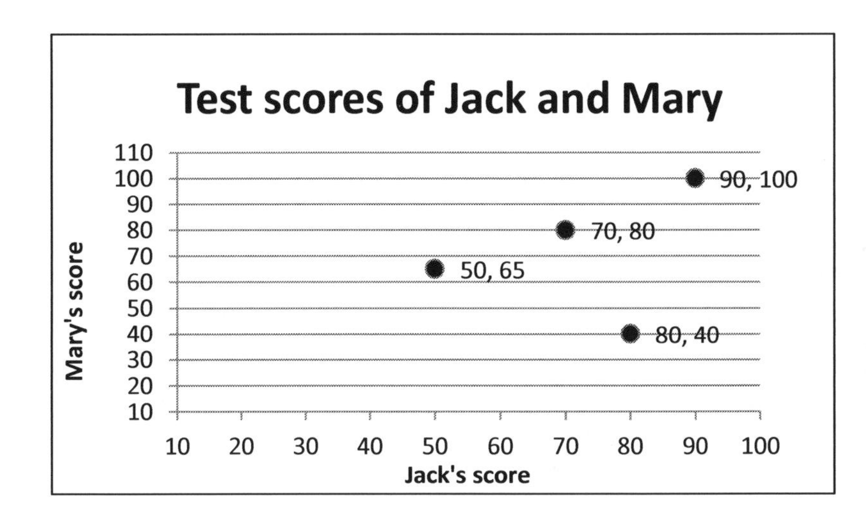

In this scatter plot, both the x axis and y axis represent the scores. The x coordinate of each point represents Jack's score and the y coordinate represents Mary's score.

You can infer from this scatterplot that there were 4 tests in total and Mary scored more than Jack in 3 tests.

Q4 I find a positive correlation between the two variables in my scatterplot. How do I fit a curve?

A4 You can fit several types of curves into a scatterplot depending on the type of correlation.

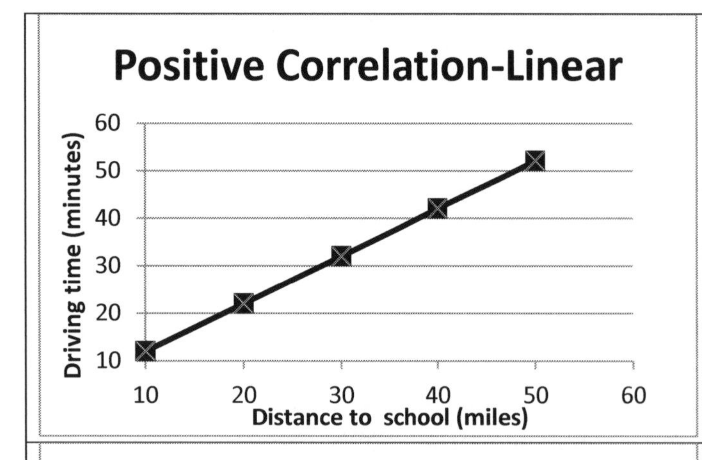

In this scatterplot, a straight line can be fit to connect the points.

You can model this line as $y = mx + b$ where m is the slope and b is the y-intercept.

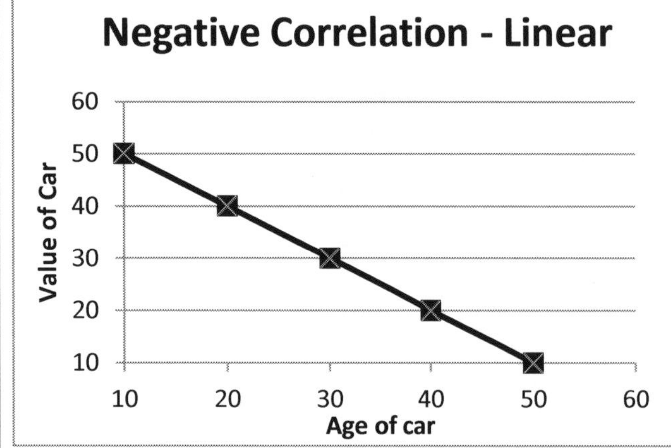

In this scatterplot, a straight line can be fit to connect the points. Note that the line has a negative slope. You can model a straight line as y=$mx + b$ where m is the slope and b is the y-intercept.

Sometimes, you may not be able to fit a line connecting all the points. In that case, connect as many points as possible. Sometimes, you may only be able to fit a line in such a way that all the points lie on either side of the line but none of them lie on the line.

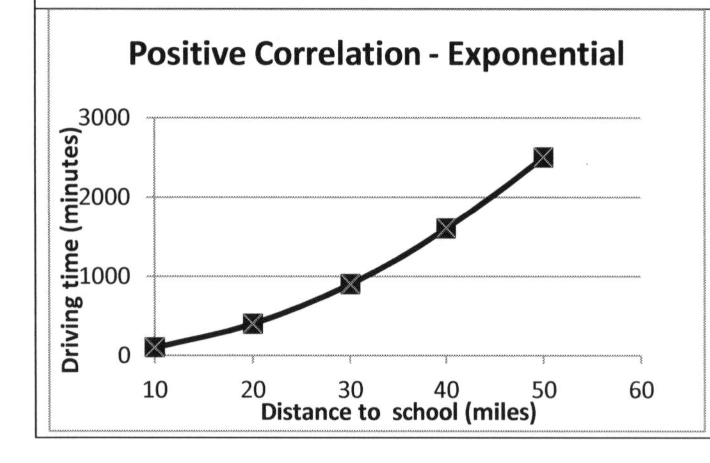

In this scatterplot, an exponential curve can be fit to connect the points.

Exponential curves take the form of $y = ab^x$.

Review the lesson on Growth and Decay for more information on Exponential functions.

PROBLEM SOLVING AND DATA ANALYSIS		
Lesson 7	Scatterplots	Practice

CALCULATOR SECTION

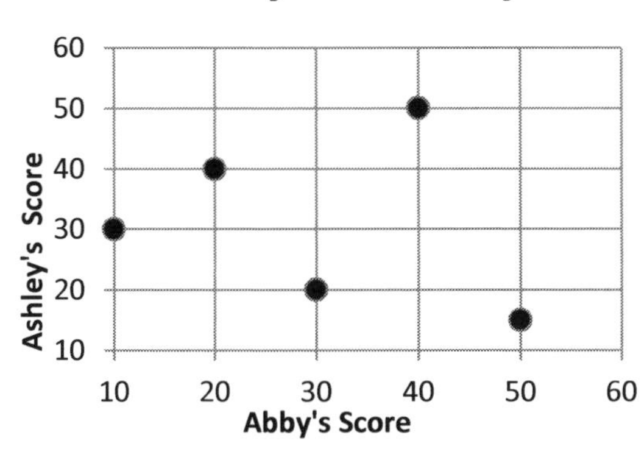

1. The scatterplot above shows the scores of two students in five games. A student with a higher score wins. What percentage of games did Ashley win?
(A) 20%
(B) 40%
(C) 60%
(D) 90%

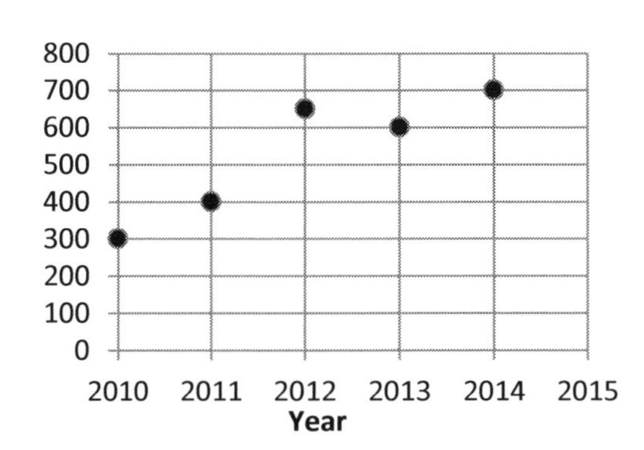

2. The scatterplot above shows the car sales at a dealership. How many cars can the dealer expect to sell in 2015?
(A) 700
(B) 750
(C) 800
(D) 850

CALCULATOR SECTION

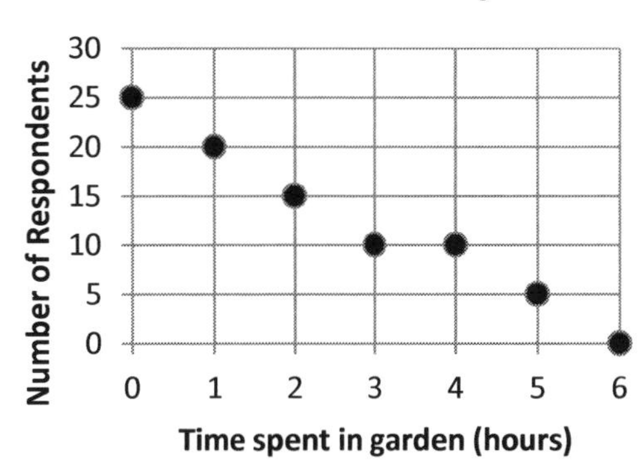

3. A botanist did a survey to find out how much time people spend every week in their gardens. The scatterplot above shows the results of the survey. Which of the following is true?

(A) The total number of people spending 3 and 4 hours at the garden is the same as the total number of people spending 0 hours at the garden.
(B) More than half of the respondents spend less than 3 hours at the garden.
(C) 5 respondents spend more than five hours at the garden.
(D) Everyone surveyed spends at least one hour at the garden.

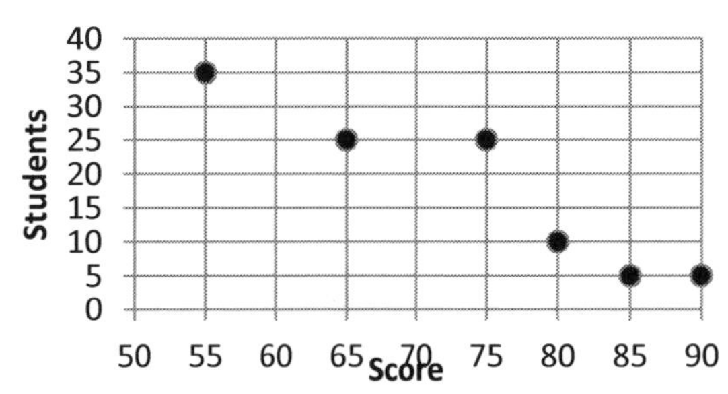

4. The scores obtained by students in a geography test are shown in the scatterplot above. What is the average score for this test?
(A) 55
(B) 57.62
(C) 63.05
(D) 67.62

CALCULATOR SECTION

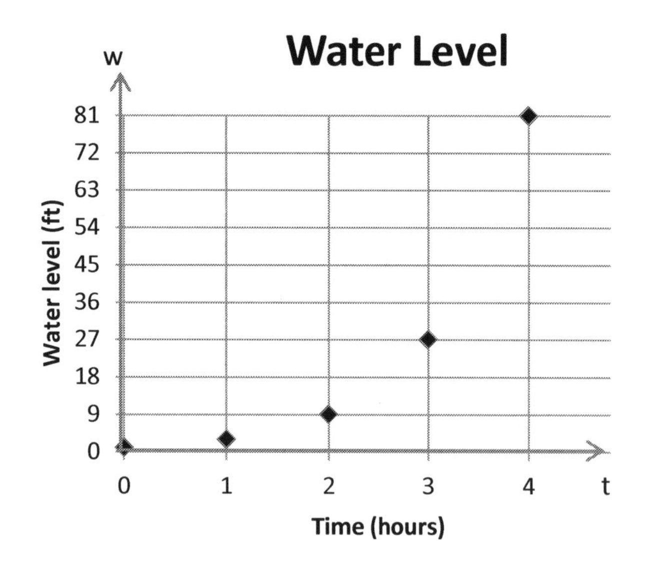

Use the scatterplot above to answer questions 5 and 6 below.

5. A hydrologist began tracking the water level in a dam as soon as heavy rain started. The plot of the water level after four hours of rain is shown above. Which of the following functions best describes the relationship between the water level (w) and the time (t)?

(A) $w = 2^t$

(B) $w = 2.5^t$

(C) $w = 3^t$

(D) $w = 5^t$

6. Assuming that the rain continues for several hours, what would be the water level (ft) in the dam after 5 hours?

(A) 32

(B) 52.52

(C) 97.66

(D) 243

NO CALCULATOR SECTION

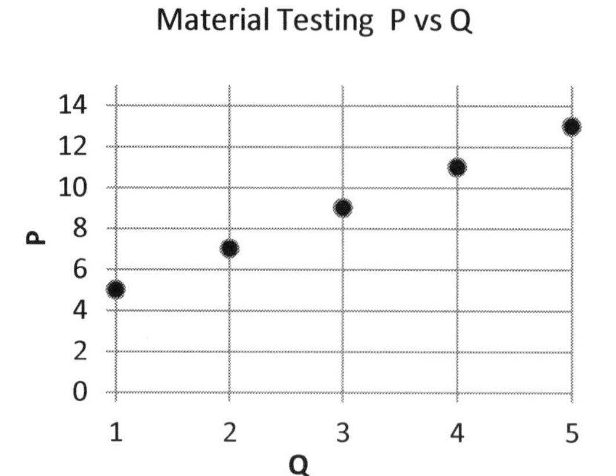

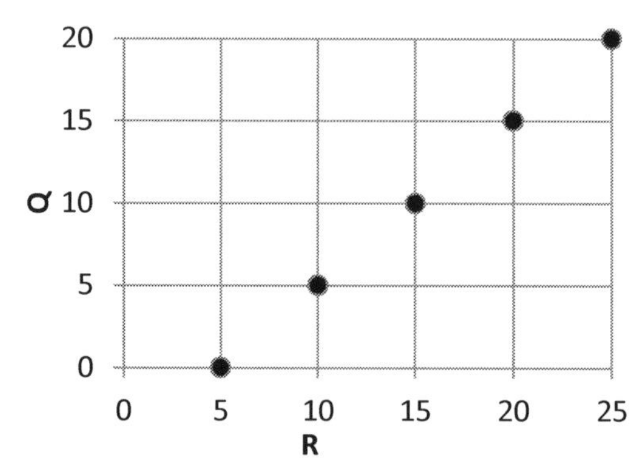

7. A materials engineer is testing three properties P, Q, and R of a new alloy. All of them have the same units of measurement. Scatterplots showing the relation between P and Q and the relation between Q and R are shown above. Which of the following models best describe the relation between P and R?

(A) $\mathrm{P} = 7 - 2\mathrm{R}$

(B) $\mathrm{P} = 2\mathrm{R} - 7$

(C) $\mathrm{P} = \mathrm{R} + 5$

(D) $\mathrm{P} = \mathrm{R} - 5$

8. If the property $\mathrm{Q} = 6$ units, then what is the ratio of R to P?

GRID IN

PROBLEM SOLVING AND DATA ANALYSIS

Lesson 7	Scatterplots	Answers

<table>
<tr><th>#</th><th>Explanation</th><th>Comments</th></tr>
<tr><td>1 C</td><td>List out the score pairs of Abby and Ashley. They are (10,30), (20.40,),(30,20),(40,50),(50,15). From this list it is clear that Ashley won 3 games out of a total of 5 games. So the percentage is $\frac{3}{5} \cdot 100 = 60\%$</td><td>Remember that a scatterplot can be used to compare values of the same type - in this problem it is the scores of two students.</td></tr>
<tr><td>2 C</td><td> 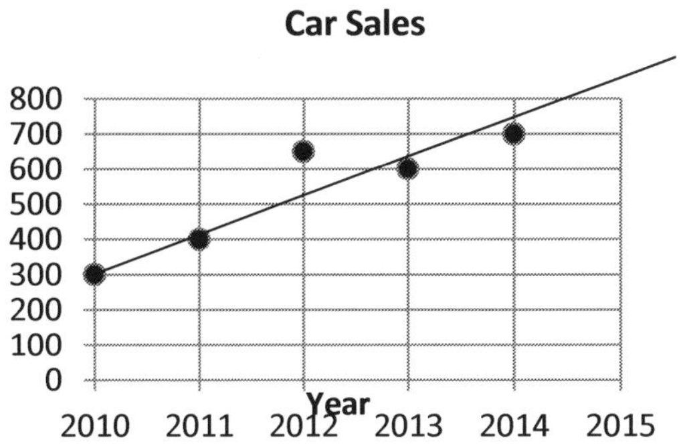Car Sales
800
700
600
500
400
300
200
100
0
2010 2011 2012 2013 2014 2015
Year
Fit a curve connecting the points. Except for 2012 (outlier), you can connect the data using a straight line. In this line, observe that there is an increase in sales of 100 units for every 1 year increment. So, from a car sale of 700 units in 2014, the dealer can expect to sell 100 more cars in 2015. The answer is 700+100=800</td><td>When you fit a line, you may not be able to connect all the points.

It is possible that in some problems, none of the points fall on the line. In that case, draw a line such that it divides the points on either side of the line, as much as possible. You can then find the slope of the line and extrapolate the data.</td></tr>
<tr><td>3 B</td><td>There are a total of 85 respondents (25+20+15+10+10+5+0). A total of 60 survey respondents spend less than 3 hours (0,1 and 2 hours) at the garden (25+20+15). This is more than half the respondents.</td><td></td></tr>
<tr><td>4 D</td><td>The average score is the sum of all scores divided by the number of students. From the scatterplot, you can see that 35 students obtained a score of 55, 25 students got 65 and so on. So, the average is calculated as (35 · 55+25 · 65+25 · 75+10 · 80+ 5 · 85+5 · 90)/105 =67.62</td><td>Note carefully that there are multiple students who have the same scores.</td></tr>
<tr><td>5 C</td><td>When you fit a curve on the data points, it appears that the curve is exponential. To find the function that fits the curve, create a table with x and y points and see if you can find a model or plug in the choices to see which one fits the data. From the scatterplot, you get the following table of values for t and w.
<table><tr><td>t</td><td>0</td><td>1</td><td>2</td><td>3</td><td>4</td></tr><tr><td>W</td><td></td><td></td><td>9</td><td>27</td><td>81</td></tr></table></td><td>The water level at $t = 0$ and $\mathrm{t} = 1$ are not clearly readable but other points are readable.

When the answer choices list the models, apply them against the data.</td></tr>
</table>

<table>
<tr>
<td></td>
<td>Since the curve appears to be exponential , try the exponential choices against the data. When $t = 2,3,$ and 4 you can see that $w = 3^t$. So the model is $w = 3^t$.</td>
<td>Note that the general form of an exponential model/function is $y = ab^x$.</td>
</tr>
<tr>
<td>6 D</td>
<td>After 5 hours, the water level would be $w = 3^5 = 243$ ft.</td>
<td></td>
</tr>
<tr>
<td>7 B</td>
<td>First, find the relationship between P and Q by listing the scatterplot values for P and Q.
<table>
<tr><td>Q</td><td>1</td><td>2</td><td>3</td><td>4</td><td>5</td></tr>
<tr><td>P</td><td>5</td><td>7</td><td>9</td><td>11</td><td>13</td></tr>
</table>
The relation can be expressed as $P = 2Q + 3$.
Now find the relation between Q and R.
<table>
<tr><td>R</td><td>5</td><td>10</td><td>15</td><td>20</td><td>25</td></tr>
<tr><td>Q</td><td>0</td><td>5</td><td>10</td><td>15</td><td>20</td></tr>
</table>
The relation between Q and R is $Q = R - 5$.
The question asks for the relationship between P and R. You have $P = 2Q + 3$ and $Q = R - 5$.
So, $P = 2(R - 5) + 3 = 2R - 10 + 3 = 2R - 7$</td>
<td>Note that you need to extract the models out of the data in the scatterplots and then derive a new model connecting P and R.

When making the table, place the variable in the x axis in the first row and the variable in the y axis in the second row, so that as you visually browse through the values in the x axis, you may get an idea about the model values in the y axis.</td>
</tr>
<tr>
<td>8
0.73</td>
<td>When $Q = 6, R = Q + 5 = 6 + 5 = 11$
$P = 2Q + 3 = 2 \cdot 6 + 3 = 15$
The ratio of R to P $= \frac{11}{15}$.</td>
<td></td>
</tr>
</table>

PROBLEM SOLVING AND DATA ANALYSIS		
Lesson 8	Graphs and Tables	Review

FOCUSPREP CHEKLIST

- What are the different types of graphs?
- What are the different parts of a graph?
- Workout practice problems in Graphs and Tables

Q1 What are the different types of graphs?

A1 Graphs such as Bar Graphs (vertical or horizontal), Line Graphs, Circle Graphs, and Pictographs will appear in the problems. Related data may be presented in tables and in textual descriptions of data.

Q2 What kind of questions are asked in problems with graphs and tables?

A2 You will be asked to calculate percentage increase and decrease, make inferences from data, extrapolate to the next data point, calculate difference between two data points, correlate information from multiple graphs, calculate ratio between two values obtained from the graphs, correlating data in graphs and tables, etc.

Q3 What are the parts of a graph?

A3 Pay careful attention to the different parts of a graph described below. A sample graph is shown.

<u>Title:</u> Title will indicate the subject of the graph – what exactly is being plotted. For example, Rainfall, Rocket Speed, Test Scores, Tiger Population, etc. Sometimes, title will indicate the scale and unit of measure of the numbers – for example Population (millions), Students (thousands), Water Level (ft).

<u>X axis label:</u> The X axis label indicates the data that is plotted on the X axis. The label will indicate the unit of measure. For example, Time (minutes), Speed (miles/hr) etc.

<u>X axis major and minor units:</u> You need to figure this out yourself from the value labels and their increment. Sometimes, you will be required to read a data point that falls between two major units. Minor units, if present, are the ticks between two major unit labels on the X-axis.

<u>Y axis label:</u> The Y axis label indicates the data that is plotted on the Y axis. The label will indicate the unit of measure. For example, Salary (US$), Temperature (Fahrenheit).

<u>Y axis major and minor units:</u> You need to figure this out yourself from value labels and their increment. Sometimes, you will be required to read a data point that falls between two major units on the Y-axis. Minor units, if present, are the ticks between two major unit labels on the Y-axis.

<u>Legend:</u> When more than one data series is shown in the graph, the legend shows the description of the data series and their corresponding markers. Read the legend carefully to identify the marker that corresponds to the relevant data series. Markers are typically shapes like squares, diamonds, circles, etc.

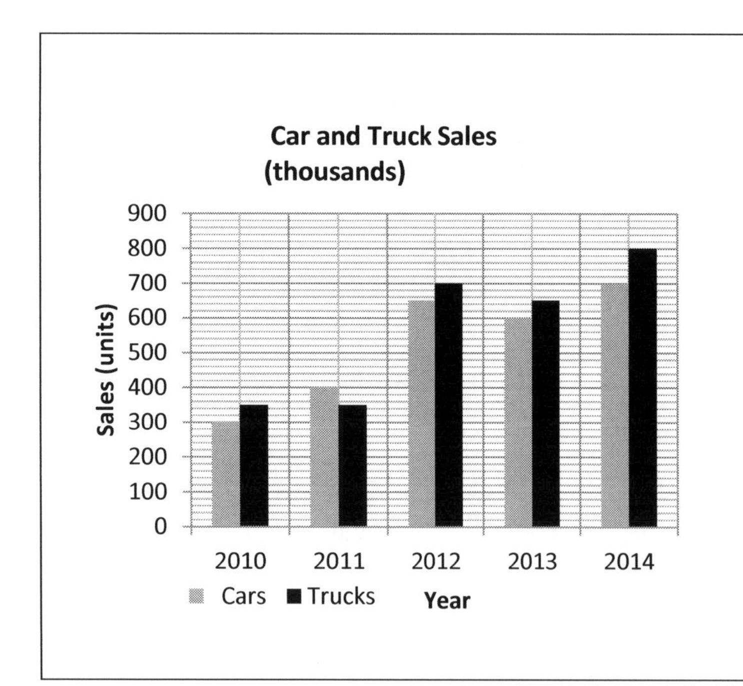	Title: Car and Truck Sales; thousands refers to the scale of the numbers in the Y-axis. For example, the sales of cars in 2010 = 300,000. Read 300 from the graph and multiply by 1000. X-axis label: Year Y-axis label: Sales (units) (in thousands) Legend (shown at bottom): Grey bars indicate Cars and Black bars indicate Trucks Y-axis major unit: 100 units (increment is 100 for every horizontal line) Y-axis minor unit: 100/5=20; the gap between two major unit labels is split into 5 sections by minor grid lines X-axis major unit: 1 year X-axis minor unit: Not relevant for bar graphs

Q4 What are the different graphs used for and how do they look?

A4 Several types of graphs are shown and described below.

Scatterplots are used for identifying the correlation between data. Scatterplots are reviewed in a separate lesson.

Line Graphs are used for showing the progression of a series over time or some other variable.

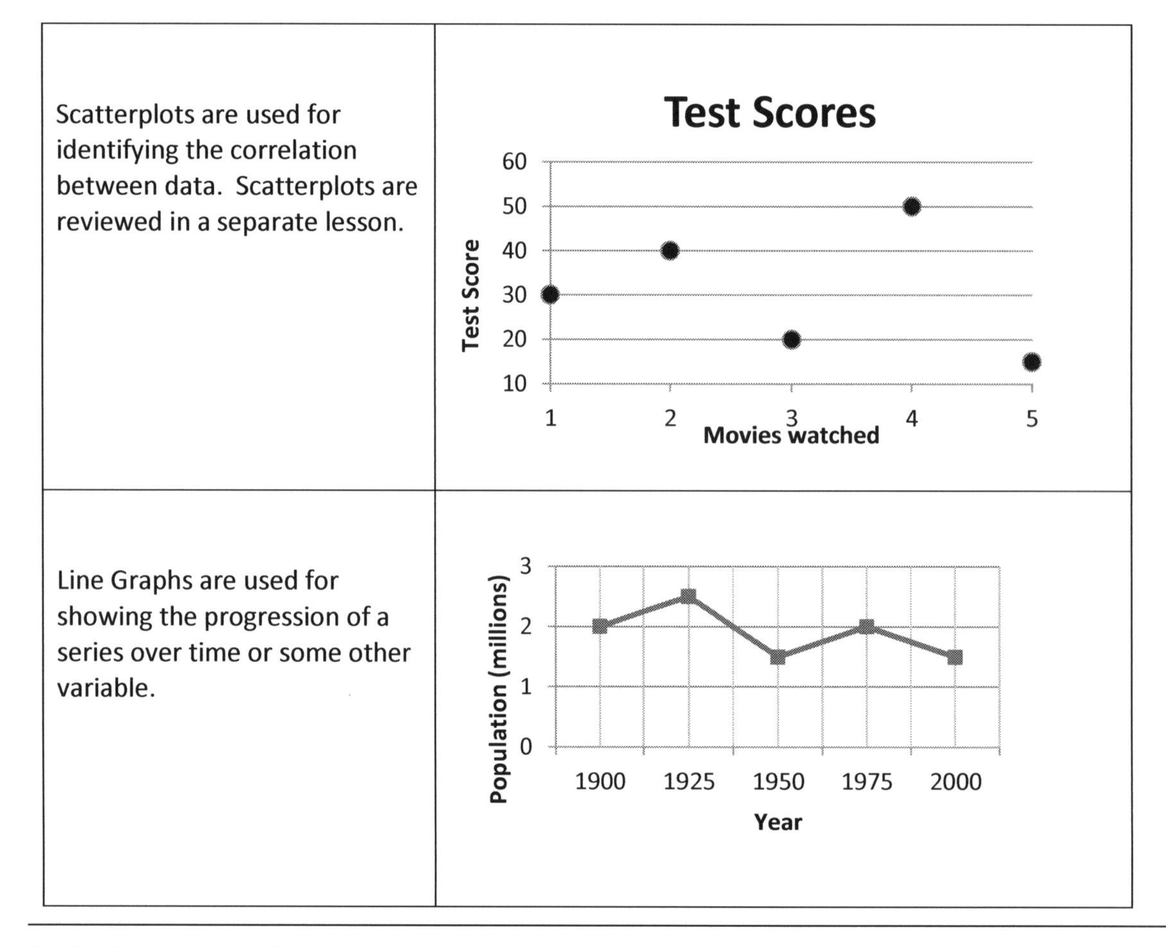

Dotted Line Graphs are used to show the progression of multiple series over time or some other variable.

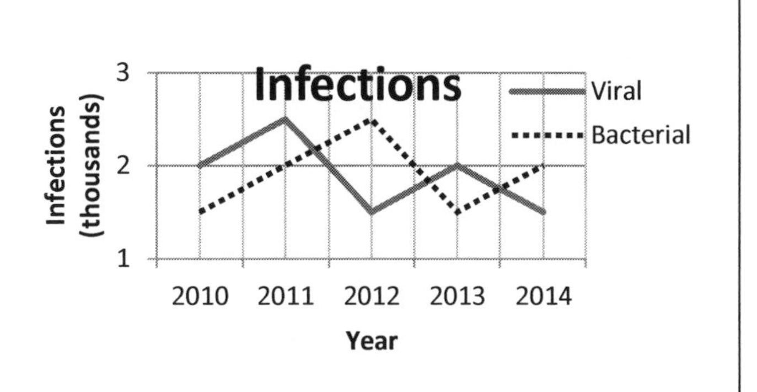

Bar graphs show the data values in bars so that it is easy to visualize the difference in data values. They can appear in horizontal or vertical formats.

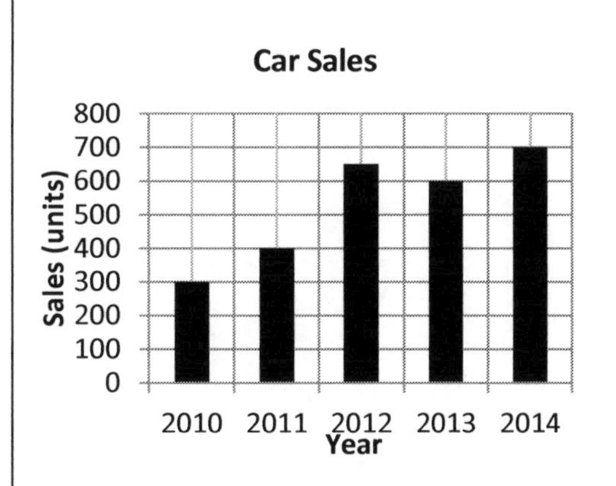

Stacked Bar Graphs are used to show the values of two sets of data on top of each other so that they can be compared using their relative heights.

Pay attention to the legend to identify the correct bar that corresponds to a series. Grey bar indicates Cars and Black bar indicates Trucks.

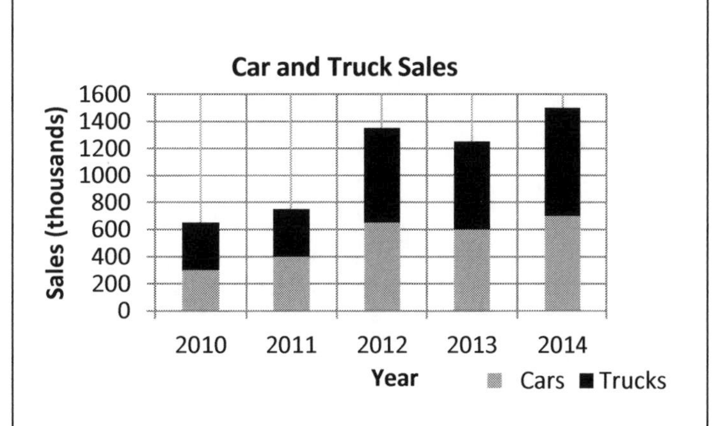

Circle Graphs, also called Pie Graphs or Pie Charts, are used to show the percentage of the parts with respect to the whole.

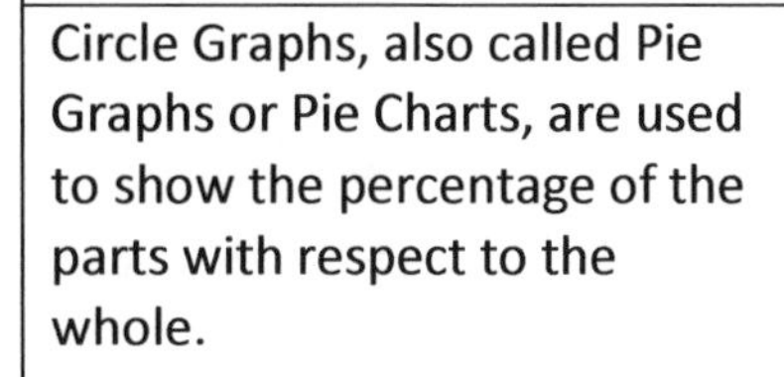

Pictographs represent data using pictures. The legend will indicate the numeric quantity that corresponds to each picture. Half sized pictures may also appear in this graph. You should account for all pictures in the pictograph.

Animal Population in a Farm

Dogs

Cats

Cows

= 40 animals

Tables are used when the data is best represented in rows and columns.

Expense Breakdown by Category				
Category	1st Qtr	2nd Qtr	3rd Qtr	4th Qtr
Salary	30%	25%	25%	25%
Materials	60%	65%	70%	40%
Legal	10%	10%	5%	35%

Histograms are bar graphs showing the distribution of data. In the histogram shown, the x-axis shows the cars owned and the y-axis shows the frequency. 10 people did not own a car, 70 people owned 2 cars, nobody owned 5 cars and 20 people owned 6 cars. There are 175 data points – so the median is the 88th data point – which is 2 cars. The mean of the distribution is

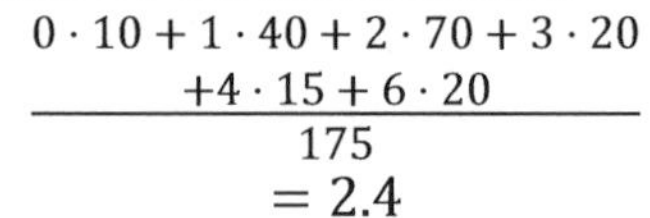

$$\frac{0\cdot 10+1\cdot 40+2\cdot 70+3\cdot 20+4\cdot 15+6\cdot 20}{175}=2.4$$

Frequency: 0, 10, 20, 30, 40, 50, 60, 70, 80

Cars Owned: 0, 1, 2, 3, 4, 5, 6

Histograms can also show the frequency of **grouped data**. The groupings are called buckets or bins. This histogram shows the cumulative frequency of 4 groups of car ownership. From this histogram, you cannot tell how many people owned 2 cars only or 3 cars only, but you can tell that a total of 90 people own either 2 cars or 3 cars. You cannot calculate the mean but you can tell that the median could be either 2 or 3 depending on the value of the 88th data point (175/2=87.5).

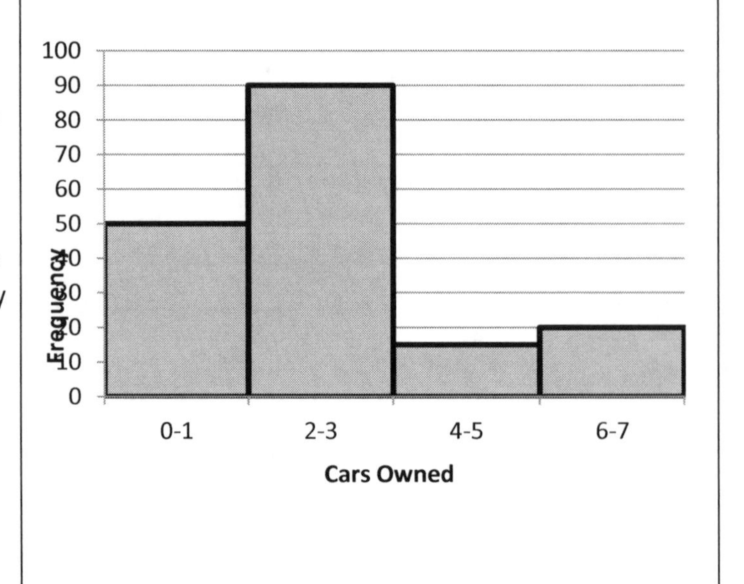

PROBLEM SOLVING AND DATA ANALYSIS		
Lesson 8	Graphs and Tables	Practice

CALCULATOR SECTION

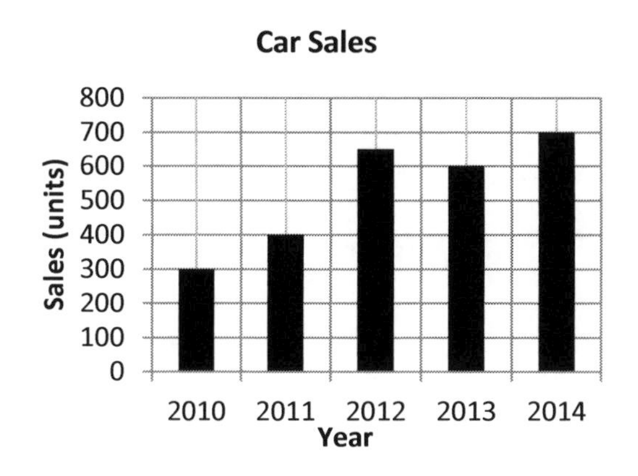

Questions 1 and 2

1. The graph above shows the car sales at a dealership. Between which two years did the car sales increase the most percentage?
(A) 2010-2011
(B) 2011-2012
(C) 2012-2013
(D) 2013-2014

2. How much more or less is the percentage increase from 2013 to 2014 when compared to the percentage increase from 2010 to 2011?
(A) 12.67%
(B) 14.67%
(C) 16.67%
(D) 33.33%

CALCULATOR SECTION

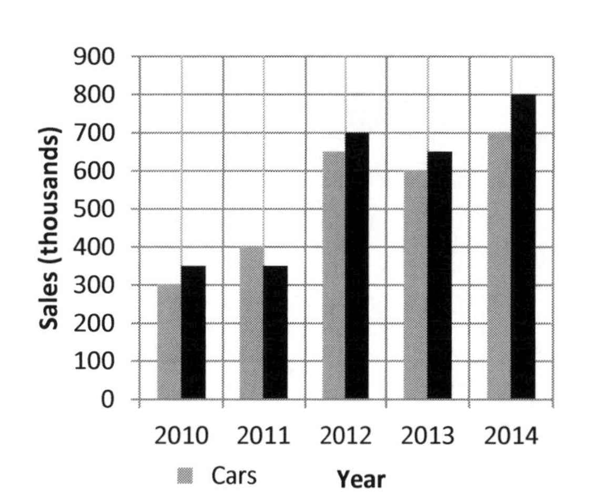

Questions 3 and 4

3. The graph above shows the car and truck sales at a dealership. From 2010 to 2014 what is the approximate ratio of total cars sold to total trucks sold?
(A) 0.65
(B) 0.93
(C) 1.08
(D) 1.80

4. In which year did the sales of trucks exceed the sales of cars the most?
(A) 2010
(B) 2011
(C) 2012
(D) 2014

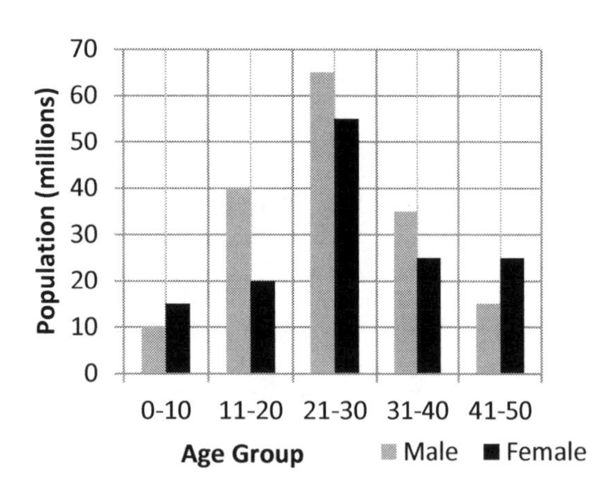

Questions 5 and 6

5. The bar graph above shows the population of different age groups in Space City. In which age group is the difference between male and female population the least?
(A) 0-10
(B) 21-30
(C) 31-40
(D) 41-50

6. How much more is the population of the 31-40 age group compared to the population of the 41-50 age group, in millions?
(A) 10
(B) 20
(C) 30
(D) 40

CALCULATOR SECTION

Age	Male	Female
0-10	10	15
11-20	40	20
21-30	65	55
31-40	35	25
41-50	15	15

7. The table above shows the male and female animal population in a zoo. Which of the following graphs describes the data accurately?
A)

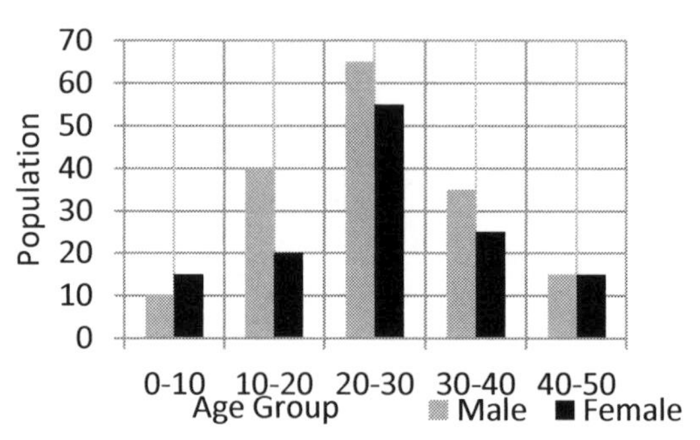

B)

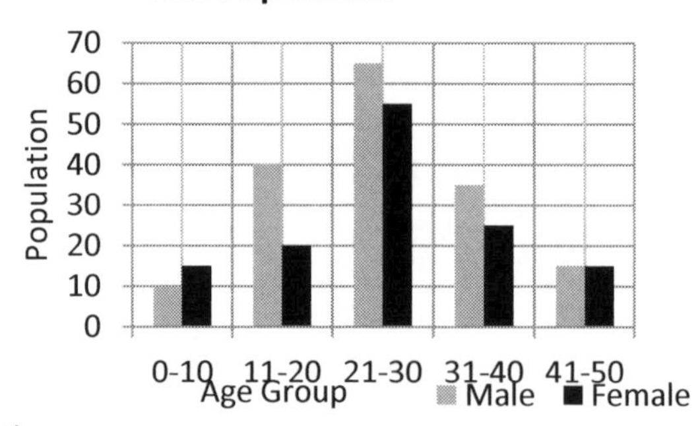

C)

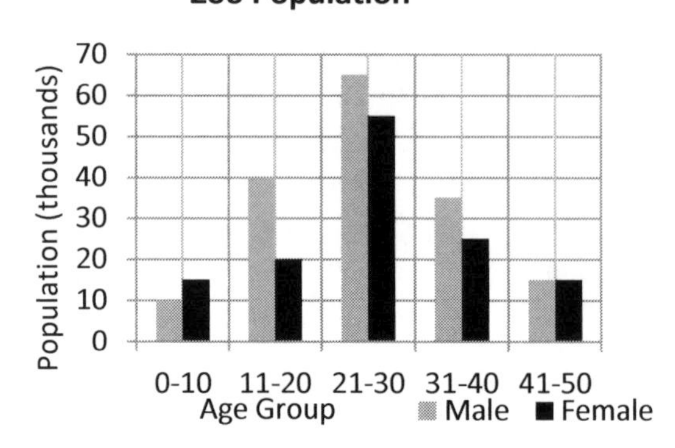

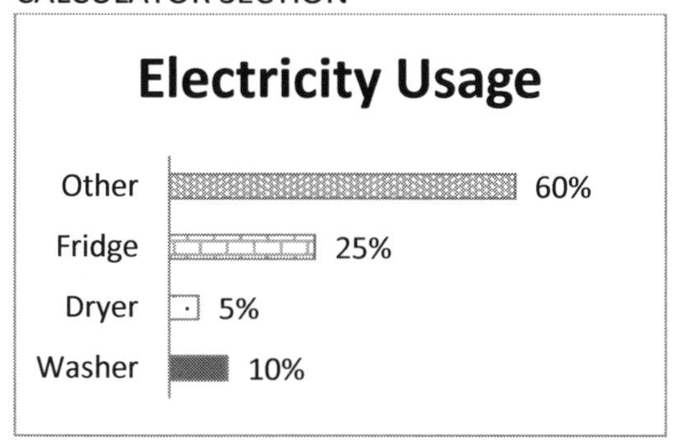

8. Electricity consumption at the McDonald household is shown above. Which of the following circle graphs most accurately depicts the data above?

(A)

(B)

(C)

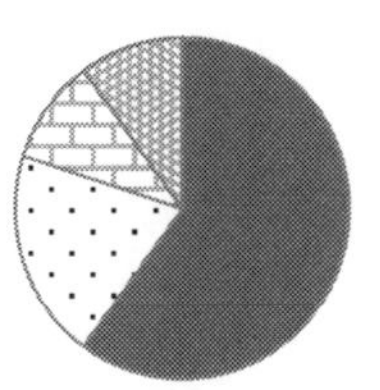

(D)

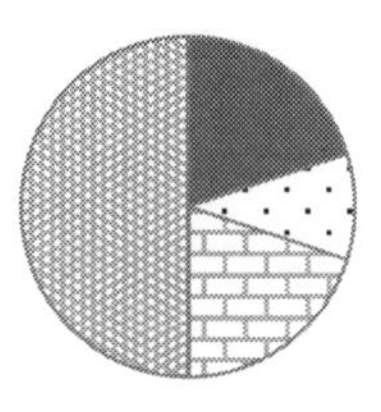

CALCULATOR SECTION

9 MORGANTOWN POPULATION DATA

Age	Male	Female
0-25	3000	4000
25-50	5800	6200
50-75	800	1200

Questions 9 and 10.

9. The table above shows the population breakdown of Morgantown. What is the ratio of male population to female population in the 25-75 age group?
GRID IN

10. How many more people are there in the 25 to 50 age group than there are in the other age groups combined?
(A) 2000
(B) 3000
(C) 6000
(D) 7000

VOLCANO HIGH SCHOOL			
	Score 0-50	Score 51-100	Total
Boys		40	
Girls	30		
Total		120	200

Questions 11 and 12

11. The table above shows partial information about the scores of boys and girls in a History test. How many boys scored in the 0-50 range?
(A) 30
(B) 40
(C) 50
(D) 120

12. What is the ratio of boys to girls at Volcano High School?
(A) 0.60
(B) 0.82
(C) 0.92
(D) 1.22

CALCULATOR SECTION

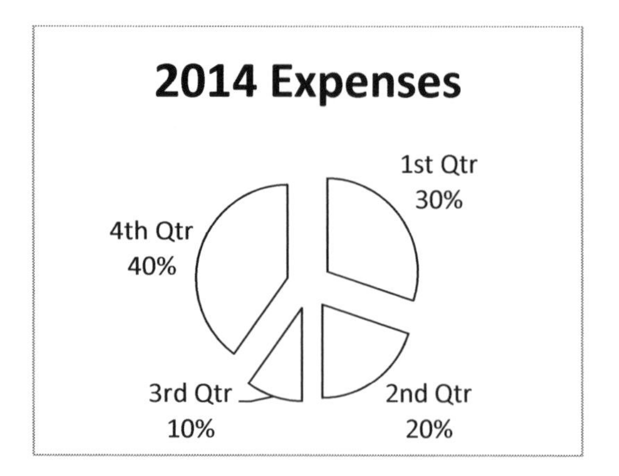

An expense of $20 million in four quarters of 2014 for a cellphone manufacturing company is shown above. A further breakdown of each quarter is shown below.

Expense Breakdown by Category				
	1st Qtr	2nd Qtr	3rd Qtr	4th Qtr
Salary	30%	25%	25%	25%
Materials	60%	65%	70%	40%
Legal	10%	10%	`5%	35%

13. How much expense did the cell phone company incur in 2014 for materials only?
(A) 2 million
(B) 4 million
(C) 10.8 million
(D) 12.8 million

14. What amount, expressed in millions was spent for paying employee salary in the 3rd quarter?

GRID IN

Restaurant Bill

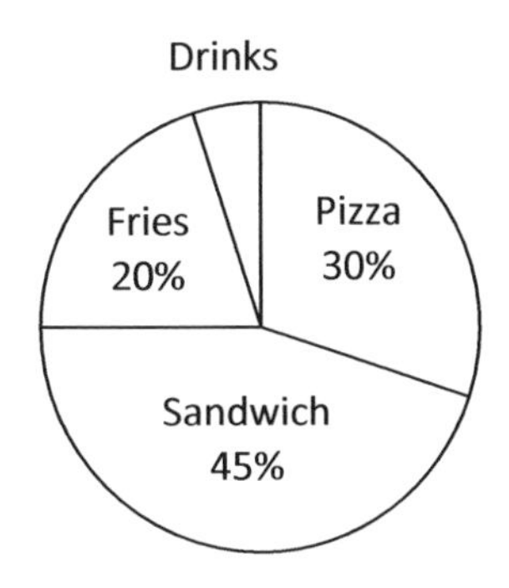

15. A restaurant bill is split up as shown above. If \$12 was spent on Pizza, how many dollars was spent on Drinks?
GRID IN

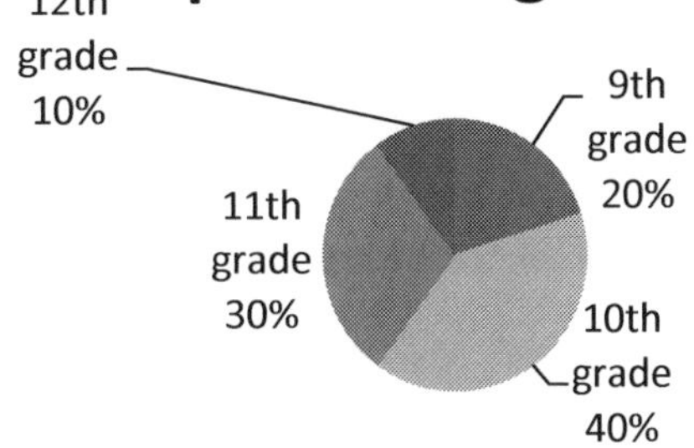

16. The students in four grades in the TopTalent High School are shown above. If the difference between the total number of students in 11th and 12th grades and the total number of students in the 9th and 10th grades is 100, how many students are there at the school?
(A) 100
(B) 200
(C) 300
(D) 500

CALCULATOR SECTION

Alicia's Portfolio

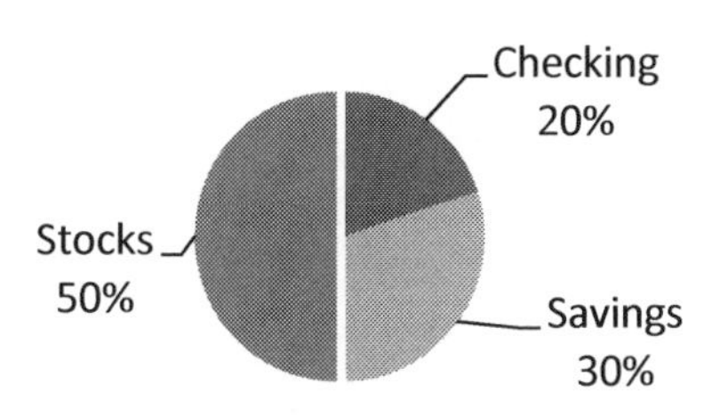

17. Alicia's portfolio of \$500,000 is shown above. If she reduces her Stocks to 20% and deposits the amount in her savings account, what percent of her portfolio now will be in Savings?
(A) 50
(B) 60
(C) 70
(D) 90

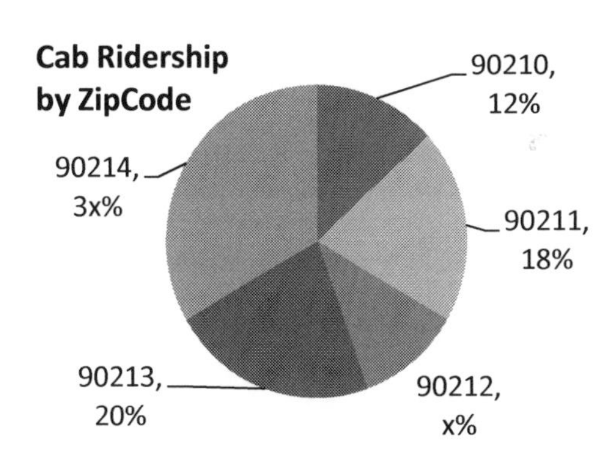

18. A cab company's ridership in various zip codes is shown above. If the total ridership is 3000, what is the ridership in zip code 90214?
(A) 1125
(B) 1375
(C) 1750
(D) 2025

CALCULATOR SECTION

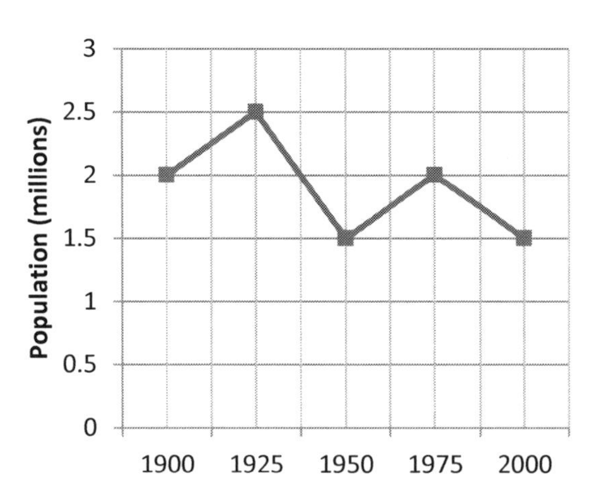

Population of Pearl City

Questions 19 and 20

19. The percentage decrease in population from 1925 to 1950 is more than the percentage decrease from 1900 to 2000 by what percent?
(A) 10
(B) 15
(C) 25
(D) 40

20. From 2000 to 2014, the population increased at the same percentage as the population decrease from 1925 to 1950. What is the population in millions in 2014?
(A) 2.1
(B) 1.2
(C) 1,500,000
(D) 2,100,000

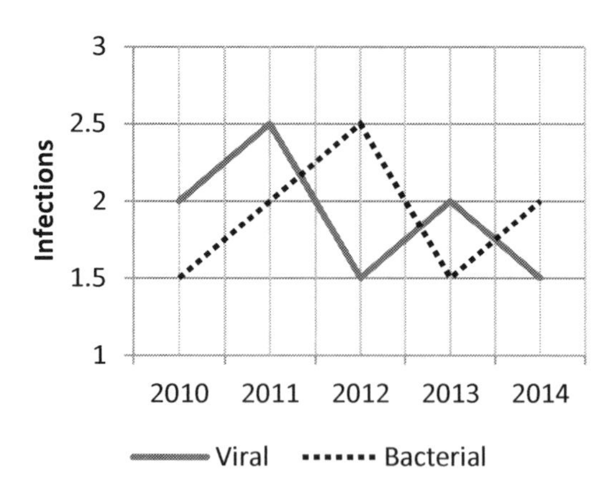

Viral vs. Bacterial Infections in Danger County – thousands

21. The set of numbers that indicates the infections at the three points in time when they were the same is which one of the following?
(A) 2.2, 1.8, 1.8
(B) 2200, 1800, 1700
(C) 1500, 2500, 1500
(D) 1.5,2.5,1.5

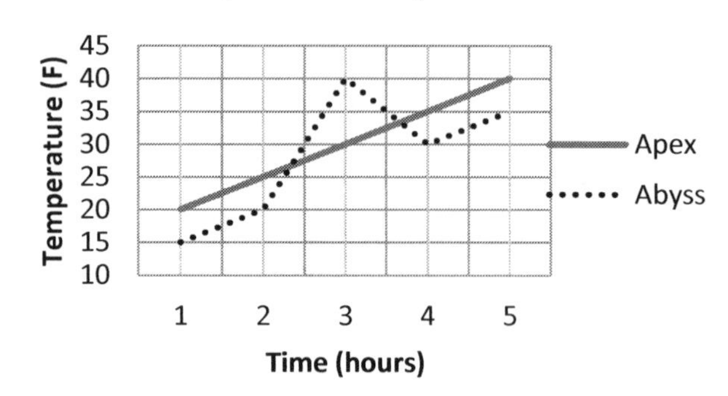

22. The temperature readings for five hours in two cities are shown above. What is the ratio of difference in maximum and minimum temperatures of Apex to Abyss?
(A) 0.1
(B) 0.5
(C) 0.7
(D) 0.8

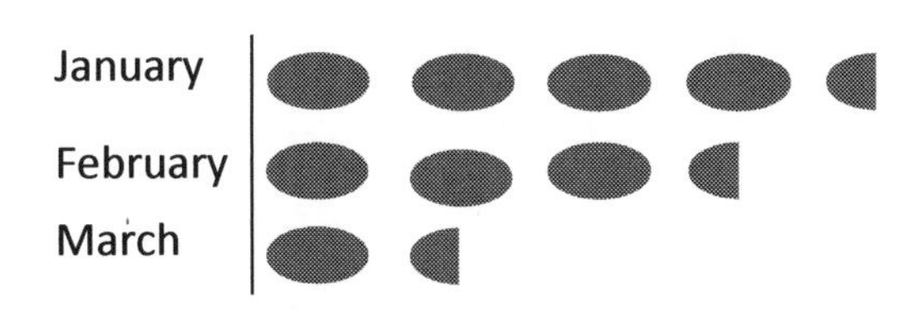

= 10,000 tiles

23. The production of tiles in a company for three months is shown above. How many more tiles must be made during the rest of the year to reach a target of 100,000 tiles?

(A) 5,000
(B) 10,000
(C) 15,000
(D) None of the above

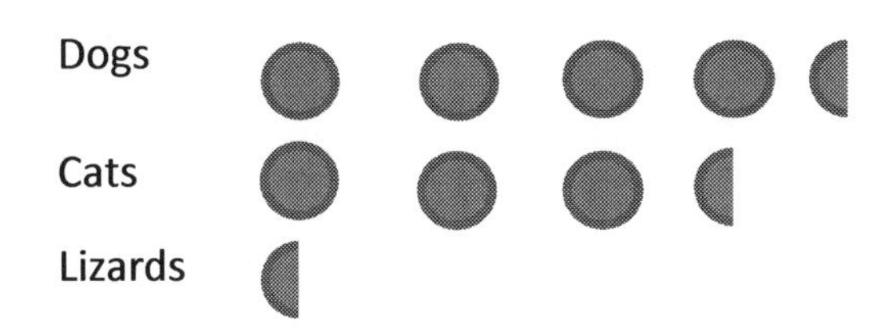

= 40 animals

24. The number of dogs, cats, and lizards in a pet shop is shown above. What is the ratio of cats to dogs to lizards?

(A) 9:7:2
(B) 7:9:1
(C) 2:7:9
(D) 7:2:9

CALCULATOR SECTION

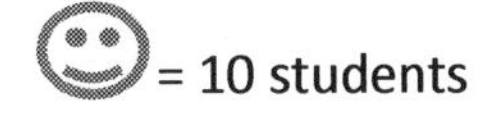
= 10 students

25. The pictograph above shows the number of students advised by two professors for their PhD thesis. If twenty students of professor A switch to professor B, which one of the following pictographs will accurately describe the switch?

A)

B)

C)

D)

PROBLEM SOLVING AND DATA ANALYSIS		
Lesson 8	Graphs and Tables	Answers

#	Explanation	Comments
1 B	There is an increase in car sales between 2010-2011, 2011-2012 and 2013-2014. Calculate the increase in sales for these three years. 2010-2011 400-300/300 · 100 = 33.33% 2011-2012 650-400/400 · 100 = 62.50% 2013-2014 700-600/600 · 100 = 16.66% So, the car sales increased the most in 2011-2012.	Review the lesson on percentages. Note carefully that the question asks for percentage increase. This is different from asking "between which two years did the car sales increase the most?" – in which case you have to only calculate the sales numbers but not the percentage.
2 C	Note that the question asks "how much more or less". Based on our calculation, you see that the percentage increase for 2013-2014 is less than the percentage increase for 2010-2011 by $16.66 - 33.33 = -16.67$. The negative sign is accounted for when the question asks "more or less".	
3 B	Total number of cars sold= 300+400+650+600+700 =2650 Total number of trucks sold= 350+350+700+650+800 =2850 The ratio of cars to trucks = $\frac{2650}{2850} = 0.93$	Numbers between the major units must be carefully read.
4 D	Looking at the bar graphs, it is clear that in 2010, 2012, and 2014, the sales of trucks exceeded cars. In 2010, trucks-cars= 350-300=50 In 2012, trucks-cars= 700-650=50 In 2014, trucks-cars= 800-700=100 So, in 2014, the number of trucks sold exceeded the cars the most.	
5 A	Look at the age groups to see where the difference might be the least. Age group 11-20 has a large difference and so it is not going to have the least difference. For age groups 0-10, 21-30 and 41-50, the difference seems to be the same. For age groups 0-10, the difference is 15-10=5 For age groups 21-30, the difference is 65-55=10 For age groups 31-40, the difference is 35-25=10 For age groups 4-50, the difference is 25-15=10 So the difference is the least in age group 0-10.	
6 B	Population of 31-40 age group = 35+25=60 Population of 41-50 age group = 15+25=40 The difference=60-40=20.	Remember to add both male and female populations.
7 B	Pay careful attention to the axes labels. Choice A has the data values from the table plotted correctly in the bar graph but the x axis data points are 0-10, 10-20, etc. – this is	This problem correlates a table and a graph.

<table>
<tr><td></td><td>incorrect; the correct axis data points must be 0-10, 11-20, 21-30 and so on. Choice B has the correct axis values and title. Choice C is incorrect because the Y axis says Population (thousands) whereas the table does not indicate that the values are in thousands.</td><td></td></tr>
<tr><td>8 A</td><td>You need to answer this question by carefully looking at the data label, values, and the shading pattern for the data point. Note that the question is presented as a bar graph but the answers are in circle graphs. "Other" is the largest data point with 60%, whereas Dryer is the least with 5%. 60% must translate to more than half the circle in the circle graph. Choices A and B have the shaded portion corresponding to 'other' drawn with a little more than 50%. Within choices A and B, look for the one with Dryer being smaller than the Washer. This indicates that the correct choice is A.</td><td>Note that each of the bars has a pattern – this pattern must be represented in the circle graphs. Choice C has 60% represented by a dark-shade pattern but the dark-shade pattern corresponds to a Washer in the bar graph which is only 10%.

Both percentages and shades must match when representing bar graphs as circle graphs.</td></tr>
<tr><td>9
0.89</td><td>Male population in the 25-75 age group = 5800+800=6600
Female population in the 25-75 age group =6200+1200=7400
The ratio = 6600/7400=0.89</td><td></td></tr>
<tr><td>10 B</td><td>Population in the 25-50 age group = 5800+6200 =12000
"other age groups combined" – indicates age groups 0-25 and 50-75.
Population in the 0-25 age group = 3000+4000 =7000
Population in the 50-75 age group = 800+1200=2000
Population in the 0-25 and 50-75 age groups = 7000+2000=9000
So, there are 12000-9000=3000 more people in the 25-50 age group than in the other groups combined.</td><td>Pay close attention to the age groups that you are comparing.</td></tr>
<tr><td>11 C</td><td>You need to look at the totals and work backwards.
There are 200 students in total. 120 of them scored in the 51-100 range. So 200-120=80 students scored in the 0-50 range. Of these, 30 students are girls. So, 80-30=50 are boys in the 0-50 score range.</td><td>Familiarize yourself with problems where you to work backwards starting with the totals.</td></tr>
<tr><td>12 B</td><td>You need to find the number of girls. You know that there are 200 students and 90 boys (from previous problem). So 200-90=110 are girls. So the ratio of boys to girls is 90/110 =0.82
<table>
<tr><th colspan="4">VOLCANO HIGH SCHOOL</th></tr>
<tr><td></td><td>Score 0-50</td><td>Score 51-100</td><td>Total</td></tr>
<tr><td>Boys</td><td>50</td><td>40</td><td>90</td></tr>
<tr><td>Girls</td><td>30</td><td></td><td>110</td></tr>
<tr><td>Total</td><td>80</td><td>120</td><td>200</td></tr>
</table></td><td></td></tr>
</table>

13 C	Note that you need to find the material expenses for 2014, which means for all four quarters. Carefully note that the table gives the material expense percentages for each of the four quarters, but this percentage is quarter specific. For example, 60% of 1st quarter expense was spent on materials, but the first quarter expense itself is obtained from the circle graph – 30% of 20 million. So, the total material expense is calculated by adding up the material expense for each of the 4 quarters. 1st quarter material expense = $\frac{60}{100} \cdot \frac{30}{100} \cdot 20 = 3.6$ million 2nd quarter material expense = $\frac{65}{100} \cdot \frac{20}{100} \cdot 20 = 2.6$ million 3rd quarter material expense = $\frac{70}{100} \cdot \frac{10}{100} \cdot 20 = 1.4$ million 4th quarter material expense = $\frac{40}{100} \cdot \frac{40}{100} \cdot 20 = 3.2$ million So the total is $3.6 + 2.6 + 1.4 + 3.2 = 10.8$ million	Circle graph and Table are correlated/linked in this problem.
14 0.5	From the table, the salary for 3rd quarter is 25% of expenses of 3rd quarter. From the circle graph, the expense for 3rd quarter is 10% of total expense of $20 million. $\frac{25}{100} \cdot \frac{10}{100} \cdot 20 = 0.5$ million	
15 2	Note that the percentage of Drinks portion is not indicated in the graph. Let the total bill be x. Pizza is 30% of the total bill. $12 was spent on pizza. So, Pizza=12=$\frac{30}{100} \cdot x$ $x = \frac{1200}{30} = 40$ = total bill. The circle graph does not indicate what percentage is Drinks. Since the total percentage must be 100%, Drinks makes up $100 - (30 + 20 + 45) = 5\%$ of the total bill. So $\frac{5}{100} \cdot 40 = 2$.	Read the question carefully – how much was spent on drinks is different from what percentage was spent on drinks. This question does not ask for pizza percentage.
16 D	Let the total number of students be x. Total number of students in 11th and 12th grades = $0.3x + 0.1x = 0.4x$ Total number of students in 9th and 10th grades = $0.2x + 0.4x = 0.6x$ Difference = 100. $0.6x - 0.4x = 100$ $0.2x = 100$ $x = \frac{100}{0.2} = 500$	
17 B	Note that Alicia has 50% of her portfolio in stocks but she reduces her stocks to 20%, This means she sells 30%. So, $\frac{30}{100} \cdot 500{,}000 = 150{,}000$ and this amount is deposited in the saving account. Savings account before this deposit was 30% =$\frac{30}{100} \cdot 500000 = 150{,}000$. Now with the additional deposit, savings account = $150{,}000 + 150{,}000 = 300{,}000$. This new savings total is $\frac{300{,}000}{500{,}000} \cdot 100 = 60\%$ of her portfolio	A person's financial portfolio is a list of accounts where money is saved – checking accounts, saving accounts, stocks, bonds, etc.

18 A	Note that the cab ridership in zip code 90212 is $x\%$ and in zip code 90214 is $3x\%$. The total ridership is 3000. The percentages must add up to 100. $12 + 18 + 20 + x + 3x = 100$ $4x = 50;\ x = 12.5$ In zip code 90214, the ridership share= $3x = 3 \cdot 12.5\% = \frac{37.5}{100} \cdot 3000 = 1125$	
19 B	Population in 1925 is 2.5 (million) and Population in 1950 is 1.5 (million). Percentage decrease = $\frac{1.5-2.5}{2.5} \cdot 100 = 40\%$ Population in 1900 is 2 (million) and Population in 2000=1.5 (million). Percentage decrease = $\frac{1.5-2}{2} \cdot 100 = 25\%$ So, the answer to this question is 40-25=15%	In this question, you have to calculate 2 percentages and then find the difference of these percentages.
20 A	Note that the question talks about 2000-2014 – this is not in the graph. The population decrease from 1925 to 1950=$\frac{1.5-2.5}{2.5} \cdot 100 = 40\%$. From 2000 to 2014, the population increased at 40%. So the population in 2014= $1.5 + \frac{40}{100} \cdot 1.5 = 2.1$ million Note that the question asks for the population in millions. So, the answer is 2.1, not 2,100,000.	Be alert to questions that extrapolate data to points that are not shown in the graph.
21 B	Read the question carefully. It asks for the set of numbers that indicates the actual number of infections. It does not ask for the answer in thousands. When the viral and bacterial infections were the same, the infections were 2.2, 1.8 and 1.7, in thousands. So, the actual number of infections is $2.2 \cdot 1000, 1.8 \cdot 1000, 1.7 \cdot 1000$ respectively. $(2200,1800,1700)$ is the answer.	
22 D	For Apex city, the maximum temperature is 40 and the minimum is 20. For Abyss city, the maximum temperature is 40 and the minimum is 15. So the ratio of the difference in temperature in Apex to that in Abyss = $\frac{40-20}{40-15} = 0.8$	
23 A	Note that the pictograph's legend indicates that one picture represents 10,000 tiles. Note also that there are half tiles as well. Each half tile represents 5000 tiles. Totally there are 9.5 tiles. $9.5 \cdot 10000 = 95{,}000$ tiles. To reach a target of 100,000 tiles, it must make 100,000-95,000=5000 tiles	
24 B	Dogs= 4.5·40=180; Cats=3.5·40=140; Lizards=0.5·40=20 Cats:Dogs:Lizard = 140:180:20 This ratio can be simplified as 7:9:1 by dividing them by 20. Note that the ratio calls for cats to be the first item in the ratio.	Pay attention to the order of items in the ratio.
25 C	When 20 students switch from professor A to professor B, professor A will have 50-20=30 students and professor B will	Read the legend to figure out how many students correspond

	have 40+20=60 students. Since each picture represents 10 students, now the students will be represented by 3 pictures for professor A and 6 pictures for professor B.	to one picture in the pictograph.

PROBLEM SOLVING AND DATA ANALYSIS		
Lesson 9	Growth and Decay	Review

FOCUSPREP CHECKLIST

- How are linear growth and linear decay modeled?
- How are exponential growth and an exponential decay modeled?
- Workout practice problems in Growth and Decay

Q1 What does Linear Growth and Linear Decay mean?

A1 Linear growth is increase and linear decay is decrease at the same rate from one time period to another. When plotted, the linear growth is a straight line with a positive slope and a linear decay is a straight line with negative slope.

For example, if a reservoir gets rain at a constant rate, then its level will grow linearly with a positive slope as shown. On the other hand if the reservoir is drained at a constant rate, it will decay(decrease) linearly with a negative slope as shown.

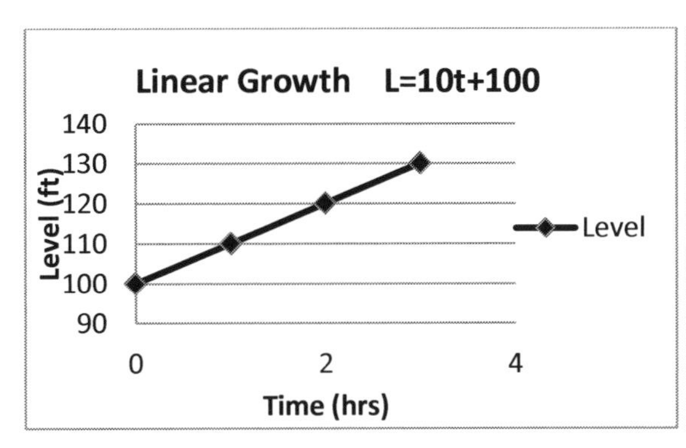

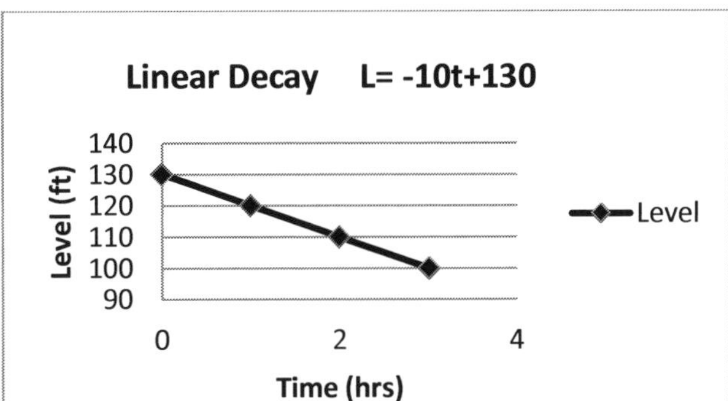

Q2 How are linear growth and decay modeled?

A2 Linear growth and decay are modeled using a linear equation of the type $y = mx + b$ where y is the dependent variable, x is the independent variable, m is the slope, and b is the y intercept.

Q3 How is a linear model developed from scratch?

A3 Depending on whether the data is in a table or graph, follow the steps below to create a linear model.

Step 1:
If the data is in a scatterplot graph, draw a line of best fit that connects the points as much as possible. Sometimes, points may be above or below the line of best fit. If the data is in a table, you do not need to draw a scatterplot. Proceed to step 2.

Step 2: Pick two data points $(x_1, y_1), (x_2, y_2)$ from the table or the graph, and calculate the slope m using $\frac{y_2 - y_1}{x_2 - x_1}$.

Step 3: If the data is in a graph, find the y-intercept (b) from the graph and then use the slope intercept formula $y = mx + b$ to create the linear model. Verify the model for different values of x.

If the data is in a table, use the point slope formula $y - y_1 = m(x - x_1)$ to develop the linear model. Some examples of linear models are: $y = 2x$, $y = 4.5x + 3.25$, $y = -8.92x + 1000$. Verify the model for different values of x.

Q4 What does correlation coefficient mean?

A4 Correlation coefficient r indicates how well the line fits the data. It can take a value from -1 to 1. ($-1 \le r \le 1$). $r = 0$ indicates no fit, $r = 1$ indicates perfect fit with positive slope, and $r = -1$ indicates perfect fit with negative slope. If the slope is positive, r is positive, and if the slope is negative, r is negative.

Q5 After developing the linear model, how do I use it?

A5 After a linear model of the form $y = mx + b$ is developed , it is used for making **predictions** for future values. In the following two examples, you will develop a linear model from a table and a graph. The process is slightly different in each case.

Example: The water level in a reservoir increases every hour as shown. Develop a linear model that fits the data. What will be the water level in the reservoir at 15 hrs? When will the water level be 420 ft?

Time (hr)	0	1	2	3
Level (ft)	100	110	120	130

Solution: Note that the problem asks you to develop a linear model. So you can start off by assuming that the model will be of the form $y = mx + b$ and go on to find m and b.

Calculate the slope using any two data points:

Using $(x_1, y_1) = (1{,}110)$ and $(x_2, y_2) = (2{,}120)$, $m = \frac{y_2 - y_1}{x_2 - x_1} = \frac{120-110}{2-1} = 10$

Use the point slope formula to develop the linear model. Pick any point say $(x_1, y_1) = (3{,}130)$. $y - y_1 = m(x - x_1)$. So, $y - 130 = 10(x - 3)$. Simplifying, you get the linear model: $y = 10x + 100$. Verify the model for different values of x. When $x = 2, y = 10 \cdot 2 + 100 = 120$.

Using this model $y = 10x + 100$, where y is the level of reservoir and x is the time in hours, you can calculate the water level in the reservoir at $t = 15\ hrs$. $y = 10(15) + 100 = 250$ ft.

Using this model, you can also, predict when the water level in the reservoir will reach 420 feet. Substitute 420 into the model.

$420 = 10x + 100$. $x = \frac{320}{10} = 32$ hours. The water level will be 420 feet after 32 hours.

Example The same problem discussed above is given in the form of a scatterplot graph. Find the linear model.

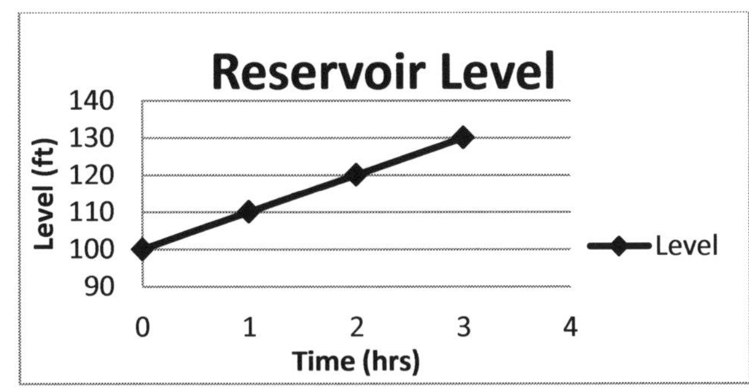

Solution: Step 1: Draw a line of best fit through the points. In this case, the line passes through all the points. In problems where all the data points do not fall on a line, draw a line that connects as many points as possible. A line of best fit may also approximately divide the points such that about half of them are above and half of them are below the line.

Step 2: Pick two points and find the slope. $(x_1, y_1) = (1{,}110)$, $(x_2, y_2) = (2{,}120)$. So the slope $m = \frac{y_2 - y_1}{x_2 - x_1} = \frac{120-110}{2-1} = 10$.

Step 3: Read the y-intercept= $b = 100$. So, the linear model = $y = mx + b = 10x + 100$. Verify the model. For $x = 3$, $y = 10 \cdot 3 + 100 = 130$. This point falls in the line. So, in both examples, the same model is obtained.

Q6 What does Exponential growth mean?

A6 Exponential growth or decay is much quicker than linear growth or linear decay. For example if something doubles or triples in value from one time period to another, then this growth is much faster than linear growth. Certain things (such that the value of a car) can decrease (decay) exponentially. When plotted, the exponential growth is a curve. Bacteria is famous for growing exponentially – for every time period, it will double in quantity over the previous time period.

Q7 How do I model exponential growth or decay?

A7 Exponential growth or decay are modeled as $y = a \cdot b^x$

When $a > 0 \; and \; b > 1$ it is Exponential growth model

When $a > 0 \; and \; 0 < b < 1$ it is Exponential decay model

When $a = 1, b = 2$, the model becomes $y = 2^x$; A table that shows the values of this model is shown below. The value of y doubles over its previous value. Compare this with linear model $y = 2x$ where the values of y do not double over their previous values. Also, note carefully the graphs of linear and exponential functions. A table and a graph of an exponential decay model is also shown.

Linear Growth $y = 2x$				
x	0	1	2	3
y	0	2	4	6

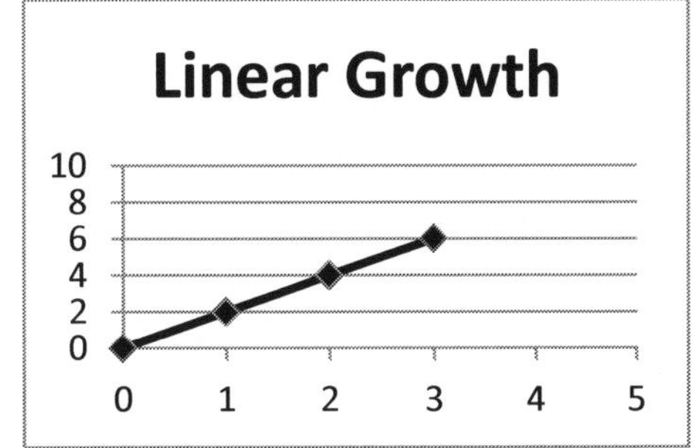

Exponential Growth $y = 2^x$					
x	0	1	2	3	
y	1	2	4	8	

Exponential Decay $y = 0.5^x$					
x	0	1	2	3	
y	1	0.5	0.25	0.125	

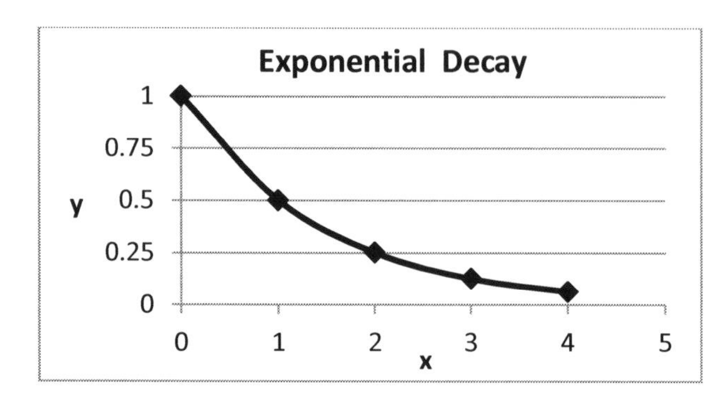

Q8 Apart from $y = 2^x$ are there other exponential models?

A8 While $y = 2^x$ is a popular exponential growth model, there are other exponential growth models and exponential decay models that are different.

Recall that the general form of an exponential model is $y = ab^x$. In this model, b is the base and x is the exponent. b can take on any value greater than zero other than 1. For example, when $b = 3$, you have $y = 3^x$, when $b = 4$, $y = 4^x$ and these are exponential growth models too. Similarly, when $b < 1$, say when $b = 0.8$, $y = 0.8^x$ – this is an example of an exponential decay model.

Q9 In exponential models, is b always given?

A9 Not necessarily – you will have to calculate b sometimes and it is easy to do so.

Example

The value of some antique furniture grows at the rate of 18% every year. What is an exponential model that will model this growth?

Answer

At the beginning, assume that the value of the furniture is P dollars.

After 1 year, the value would be P + $\frac{18}{100}$ · P = 1.18 P

After 2 years, the value would be 1.18P + $\frac{18}{100}$ · 1.18 P = 1.18·P(1+0.18) = P · 1.18^2

After n years, the value would be P · 1.18^n. This is the model that describes the growth in value of the antique furniture. This is an exponential model too, since it is of the form $y = a \cdot b^x$.

Note that the general formula for an exponential model, y= ab^x can be expanded to include more details about calculating b (in cases where b is not given explicitly) as follows:

$y = a(1 \pm r)^t$ where a is the initial value, r is the rate of increase or decrease, and t is the time period.

Example

The value of a car decreases exponentially at the rate of 20% every year. If its initial value is $20,000, what will be the value of the car after 3 years?

Using $y = a(1 \pm r)^t$, $y = 20000(1 - 0.2)^t = 20000 \cdot 0.8^t$ After 3 years, the value of the car will be $20000 \cdot 0.8^3$= $10,240. Learn to use your calculator to find this value correctly.

CALCULATOR SECTION

1. A physics professor performs an experiment to measure the friction of a wooden surface. He applies forces on a brick and measures the displacement of the brick. His measurements are shown below.

Force and Displacement

Force f	0	10	15	20
Displacement d	0	3	4	4.5

Which of the following models best describes the displacement as a function of the force applied on the brick?

A) $d = 0.3f$
B) $d = 0.2f$
C) $d = 0.2f + 1$
D) $d = 0.3f + 1$

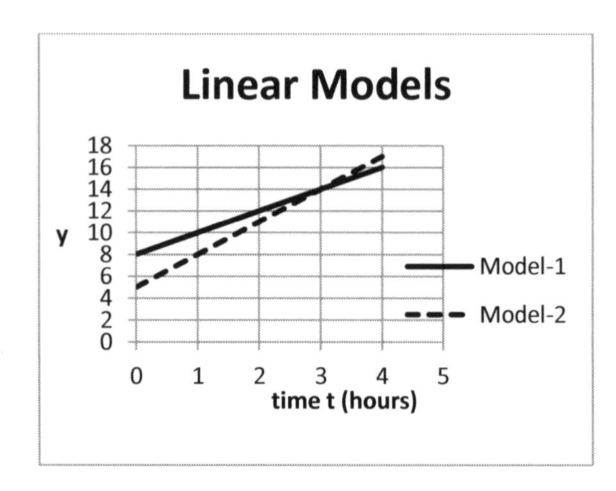

2. Two linear models are graphed above. How many hours after both the linear models have the same value will Model-2 have a value of 62?
GRID IN

CALCULATOR SECTION

An ornithologist spends a significant amount of money to restore a marshy land in order to attract more birds. His recordings for 5 months after the restoration are as follows.

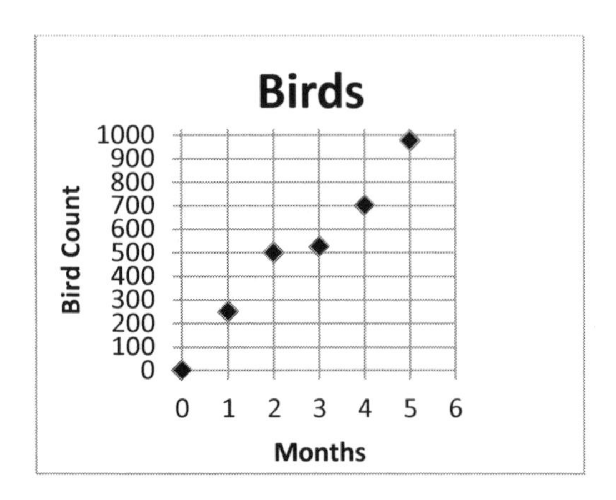

3. What is the average monthly increase in the number of birds visiting the marshland?
GRID IN

4. A nurse was tasked to inject 250 mL of saline water into a patient at the rate of 10 mL every 5 minutes. After how many minutes will the entire saline solution be injected into the patient?
GRID IN

5. The value of a boat that Jim bought for \$50,000 depreciates according to the table below.

BOAT'S VALUE IN THOUSANDS

Year y	0	1	2	3
Value v	50	40	32	25.60

Which of the following models describes the depreciation value of the boat, in thousands, over time accurately?

A) $v = 50 \cdot 0.8^y$
B) $v = 50 \cdot 1.2^y$
C) $v = 0.8^y$
D) $v = 1.2^y$

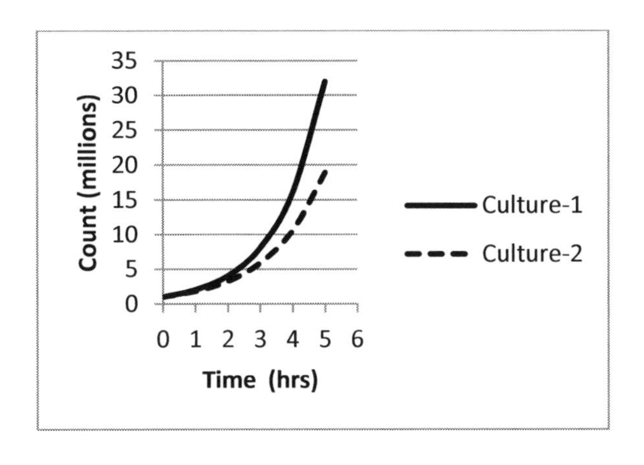

6. Bacterial culture-1 is modeled as $y = 2^x$ and bacterial culture-2 is modeled as $y = 1.8^x$ as shown in the graph. What is the difference in the bacterial count after 7 hours of growth?

A) 6.12 thousand
B) 61.22 thousand
C) 66.78 million
D) 76.84 million

CALCULATOR SECTION

7. Money deposited in the Bank of Generous will get you a 5% interest compounded yearly whereas the Bank of Stingy offers only 3% interest compounded yearly. If \$3500 is deposited in both banks, what will be the difference in amounts in the two banks after 8 years?
GRID IN

8. Brandi has to payback a loan of \$300,000 at the rate of 8% of the loan every year. How many years will she take to pay off her loan?
GRID IN

PROBLEM SOLVING AND DATA ANALYSIS		
Lesson 9	Growth and Decay	Answers

#	Explanation	Comments
1 C	Note that the question stem says ".. best describes". In this problem , you are given a table and a set of linear models. You do not have to develop the models from scratch by using the point slope formula. Fit the model to the data and see which model "best fits" the data. Choice C, $d = 0.2f + 1$ fits the data at 3 points accurately but on the 4th point, $d = 0.2 \cdot 20 + 1 = 5$, which is very close to 4.5. Other models do not fit the data points closely.	In this problem, you don't need to develop the linear model from scratch since the models are given in the answer choices.
2 16	The question is – how many hours after the models have the same value does model 2 have a value of 62? From the graph, it is clear that the models have the same value at 3 hrs. Now, find when the model-2 will have a value of 62. y intercept=$b = 5$, pick any 2 points to find the slope, $(x_1, y_1) = (0,5)$ and $(x_2, y_2) = (1,8)$. slope = $(8 - 5)/(1 - 0) = 3$. So, the model-2 is $y = 3t + 5$. You need to find when y will be equal to 62. $62 = 3t + 5;\ t = \frac{57}{3} = 19$ hrs. So with the models being the same at 3 hours, it will take $19 - 3 = 16$ more hours for model-2 to have a value of 62.	Pay attention to the legend – when there are multiple models in the graph, they can be shown as dashed lines.
3 200	What is the average monthly increase in the number of birds? This is the same as the slope of the line. Since this is a scatterplot, draw a line of best fit as shown. 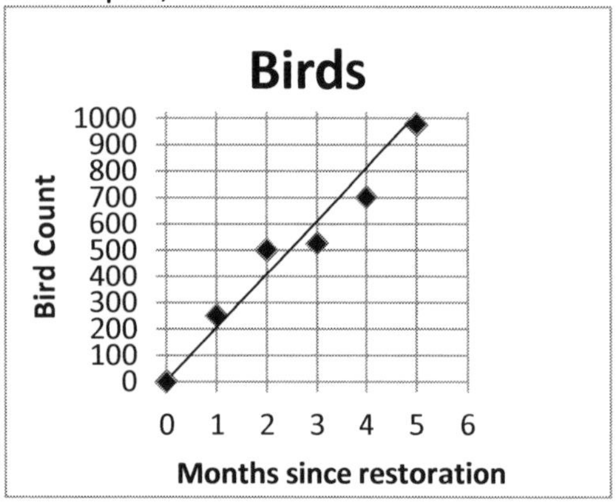 Birds Bird Count: 0, 100, 200, 300, 400, 500, 600, 700, 800, 900, 1000 Months since restoration: 0, 1, 2, 3, 4, 5, 6 Pick 2 points, $(0,0)$ and $(1,200)$. The slope is $\frac{200 - 0}{1 - 0} = 200$.	Draw a line of best fit connecting the data points. Not all points will always fall on the line. About half the points are above and the other half are below the line. That is the best fit you can get for these points. For linear models, the average increase or decrease in y for corresponding increase in x is the slope of the line. Be alert for questions that test your understanding of this concept.

4 250	250mL initially; injection rate is 10 mL/5mins = 2mL/minute. So, imagine a linear decay model that starts at y intercept of 500 and with negative slope of -2. Slope is -2 because the injection rate is 2 – so the saline depletion rate is -2 mL/min. $s = 500 - 2t$ or $-2t + 500$ is the linear model, where s is the saline left. When the entire solution is injected, $s = 0$; so $0 = 500 - 2t$ $2t = 500$ $t = \frac{500}{2} = 250 \text{ mins}$	
5 A	Note that the values are in thousands. Note that the value of the boat at $y = 0$, is 50. Plug in the models to the data. When $y = 0$, the value given by the first 2 models is $v = 50 \cdot 0.8^0 = 50$. Since the value decays, the model is likely to be choice A which is $50 \cdot 0.8^x$. Use your calculator to plug in the other data points; $y = 1,2$, and 3 and verify that the model gives you the value v of the boat correctly. $50 \cdot 0.8^1 = 40, 50 \cdot 0.8^2 = 32, 50 \cdot 0.8^3 = 25.60$.	Learn to use your calculator to find exponential values such as $50 \cdot 0.8^3$ quickly and accurately.
6 C	The graph does not have values at $t = 7$ hours, but the textual information gives you the model. At $t = 7$, culture-1 has 2^7 and culture-2 has 1.8^7. So the difference is $2^7 - 1.8^7 = 66.78$. Note that the graph provides useful information about the scale of the bacterial count – it is in millions. So, the answer is 66.78 million.	
7 735	Since money is compounded yearly, this is a case of exponential growth. Recall that the formula for growth is $P(1+r)^t$. So, 3500 will become $3500(1.05)^8$ in one bank and $3500(1.03)^8$ in another bank. The difference is $3500(1.05^8 - 1.03^8) = 3500(1.48 - 1.27) = \$735$.	Pay attention to parenthesis – the correct answer is not $3500(1.08 - 1.03)^8$.
8 12.5	Note that the problem says she has to pay at the rate of 8% of the loan every year. This indicates a linear decay(decrease) in the amount of 8% of 300,000= $0.08 \cdot 300{,}000 = 24{,}000/year$. So, the linear model is: balance= $300000 - 24000t$. When the amount is paid in full, the balance is 0. $300000 - 24000t = 0$ $24000 \cdot t = 300{,}000$ $t = \frac{300000}{24000} = 12.5$ years	Read the problem carefully but don't assume anything other than what is stated. The linear model can have large numbers in them and that should not be an issue.

PROBLEM SOLVING AND DATA ANALYSIS		
Lesson 10	Statistics	Review

FOCUSPREP CHECKLIST

- How do I calculate the mean, median, mode, and range?
- How do I calculate the weighted average?
- What is standard deviation? How is it calculated?
- How do I read a box and whisker plot?
- Workout practice problems in Statistics

Q1 How are the mean, median, mode, and range of a set of numbers calculated?

A1 For a set of numbers, $x_1, x_2, x_3 \ldots . x_n$ you can calculate the following:

Mean (Average, or Arithmetic mean)= $\frac{x_1+x_2+x_3+\ldots x_n}{n}$

For example, the mean of 1,2,3,4,5 is $\frac{1+2+3+4+5}{5} = \frac{15}{5} = 3$

Median: The middle number in the set, when the set is arranged in ascending order. If there is even number of items, then there will be two numbers in the middle. In that case, the median is the average of the two middle values. For example, if there are four numbers in a list, the median is the average of the 2nd and 3rd numbers. The median of 1, 2, 3 is 2, the middle number in the set, and the median of 1,2,3,4 is $\frac{2+3}{2} = 2.5$, the average of the 2nd and 3rd numbers in the set.

Mode: The number that appears the most number of times. You can have no mode, one mode or multiple modes. For example, in the set 1,3,3,4 the mode is 3 whereas in the set 1,2,2,3,3 the mode is both 2 and 3. In the set 1,2,3 there is no mode.

Range: The difference between the largest and the smallest number of a data set .

Q2 What does the median indicate?

A2 The median of a set of numbers indicates the value above and below which equal numbers of values exist. For example, the values of 4 toys are $10, $20, $30 and $40. The median is $\frac{20+30}{2} = 25$. This indicates that half the toys are below $25 and half are above $25. In Beverly Hills, the median price of homes is $3 million. This means that 50% of the homes there are below $3 million and 50% are above $3 million.

Q3 What does weighted average mean? When will I need to use it?

A3 Weighted average is also called Expected Value. When you know the frequency of specific data values, you can find which data value can be "expected". If there are n values, $v1, v2, v3$ ... and each value occurs $n1, n2, n3$.... times respectively, then

Weighted Average (Expected value) = $\frac{v1 \cdot n1 + v2 \cdot n2 + \cdots}{n1+n2+\cdots}$

Q4 What is central tendency and how is it measured?

A4 Central tendency is a number that indicates the central value of data. It can be the mean or median or mode of the data set, depending on the type of data and the distribution of data. When the data does not have outliers, the mean is a good indicator of central tendency. When the data has outliers, the median is a good indicator of central tendency. When a data is categorical, the mode (the value that occurs most number of times than other values) is a good indicator of central tendency.

Example 1: Mean is the central tendency: The ages of 5 adults are: 28,37,49,61,75. The data values are close and do not have outliers. The mean is 50 and is a good indicator of central tendency.

Example 2: Median is the central tendency: The ages of 5 adults are: 23,25,28,92,99. Three data values are less than 30 and two values in nineties are very high outliers. The mean is 53.4 and the median is 28. Two adults are older than 28 and two are younger than 28.The median is a better measure of central tendency in this case. When there are outliers, the median is a better indicator of central tendency.

Example3: Mode is the central tendency: Students in a daycare were asked which tour they wanted to take and the results were as follows: Zoo:10 Waterpark:25 Movie:12 Museum:16. In this scenario, the waterpark option is the best measure of central tendency since most students want to go there. Mean or Median will not make sense in deciding the central tendency for this data. Mode is a good indicator of central tendency in situations where you have to choose between several options.

Q5 What are the measures of spread (variance) of data?

A5 The range, standard deviation, and quartile are the commonly used measures of variance.

Q6 What is standard deviation and how is it calculated?

A6 The standard deviation of a set of numbers indicates how much deviation is there from the mean, on an average, considering all data in the set. It is an important measure of the spread or variance of data from the mean. It is represented by the Greek symbol Sigma, written as σ.

For a set of n numbers, $x_1, x_2, x_3 \ldots . x_n$ where $\bar{x}$ as the mean, the standard deviation is calculated as follows:

$$\sigma = \sqrt{\frac{(x_1-\bar{x})^2+(x_2-\bar{x})^2+(x_3-\bar{x})^2+\cdots.(x_n-\bar{x})^2}{n}}$$

Calculating σ is easy – take the difference of each value from the mean, square and sum them, and then average the sum over the number of data values.

The variance is the number inside the square root. It is written as σ^2.

$$\text{Variance} = \sigma^2 = \frac{(x_1-\bar{x})^2+(x_2-\bar{x})^2+(x_3-\bar{x})^2+\cdots.(x_n-\bar{x})^2}{n}$$

The standard deviation is the square root of variance. The College Board says that you will not be required to calculate standard deviation, but you are expected to know what it is and answer questions about it. It is important to know how it is calculated so that you can be better prepared to answer questions.

Remember that when the data is clustered around the mean, the standard deviation is close to 0, whereas if the data is spread out, the standard deviation is greater than 0. Learning to calculate standard deviation using the calculator can be valuable sometimes even though SAT questions will not ask you to calculate it. See the calculator section for instructions.

Example 1: The heights of 5 students in a school are as follows: 6, 5, 4, 7, 6. What is the standard deviation of this set of data?

Solution:

Calculate the mean: $\bar{x} = \frac{6+5+4+7+6}{5} = 5.6$

Calculate the variance: $\sigma^2 =$

$$\frac{(6-5.6)^2+(5-5.6)^2+(4-5.6)^2+(7-5.6)^2+(6-5.6)^2}{5} = \frac{(0.4^2)+(-0.6)^2+(-1.6)^2+(1.4)^2+(0.4)^2}{5} = 1.04$$

Calculate the standard deviation: $\sigma = \sqrt{1.04} = 1.02.$

Example 2: In a high school, the average height of students is 5 feet and the standard deviation is 0 feet. This means that there is no deviation from the mean and so all the students are 5 feet tall.

Example 3: In a high school, the average height of students is 5 feet and the standard deviation is 2 feet. This means that the average deviation of the height of students from their mean height is 2 feet.

Example 4: A high school math teacher wishes that all of her students have almost the same scores in a test. Which one of the following choices of mean and standard deviation will satisfy the teacher's wish?

(A) Mean 75, Standard Deviation = 1.21
(B) Mean 52, Standard Deviation = 0.52
(C) Mean 75, Standard Deviation = 5.67
(D) Mean 69, Standard Deviation = 22.78

Solution: Choice B is the answer. If the students have almost the same scores, then the mean $\bar{x}$ will be almost the same as the individual scores, so $(x_1 - \bar{x})^2$ will be almost 0. So, the standard deviation will be close to 0. The standard deviation in choice b is 0.52 which is the closest to 0.

Q7 How do I calculate the standard deviation using a calculator?

A7 The College Board says that you will **not** be required to calculate standard deviation. Regardless, it is easy to do so using your calculator. Refer to the calculator section for instructions. Knowing how to calculate standard deviation using your calculator can be of help.

Q8 What is an outlier? How does it impact the mean, median, and standard deviation?

A8 An outlier is a value that is very high or very low compared to other values in the data set. Scatterplots and box and whisker plots are used to visually identify outliers in data.

Example 1: In the data set 1,45,48,52,61 the value of 1 is an outlier since it is very much less than rest of the data.

Example 2: In the data set 1,50,53,59,500 the values of 1 and 500 are outliers since they are very distant from the rest of the data.

If you remove the outlier and analyze data, you will see that the mean and standard deviation are impacted significantly but the median is not impacted significantly. In Example 2, the mean with the outliers is 132.6 whereas the mean without the outliers is 54. The median with outliers is 53 and the median without the outliers is also 53. The standard deviation with the outliers is 184.76 whereas it is 3.74 without the outliers.

Q9 What is a quartile?

A9 Quartiles are numbers that divide a list of numbers into four parts. There are three quartiles for any data set. The first quartile Q1, the second quartile Q2 , and the third quartile Q3. The second quartile is the median of the data set. The first quartile is the median of the lower half of the data set. The third quartile is the median of the upper half of the data set. In terms of percentiles, the first quartile is the 25th percentile, the second quartile is the 50th percentile, and the third quartile is the 75th percentile. The first quartile is also called the lower quartile and the third quartile is also called the upper quartile. The interquartile range is $Q3 - Q1$, that is, the difference between the first and third quartiles. Data that falls in the interquartile range are above the 25th percentile and below the 75th percentile.

Example 1: Consider the data set 1,5,8,10. The median of the data set is (5+8)/2= 6.5. The median of the lower half is (1+5)/2=3. The median of the upper half is (8+10)/2=9. So, the first quartile Q1 is 3, the second quartile Q2 is 6.5 and the third quartile Q3 is 9. The interquartile range is Q3-Q1=0-3=6.

Example 2: Consider the data set 1,5,8,10,15. The median of the data set is 8. The median of the lower half is (1+5)/2=3. The median of the upper half is (10+15)/2=12.5. So, the first quartile is 3, the second quartile is 8 and the third quartile is 12.5. In terms of percentiles, the third quartile value of 12.5 corresponds to 75th percentile. This means that 75% of the data values are below 12.5.

Q10 What is a box and whisker plot used for?

A10 A box plot is used to show the distribution of data. It shows the minimum value, the first quartile, second quartile, third quartile, and the maximum value of the data. The quartiles are shown in a box and the minimum and maximum values are shown in lines that look like whiskers. The range of the data is the difference between the maximum and minimum values.

When two data sets are compared, two box plots are presented together.

Example: The box plot below shows the data obtained from the Electricity bills (in Dollars) of two families over a 12 month period. Several questions can be answered from this box plot as shown below.

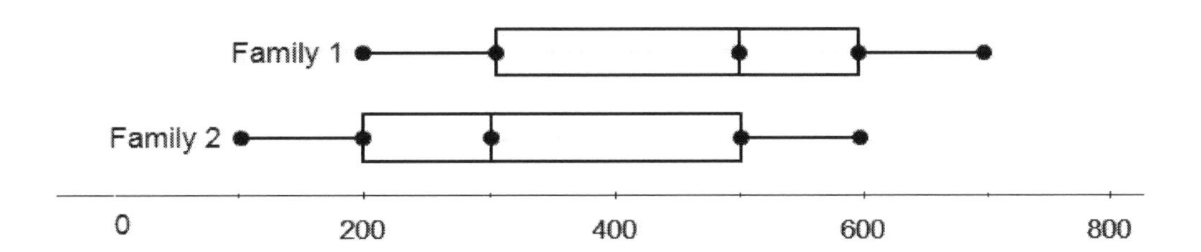

- Which family had the lowest electricity bill?
  Family 2–$100
- Which family had the highest electricity bill?
  Family 1– $700
- 50% of the bills of Family 2 were below what amount?
  $300–50% corresponds to the second quartile.
- What is the median expenditure on electricity for Family 1?
  $500–read the dollar value for the second quartile(50th percentile).
- What percentage of bills of Family 1 is above $200?
  100%–all the values are above the minimum value.
- What is the range of expenditures for Family 2?
  Range=max-min=600-100=500
- What percentage of bills for Family 2 is between 200 and 500 dollars?
  75% of bills are below $500 and 25% of bills are below $200. So,75-25=50% of bills are between 200 and 500 dollars.

PROBLEM SOLVING AND DATA ANALYSIS		
Lesson 10	Statistics	Practice

CALCULATOR SECTION

1. The scores of a student in four tests are 50, 51, 52, and 53 respectively. How much should the student score in the fifth test if the average score in five tests has to be 54?

(A) 44

(B) 54

(C) 64

(D) 74

2. The average of three consecutive numbers starting with $x - 4$ is which one of the following?

(A) $x - 1$

(B) $x - 2$

(C) $x - 3$

(D) $x - 4$

3. The average of three numbers is 5. When a fourth number is added to the list, the average increases to 7. What is the value of the fourth number?

(A) 7

(B) 8

(C) 12

(D) 13

CALCULATOR SECTION

4. The average of six numbers is 15. When one number is removed, the average is 10. What is the value of the number that was removed?

(A) 15

(B) 20

(C) 35

(D) 40

5. Each of the 50 ducks in Alpha Zoo weighs 5 pounds. Each of the 40 ducks in the Beta Zoo weighs 8 pounds. What is the average weight of the ducks in both Zoos combined?

(A) 5.33

(B) 6.33

(C) 7.33

(D) 8.33

6. 50 employees in a company own an average of 2 cars each whereas the remaining 25 employees own an average of 3 cars each. What is the average number of cars owned by all the employees of the company?

(A) 1.53

(B) 1.73

(C) 2.13

(D) 2.33

7. The average of three numbers x, y, z is m. The average of y and z is n. What is the value of x in terms of m and n?
(A) $\frac{2n}{3m}$
(B) $2n + 3m$
(C) $3m - 2n$
(D) $6mn$

8. If $\frac{a}{b} = \frac{1}{4}$ and $\frac{c}{b} = \frac{3}{4}$, what is the average of a and c?
(A) $\frac{b}{2}$
(B) $\frac{b}{3}$
(C) $\frac{b}{4}$
(D) $\frac{b}{5}$

9. The median and mode are the same in which of the following choices?
(A) 11,12,13,14,15
(B) 11,12,12,14,15
(C) 11,12,13,14,14
(D) 11,11,13,14,15

CALCULATOR SECTION

Set-1: 105,106,107,108,110
Set-2: 45,46,47,47,49

10. The range of Set-1 is more than the range of Set-2 by
(A) 1
(B) 2
(C) 4
(D) 6

11. Consider the two statements below and indicate which one of the answer choices is true.

I: The average height of 50 students can be calculated by adding the average heights of two sets of 25 students each.

II: The average height of each of two sets of 25 students can be used to calculate the average height of 50 students.

(A) I only
(B) II only
(C) I and II
(D) None of the above

12. The smallest number in a data set is 5 and the range of the data set is 15. What is the largest number in the data set?
(A) 5
(B) 10
(C) 15
(D) 20

13. A shoe store recorded the following information.

Size	5	6	7
Sales (number of shoes)	85	62	21

If you randomly select a shoe that was sold, it can be expected to be of which size? (round up to the next size)
(A) 5
(B) 6
(C) 7
(D) None of the above

14. If Jana drives 6 hours at a speed of 60 miles/hour and 9 hours at a speed of 62 miles/hour, what is her average speed in miles/hour during her 15 hours of driving?
(A) 51.20
(B) 58.46
(C) 61.20
(D) 64.30

CALCULATOR SECTION

15. If x is the average of all the angles of a triangle and y is the average of all the angles of a rectangle, then $x + y =$
(A) 60
(B) 90
(C) 150
(D) 180

16. A survey asking people how many cars they owned resulted in the following histogram.

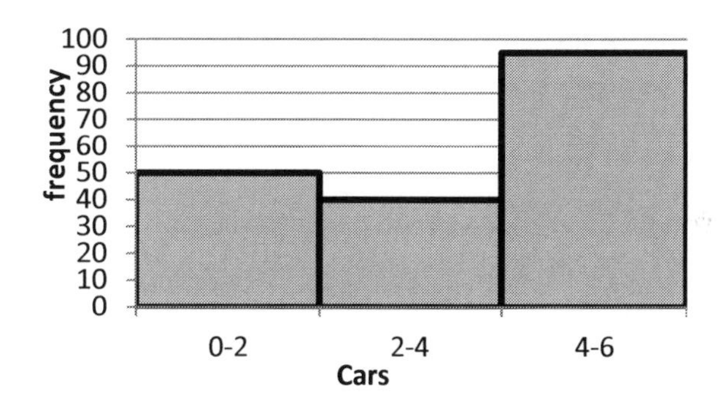

Which of the following could be the median number of cars owned by those surveyed?
(A) 1
(B) 2
(C) 5
(D) 6

17. For a given set of data, which of the following is least affected by the addition of an outlier?
(A) Standard Deviation
(B) Mean
(C) Median
(D) Range

18. The mean score in a Geography test is 74 and the standard deviation is 10. A trophy will be given to students who are at least two standard deviations more than the mean. What is the least one must score to get a trophy?

(A) 64
(B) 74
(C) 84
(D) 94

19. The interquartile range of a data set with a lower quartile of 10 and an upper quartile of 22 is
(A) 10
(B) 12
(C) 22
(D) 32

20. An opinion poll stated that 30% of the citizens of Culver City will vote for Stacy as the new governor of their state. The margin of error of the poll is $\pm 4\%$ with a 95% confidence level. If the poll in conducted again, what is the least percent of votes that Stacy can expect to get?
(A) 10
(B) 26
(C) 30
(D) 34

CALCULATOR SECTION

Set-1: 105,106,107,108,110
Set-2: 11,26,47,59,84

21. Considering the two sets above, which of the following statements below is true?

(A) Set-1 has more standard deviation
(B) Set-2 has more standard deviation
(C) Set-2 has two modes
(D) Set-1 has a range of 105

11,22,33,44,55

22. The standard deviation of the data shown above is
(A) 10.29
(B) 11
(C) 12.29
(D) 33

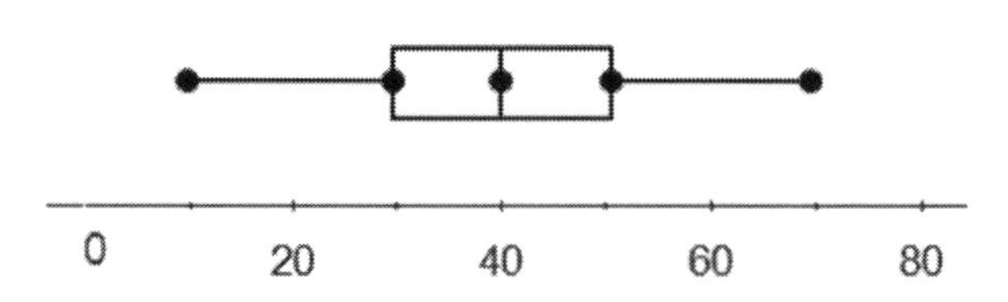

23. The minimum temperature readings in a city for 365 days are shown in the box plot above. The range and interquartile range for this data are
(A) (60,30)
(B) (60,40)
(C) (60,60)
(D) (60,20)

#	Explanation	Comments
1 C	Let x be the score that he needs in the fifth test. $\frac{50+51+52+53+x}{5} = 54$ $x = 54 \cdot 5 - 206 = 270 - 206 = 64$	This is a standard problem involving averages.
2 C	Starting with $x - 4$, three consecutive numbers are one more than the previous number $x-4, x-4+1, x-4+2$ $x-4, x-3, x-2$ The average is $\frac{x-4+x-3+x-2}{3} = \frac{3x-9}{3} = x - 3$	Some problems require you to know that for a given number x, the preceding numbers are $x-1$, $x-2$, etc and the succeeding numbers are $x+1$, $x+2$, etc.
3 D	Let a, b, c be the three numbers. $\frac{a+b+c}{3} = 5;$ So, $a + b + c = 15$ Let d be the fourth number. Average of four numbers is 7. $\frac{a+b+c+d}{4} = 7;$ So, $a + b + c + d = 28.$ Substituting $a + b + c = 15$ in the above equation, you get $15 + d = 28;\ d = 28 - 15 = 13.$	
4 D	$\frac{a+b+c+d+e+f}{6} = 15$ $a+b+c+d+e+f = 6 \cdot 5 = 90$ Let f be the number that is removed; average is now 10; $\frac{a+b+c+d+e}{5} = 10.$ $a+b+c+d+e = 50$ Substituting this equation in the first one, you get $50 + f = 90, \quad f = 90 - 50 = 40$	When an item is removed, remember to reduce the denominator by 1 when calculating the average.
5 B	Average weight= weight of all ducks/ total ducks $= \frac{50 \cdot 5+40 \cdot 8}{50+40} = \frac{250+320}{90} = \frac{570}{90} = 6.33$	Remember to account for the ducks in both zoos.
6 D	$\frac{50 \cdot 2 + 25 \cdot 3}{50+25} = \frac{100+75}{75} = \frac{175}{75} = 2.33$	
7 C	$\frac{x+y+z}{3} = m;\ \text{So}, x+y+z = 3m$ $\frac{y+z}{2} = n;\ y + z = 2n;$ substituting this in the above, you get $x + 2n = 3m;\ x = 3m - 2n$	
8 A	Note that the answers choices show the average of a and c in terms of b. $\frac{a}{b} = \frac{1}{4}; a = \frac{b}{4}; \frac{c}{b} = \frac{3}{4}; c = \frac{3}{4}b;$ $so\ \frac{a+c}{2} = \frac{1}{2}\left(\frac{b}{4} + \frac{3b}{4}\right) = \frac{b}{2}$	

9 B	In A, median=13 mode=none In B, median=12 mode=12 – both are 12 In C, median=13 mode=14 In D, median=13 mode=11	Review the definition of median and mode.
10 A	Range of set 1= 110-105=5 Range of set 2= 49-45=4 Range of set 1 is more than range of set 2 by 5-4=1	Review the definition of range.
11 B	I. is false – you cannot add averages of two sets of numbers to get the average of the combined set. II. is correct – the average height of each of two sets of 25 students <u>can be used</u> to calculate the average height of 50 students.	If the average height of one set of 25 students is a, then then the sum of their heights is 25a. If the average height of another set of 25 students is b, then the sum of their heights is 25b. You can use this to calculate the average height of 50 students as (25a+25b)/50.
12 D	Range=largest number – smallest number 15=largest number-5 Largest number=15-5=10	
13 B	The expected value is the weighted average= $\frac{5\cdot85+6\cdot62+7\cdot21}{85+62+21} = 5.6 \cong 6$	
14 C	Calculate the total distance. Average speed for the entire trip is distance / time for the entire trip $= \frac{60\cdot6+62\cdot9}{6+9} = 61.20$	
15 C	A triangle has 3 angles that add up to 180. So, x=average of the 3 angles= $\frac{180}{3} = 60$. A rectangle has 4 angles that add up to 360. So y=average of the 4 angles= $\frac{360}{4} = 90$. Hence, $x + y = 60 + 90 = 150$.	
16 C	There are 50 respondents for 0-2 cars, 40 respondents for 2-4 cars, and 95 respondents for 4-6 cars. So, totally there are 185 respondents. The median of 185 data points is the 185/2=93rd . Since there are 50 data points for 0-2 cars and 40 data points for 2-4 car range, a total of 90, the 93rd data point will lie in the 4-6 car range. You cannot accurately identify the median since the histogram only shows grouped frequency and not the frequency for the individual number of cars. The 93rd respondent could own either 4 cars or 5 cars. Since choice C is 5, it is the correct answer. Not that choice D is 6 but 6 is not included in any of the bars shown.	Note that the buckets in histograms can sometimes be single values instead of a range. For example, they could be just 0 car, 1 car, 2 cars etc. These are the simple type of histograms. When they have a grouped range like 0-2 cars, 2-4 cars, etc. they are called frequency distribution histograms. Note that since the x-axis labels overlap, like 0-2, 2-4,4-6 each bar in the histogram does not include the right limit of their range. That is, the bar for 0-2 shows the frequency for 0 and 1 cars owned, but not for 2 cars owned. Similarly, the bar for 2-4 cars shows the frequency for 2 and 3 cars owned, but not for the right limit of 4 cars.

17 C	Addition of an outlier will affect the mean, standard deviation, and range the most. It will affect the median the least.	
18 D	Two standard deviations from the mean is 74+20=94. So, one must score 94 to get a trophy.	
19 B	Interquartile is the difference of upper and lower quartiles. 22-10=12.	
20 B	Margin of error is 4%. This means that the next time the poll is conducted, Stacy can expect at least 30-4=26% of the votes and at most 30+4=34% with a confidence level of 95%.	Know how to use the Margin of Error.
21 B	Set-1 does not have a large standard deviation since the data is clustered around the average of about 107. Data in set-2 is widely distributed and hence has a large standard deviation. Set-2 does not have 2 modes and set-1 does not have a range of 105.	
22 C	Use your calculator to find the standard deviation of 12.29 for this data set.	
23 D	Range is max-min=70-10=60. Interquartile range is 50-30=20.	

FOCUSPREP CHECKLIST

- What are the different types of studies?
- What is the difference between an observational study and an experimental study?
- How is data collected for a survey?
- What is the difference between a population and a sample?
- What is a two-way frequency table?
- How do I identify the association of variables?
- Workout practice problems in Population and Sample

Q1 What are the different types of scientific studies?

A1 The two types of scientific studies are a) Observational study and b) Experimental study. Scientists design their studies using one of these methods and then collect data and analyze them using statistics. The goal of these studies is to be able to make conclusions that are statistically significant.

Q2 What are the elements of a study?

A2 A study has several elements: a) type – observational or experimental b) subjects – the people or things that are studied c) treatment – specific action applied on the subjects in the case of experimental studies only and d) response – the variable whose outcome is measured.

Q3 What is the difference between an observational study and an experimental study?

A3 An observational study and an experimental study are two different types of studies.

In an observational study, the scientist only observes the subjects and records the information. No treatment is applied to the subjects – that is, no specific experiment is performed on the subjects. Polls and Surveys are examples of observational studies. They are just data gathering exercises.

Example: A research scientist wants to measure the effect of gender on the color of cars purchased. He designs a survey asking people in his zip code what their gender is and the color of their car.

In an experimental study, the subjects are divided into a control group on which no treatment is applied and an experimental group on which treatment is applied and the response is measured from both groups. Experimental studies aim to find cause and effect relationships.

Example: A drug company claims that it has developed a drug to reduce blood sugar. To test this claim, a researcher conducts an experimental study on 50 patients. He divided them into 2 groups of 25 patients each. He does not administer the drug on the first group (control group) but gives them a fake drug (placebo), and administers the drug on the second group. He then measures the blood sugar of all the patients from both groups and analyses them. The measurements from the control group are used as a baseline to compare the results from the experimental group.

Q4 What do Population and Sample mean? How are they related?

A4 A population is the entire set of values that are being considered for study. A sample is a small subset of the population. For example, all the students in a school can be considered as population whereas the students in one specific class can be considered as a sample.

Q5 What is the difference between a population parameter and a sample statistic?

A5 The goal of a research study is to measure a population parameter. Since a population is too large to conduct a survey on, the survey is conducted on a small sample. The sample statistic (such as mean, median, standard deviation, etc) is then used to make an estimate of the population parameter. So, you have sample mean, sample median, etc and population mean, population median, etc. The population parameters are also called as true mean, true median, etc.

Example: A study aimed to find many families in the country have pets. It surveyed 1000 families and asked them if they have pets. In this example, the number of families in the country that have pets is the population parameter. The number of families that have pets in the sample of 1000 families is the sample statistic.

Q6 What is a survey?

A6 A survey aims to collect information about certain parameters of a population. Since it is often difficult to survey the entire population, a small sample of the population is selected randomly for the survey and its statistics are analyzed and used to make inferences about the entire population. A follow-up survey is a survey that is done in addition to the first survey to find out specific information about the population.

Q7 How is a survey done? How are the results documented?

A7 A survey is done by collecting sample data using unbiased, random sampling. Sampling results are recorded in tables and then analyzed.

Example: A school district administrator wants to find how well the students would perform in a math test. There are 50,000 students in the school district. He picks 300 students randomly and gives them the test. He then calculates the average score obtained by the 300 students.

In this example, the population is made of 50,000 students and the sample is made of 300 students.

Q8 Are surveys accurate?

A8 Errors do creep into surveys due to a variety of reasons – misunderstanding of survey questions, biased survey questions, etc. A survey is said to be biased if these mistakes happen. Errors in surveys are reported in terms of margin of error.

Q9 What statistical measures are used to analyze the results of a survey?

A9 Basic statistical measures such as the mean, median, mode, range, and standard deviation of the sample are used to analyze the results of a sample survey. These sample statistics, along with margin of error and confidence level are used to make estimates/projections of population parameters.

Q10 What is a margin of error? What is a confidence interval? What is a confidence level?

A10 Since the sample sizes are small compared to the population, the sample statistic cannot be applied directly to the population parameter. If a sample survey says that a candidate will get 78% of the votes in a city, you cannot say that he will get 78% of the votes in the country as well. You must take the margin of error and confidence level into account.

A correct survey result will be published as follows: An unbiased poll conducted to predict who will win the election found that the Green party candidate will win 78% of the votes. The poll has a margin of error of $\pm 3\%$ and has 95% confidence level.

The Margin of Error in this survey is $\pm 3\%$. This means that the confidence interval is 75 to 81 $(78 - 3$ to $78 + 3)$. The confidence level is 95%. This means that if the poll is conducted several times, 95% (confidence level) of the time the candidate will get votes in the (confidence interval) range of 75% $(78 - 3)$ to 81% $(78 + 3)$.

Q11 What does a two way table mean?

A11 A two way table categorizes data from a survey in rows and columns. By analyzing the results using a two way table, you can find if the variables are associated or not.

Example: The two-way table below shows the grade of students and the language spoken by them. The cells indicate the number of students in a particular grade speaking a particular language. The totals row and column sum up the data in two ways. Hence it is called a two way table. This table has two categories- grades and language. Each category is broken down into 2 groups- 9th and 10th grades and Spanish and French.

Grade	Spanish	French	Total
9	3	1	4
10	3	2	5
Total	4	5	9

Q12 What does frequency distribution mean?

A12 Data collected from survey is summarized and analyzed in frequency distribution tables and charts such as bar charts and histograms. For example, after doing a survey to find out how many cans of beverage the students in a class drink every week, you can summarize the data in a frequency distribution table and a histogram as follows.

Survey : How many cans of beverage do you drink every week?							
2	0	1	3	5	8	1	0

Frequency Distribution Table	
Cans (Buckets)	Total Number of students
0-3 (0,1,2 cans)	5
3-6 (3,4,5 cans)	2
6-9 (6,7,8 cans)	1

The histogram below showing the frequency distribution of data. Pay attention to the x-axis labels in histograms. In the histogram, the labels show groupings of beverage cans in 0-3, 3-6, and 6-8 range. The first bar represents cans from 0-2 only but not 3. The second bar shown is for groups 3-5 only, but not 5 and so on. Histograms that appear in SAT also follow this convention.

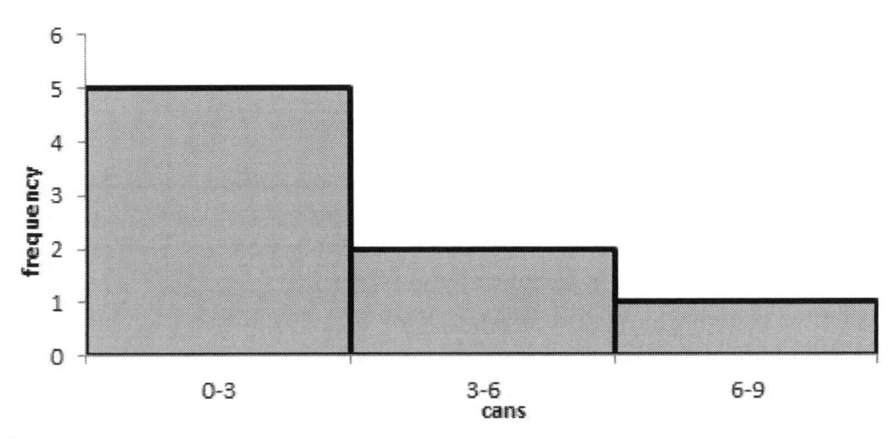

Q13 How do I calculate the mean and median from a histogram?

A13 If the histogram has grouped values in the x-axis such as 0-3, 3-6, etc then you cannot find the mean but you can estimate it. In the histogram above, there are 5 students who drink 0-3 cans – so, since we cannot say how many drank 0 or 1 or 2 cans, we can estimate that all 5 of them drank at least 0 cans. Similarly, we can estimate that 2 students drank at least 3 cans each, and 1 student drank at least 6 cans. So, the average number of cans consumed can be estimated to be at least $\frac{5 \cdot 0+2 \cdot 3+1 \cdot 6}{8} = 1.5$.

The median can also be estimated. There are 5+2+1=8 students. So there are 8 data values. The median is therefore the average of the 4th and 5th data values. Since there are 5 students in the 0-3 can group, the 4th and 5th students are in this group. So, the median will be in this group. We cannot accurately say what the median is, but we can be sure it will be between 0 and 3.

In the following histogram, the x-axis labels are not grouped. So, the mean and median can be calculated accurately as shown below.

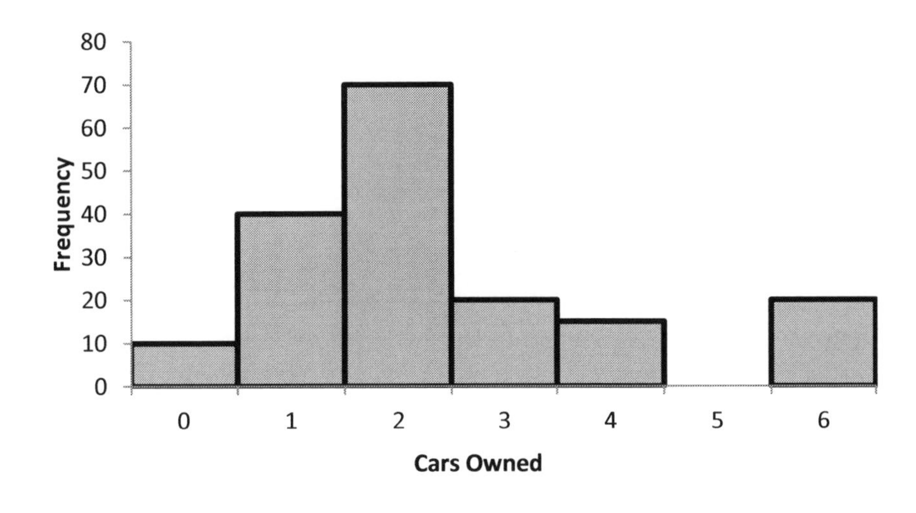

Mean = $\frac{10 \cdot 0 + 40 \cdot 1 + 70 \cdot 2 + 20 \cdot 3 + 15 \cdot 4 + 20 \cdot 6}{165} = 2.545$

There are 165 data values. So the median is the value of the 165/2=82.5=83rd data point. From the histogram, you can see that there are 10 people with 0 cars, and 40 people with 1 car – a total of 50 people. There are 70 people with 2 cars – a total of 50+70=120 people. So, the 83rd data point falls in this bar that corresponds to 2 cars. So, the median of this data set is 2.

Q14 How do I calculate the mean and standard deviation from a frequency table?

A14

You are not required to calculate standard deviation or mean from a frequency table but knowing how it is calculated can give you valuable insights. Review the lesson on Statistics for calculation of mean and standard deviation for a set of numbers. If the numbers appear several times and are presented in a frequency table, the mean and standard deviation are calculated as follows. The column f shows the frequency of data x. Calculate the column values and calculate the mean and standard deviation.

x	f	$f \cdot x$	$x - \bar{x}$	$(x - \bar{x})^2$	$f \cdot (x - \bar{x})^2$
1	8	8	-0.76	0.58	4.64
2	5	10	0.24	0.06	0.6
3	4	12	2.24	5.01	6.01
	17	30		5.65	11.25

Mean= $\bar{x} = \frac{f1 \cdot x1 + f2 \cdot x2 + \cdots fn \cdot xn}{f1 + f2 + \cdots fn} = \frac{30}{17} = 1.76.$

Standard Deviation $= \sqrt{\frac{f1 \cdot (x1 - \bar{x})^2 + f2 \cdot (x2 - \bar{x})^2 + \cdots}{f1 + f2 + \cdots . fn}} = \sqrt{\frac{11.25}{30}} = 0.61$

Q15 In a two-way table, how do I calculate the marginal probability, the joint probability and the conditional probability?

A15 Consider the data collected from a survey showing the number of people who speak Spanish and don't speak Spanish and their gender. There are two categories of data – Gender and Language. The goal of the survey is to find if there is an association between gender and people's opinion of sports.

Gender	Like sports	Don't like sports
Male	13	7
Female	3	27

Add a Total row and a Total column and calculate the row and column totals. Then, calculate the marginal, joint, and conditional probabilities as shown in the table below. Using these probabilities (also called distributions) you can make several inferences of the sample data.

Gender	Like sports	Don't like sports	Total
Male	13 (13/50=26%) joint (13/20=65%) conditional	7 (7/50=14%) joint (7/20=35%) conditional	20 (20/50=40%) marginal
Female	3 (3/50=6%) joint (3/30=10%) conditional	27 (27/54=54%) joint (27/30=90%) conditional	30 (30/50=60%) marginal
Total	16 (16/50=32%) marginal	34 (34/50=68%) marginal	50 (grand total) marginal

Marginal probability is the ratio of the marginal total with respect to the grand total.
40% of those surveyed are male; 60% of those surveyed are male.
32% of those surveyed like sports; 68% of those surveyed do not like sports.

Joint probability is the ratio of the cell value with respect to the grand total.
Of those surveyed, 26% are males who like sports; 14% are male who don't like sports.
Of those surveyed, 6% are females who like sports; 54% are females who don't like sports.
Sum of joint probabilities in all cells = 1 (100%)

Conditional probability is the ratio of the cell value with respect to the row total. It is used to find the association of categorical variables (gender and choice of sports).

65% of males like sports; 35% of males do not like sports.
10% of females like sports, 90% of females do not like sports.

Q16 How do I find out if the variables in a two-way table are dependent or independent?

A16

If the conditional probabilities are the same in all the cells in a column, then the two categorical variables are independent.

In the above example, since the conditional probabilities are not the same, the variables are dependent on each other. When there is dependence between two categorical variables, they are said to be related or associated.

The following example illustrates how conditional distributions are used to determine independence/dependence of categorical variables.

Example:

The number of students in a college taking Arts and Science classes are shown in the table below:

Gender	Arts	Science	Total
Male			88
Female			62
Total	100	50	150

A research scientist wants to know if the gender of the student is associated with the choice of classes taken. How many male students should take classes in Arts so that there is no association between gender and class choice?

Solution:

If there must be no association between the categorical variables (gender and class choice), then the conditional probabilities must be the same in both cells in one column. It should also be equal to the marginal probability of the variable in that column. For example, if a student takes Arts classes, then the conditional probability of the Arts student being male or female must be the same in the Arts column. The marginal probability that a student will take Arts classes (compared to all the students) should also have the same probability.

The two conditional probabilities and one marginal probability of the Arts column must be the same for no association to exist. If they are different, then there is an association.

In the totals row, you have $\frac{100}{150} = 0.67$. In the male row, if there are m male students that take Arts classes, then $\frac{m}{88}$ is the conditional probability. So, $\frac{m}{88} = \frac{100}{150} = 0.67$ if there should not be any association. This gives $m = 59$ students.

Summary:

A two way table shows categorical information about two variables. Each variable is divided into two groups. For example Gender is one variable that is divided into Male and Female groups. Class choice is another categorical variable that is divided into Arts and Science groups.

A two-way table has $2 \cdot 2 = 4$ cells. Additional cells are added to show the row totals and column totals. Probabilities can be calculated in marginal context, joint context, and conditional context.

Marginal probability:
What is the probability that a randomly selected student is an Arts student?
What is the probability that a randomly selected student is a female student?
Joint probability:
What is the probability that a randomly selected student is a male student taking an Arts class?
What is the probability that a randomly selected student is a female student taking a Science class?
Conditional probability:
What is the probability that a randomly selected male student will take an Arts class?
What is the probability that a randomly selected female student will take a Science class?
Association of variables:
Procedure to find whether there is an evidence of association of the two categorical variables:

1) Pick one column.
2) Find the conditional probability of the two cells in that column (cell value/row total)
3) If the conditional probabilities of the two cells are equal there is **no association.** If they are not equal, there is an **evidence of association**.
4) Use the fact that all three probabilities (two conditional and one marginal) in any one column must all be the same (in order not to have an association) to find any data that is not given. Refer to the above example to learn how to find missing data.

PROBLEM SOLVING AND DATA ANALYSIS		
Lesson 11	Population and Sample	Practice

CALCULATOR SECTION

A company that specializes in marketing research conducted a random survey in the state of Texas to find how many people agree that fracking (a method by which shale rock is broken to release natural gas) is necessary to meet the state's energy demand. The response was tabulated as shown below.

Survey Response (in thousands)

Age Group	Fracking OK	Fracking NOT OK	Not Sure	Total
16-25	8,259	2,345	925	11,529
25-50	7,680	5,250	89	13,019
50+	2,344	4,232	10	6,586
Total	18,283	11,827	1024	31,134

1. Based on the survey results, which age group does not like fracking the most?

(A) 16-25
(B) 25-50
(C) 50+
(D) 75+

2. A follow-up survey was done on the 16-25 age group to find out how many women like fracking by randomly selecting 700 people from this group. 435 respondents in this follow-up survey indicated that they are women. Based on the results of the follow-up survey and the results of the initial survey, which of the following is most likely to be an accurate estimate of how many women in the state of Texas think fracking is ok?

(A) About 3 million women in the state of Texas think fracking is OK.
(B) About 5 million women in the state of Texas think fracking is OK.
(C) About 7 million women in the state of Texas think fracking is OK.
(D) About 4 million women in the state of Texas think fracking is OK.

CALCULATOR SECTION

A soda manufacturing company conducted a random survey to find out how many boys and girls like their two brands of soda. The response was tabulated as shown below.

Age Group	Soda-1	Soda-2	Neither	Total
1-10	8,259	2,345	925	11,529
11-18	7,680	5,250	89	13,019
Total	15,939	7,595	1014	24,548

3. Based on the survey results, what percentage of 11-18 students like Soda-1 or Soda-2?
(A) 40.32
(B) 58.99
(C) 92.31
(D) 99.32

4. Of all those that like Soda-1, what percentage are in the 1-10 age group?
(A) 48.18
(B) 51.82
(C) 62.25
(D) 71.59

5. What percentage(rounded to the nearest hundredths) of those surveyed like neither soda?
GRID IN

6. A follow-up survey of boys and girls that like neither soda was conducted to find out a correlation between their weight and the reason for their dislike of soda. The average weight of the 125 boys and girls randomly surveyed in this follow-up is 85 pounds. What is most likely to be the average weight of the 1014 boys and girls that do not like soda?
GRID IN

CALCULATOR SECTION

The results of the 2010 Census taken at the city of Ventura is shown below.

Age	Asian	African	White	Hispanic
0-10	1300	2400	2000	850
11-25	2500	850	2255	4400
26-50	525	1050	1450	1940
51-100	727	550	650	640

7. What percentage of those in the 0-25 age group is African or White?
   (A) 28.74
   (B) 37.63
   (C) 45.33
   (D) 66.38

8. What percentage of Hispanic population is in the 26-100 age group?
   (A) 8.17
   (B) 24.78
   (C) 32.95
   (D) 41.38

9. A random sample of 26-50 year olds indicates that 35% of them have a Bachelor's degree. Based on this survey result, which one of the following can be inferred?

   (A) 35% of Asian American people in Ventura county have a Bachelor's degree.
   (B) 35% of Asian African American people in Ventura county have a Bachelor's degree.
   (C) 35% of Whites in Ventura county have a Bachelor's degree.
   (D) About 1060 people in the 26-50 age group have a Bachelor's degree.

10. A frequency distribution histogram showing Age buckets and Population will show which one of the following population for the 26-50 age group?
   (A) 655
   (B) 2567
   (C) 4965
   (D) 10,005

CALCULATOR SECTION

A survey done among 9th and 10th graders to find out how many learn Spanish and French produced the following results. The grade of the respondent and the language is listed adjacent to each other.

Grade	Language	Grade	Language	Grade	Language
9	Spanish	10	French	9	Spanish
10	French	9	French	10	Spanish
9	Spanish	10	Spanish	10	French

<u>Questions 10 and 11 refer to the table above</u>

11. How many 9th graders surveyed speak Spanish?
(A) 1
(B) 2
(C) 3
(D) 4

12. Which of the following two way tables represents the data shown above?

(A)

Grade	Spanish	French	Total
9	3	1	4
10	2	3	5
Total	5	4	9

(B)

Grade	Spanish	French	Total
9	2	3	5
10	3	1	4
Total	5	4	9

(C)

Grade	Spanish	French	Total
9	3	3	6
10	2	1	3
Total	5	4	9

(D)

Grade	Spanish	French	Total
9	1	3	4
10	3	2	5
Total	4	5	9

CALCULATOR SECTION

13. The table below shows the data collected from a survey that tried to find if there is an association (dependence) between types of soda by and age groups of students.

Age Group	Soda-1	Soda-2	Total
1-10	80	120	200
11-18	120	280	400
Total	200	400	600

Based on the survey results, the following conclusions can be made.

(A) There is an association between the age groups and the types of soda consumed
(B) There is no association between the age groups and the types of soda consumed
(C) The association between age groups and types of soda cannot be found from the data
(D) More data is required to find an association between age groups and types of soda

14. A two way table prepared after a survey was done on the response to headache tablets on children is shown below.

Age Group	Useful	Not useful	Total
1-10	80	120	200
11-18	120	180	300
Total	200	300	500

Based on the survey results, the following conclusions can be made.

(A) There is an association between the age groups and opinion
(B) There is no association between the age groups and opinion
(C) The association between age groups and opinion cannot be found from the data
(D) More data is required to find an association between age groups and opinion

15. Two lab tests were conducted on 12 guinea pigs. Each of them was placed in a sound proof cage. In Lab Test-1 a low decibel sound was sent into the cage through a small hole in the cage. The time it took for each guinea pig to recognize the sound was noted in seconds. In Lab Test-2 a high decibel sound was sent into the cage and the time it took for each guinea pig to recognize the sound was noted. The results are shown in the dot plots below. Which of the following inferences can be made?

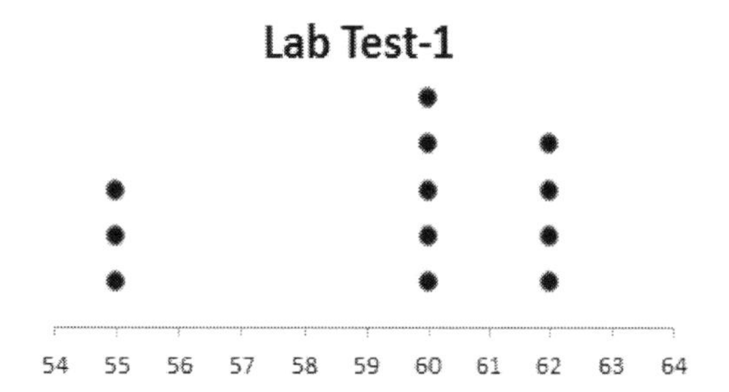

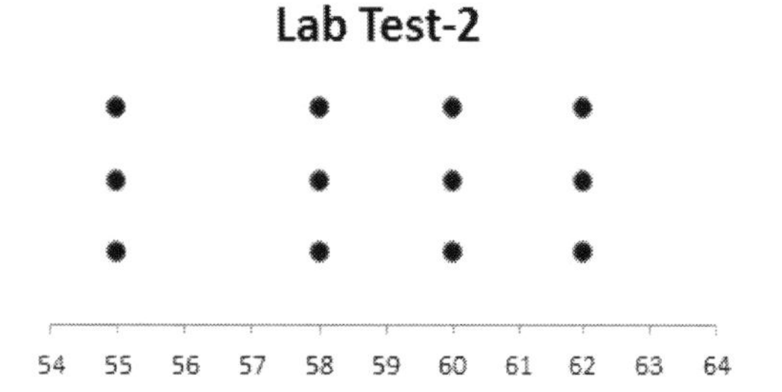

(A) Lab Test 1 has more standard deviation than Lab Test-2
(B) Lab Test 2 has more standard deviation than Lab Test-1
(C) Both tests have the same standard deviation
(D) More students should take the test in order to compare their standard deviations

16.

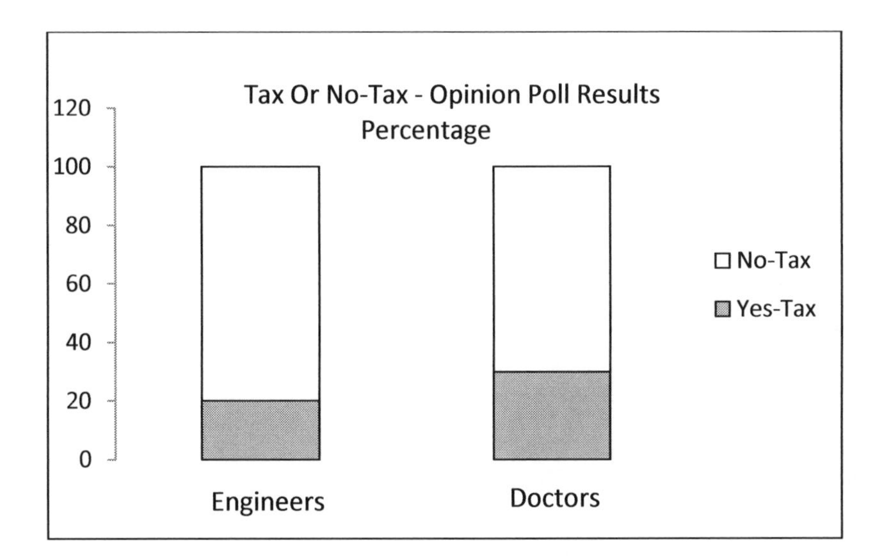

An opinion poll was conducted from Doctors and Engineers to decide if they support or oppose new taxes on their profession. The results are shown in percentages in the stacked bar chart. Which of the following inferences can be drawn from the opinion poll?

(A) Both Engineers and Doctors support taxes equally
(B) More Engineers than Doctors were polled
(C) There is no relation between professionals and their opinion on taxes
(D) There appears to be a relation between professionals and their opinion on taxes

17. A pharmaceutical company wants to test the effect of its back pain drug on 50 test subjects who work in warehouses. Which of the following choices represent the best plan of action to achieve reliable results?

(A) The company must go to warehouses across the country and observe 50 warehouse workers with back pain
(B) The company should select 50 warehouse workers from one warehouse in New York city, and administer the drug on them
(C) The company must randomly select 50 warehouse workers from the country and administer the drug on them
(D) The company must perform a controlled experiment on 50 warehouse workers with back pain selected randomly from the country, and administer the drug only to 25 of them while giving a placebo drug (that does nothing) to the rest

PROBLEM SOLVING AND DATA ANALYSIS		
Lesson 11	Population and Sample	Answers

<table>
<tr><th>#</th><th>Explanation</th><th>Comments</th></tr>
<tr><td>1 C</td><td>Even though age group 25-50 has more people that do not like fracking, as a percentage of their group, it is only 40.3% (5250/13019) whereas the age group 50+ is the one where 64.25% (4232/6586) of the respondents say they don't like fracking.</td><td>In this problem, you need to use the percentage to decide.</td></tr>
<tr><td>2 B</td><td>Follow-up survey was done on 700 people and 435 reported they are women; Percentage of women in 16-25 age group= $\frac{435}{700} \cdot 100 = 62\%$. Total of 8259 people say fracking is OK- so 62/100 ·8259 – about 5120·1000 – all numbers in the table are in thousands – approximately 5 million women think fracking is OK.</td><td>Follow-up survey is a survey that is done in addition to the main survey to find out specific information about the population.</td></tr>
<tr><td>3 D</td><td>The question asks what percentage like soda – which means both soda1- and soda-2 must be taken into account.
Soda-1+ soda-2= 7680+5250=12,930. Percentage= $\frac{12930}{13019} \cdot 100 = 99.32\%$</td><td></td></tr>
<tr><td>4 B</td><td>Total that like soda-1 is 15,939. Of these, 1-10 age group has 8259. So, the percentage is $\frac{8259}{15939} \cdot 100 = 51.82\%$</td><td></td></tr>
<tr><td>5
4.13</td><td>1014 like neither soda; 24,548 surveyed.
$\frac{1014}{24548} \cdot 100 = 4.13\%$</td><td></td></tr>
<tr><td>6
85</td><td>1014 do not like soda.
Sample of 125 students has an average weight of 85 lbs.
So, this statistic of the <u>sample</u> can be applied to the <u>population</u> and you can say that the average weight of 1014 boys and girls will also be 85 lbs.</td><td>A statistic of the sample can be used to make an inference about the population, provided that the sample is not biased.</td></tr>
<tr><td>7 C</td><td>
<table>
<tr><td>Age</td><td>Asian</td><td>African</td><td>White</td><td>Hispanic</td><td></td></tr>
<tr><td>0-10</td><td>1300</td><td>2400</td><td>2000</td><td>850</td><td>6550</td></tr>
<tr><td>11-25</td><td>2500</td><td>850</td><td>2255</td><td>4400</td><td>10005</td></tr>
<tr><td>26-50</td><td>525</td><td>1050</td><td>1450</td><td>1940</td><td>4965</td></tr>
<tr><td>51-100</td><td>725</td><td>550</td><td>650</td><td>640</td><td>2565</td></tr>
<tr><td></td><td></td><td></td><td></td><td>7830</td><td></td></tr>
</table>
Question is about the 0-25 group – this is 0-10 group + 11-25 group.
African =2400+850=3250
White=2000+2255=4255.
Total African or White= 3250+4255=7505.</td><td>Add additional columns or rows to place your subtotals there.</td></tr>
</table>

<table>
<tr><td></td><td>Total in the 0-25 group=6550+10005=16555.
So, the percentage is 7505/16555 ·100=45.33%</td><td></td></tr>
<tr><td>8 C</td><td>The age range in this question is 26-100, which is 26-50 + 51-100. Total Hispanic population in 26-100 age group =1940+640=2580. Total Hispanic population is 7830. So, the percentage is 2580/7830 ·100=32.95%</td><td></td></tr>
<tr><td>9 D</td><td>Random sample of 26-50 year olds indicate 35% of them have a Bachelor's degree. So, you can conclude that 35% of the total 26-50 year olds – 35/100 · 3025=1058 ≅ 1060 people have Bachelor's degree. Note that other choices are not true because you don't know the breakdown of the random sample among Asian, African, White, and Hispanic separately to make this inference.</td><td>Make inferences carefully by considering the type of sample obtained.</td></tr>
<tr><td>10 C</td><td>The frequency histogram showing age group 26-50 on the x-axis will correspond to a population frequency of 525+1050+1450+1940.</td><td>See the lesson on graphs and tables and statistics for a review of histograms.</td></tr>
<tr><td>11 C</td><td>Count the number of Spanish speaking 9th graders; there are 3 of them.</td><td>Get familiar with the way the survey results are recorded.</td></tr>
<tr><td>12 A</td><td>There are a total of 9 students in the survey chart; there are 3 Spanish and 1 French 9th graders, 10 Spanish and 3 French 10th graders. So table 1 is the correct choice.</td><td>Familiarize yourself with two way tables.</td></tr>
<tr><td>13 B</td><td>
<table>
<tr><th>Age Group</th><th>Soda-1</th><th>Soda-2</th><th>Total</th></tr>
<tr><td>1-10</td><td>80 (80/200=0.4)</td><td>120</td><td>200</td></tr>
<tr><td>11-18</td><td>120 (120/400=0.3)</td><td>280</td><td>400</td></tr>
<tr><td>Total</td><td>200</td><td>400</td><td>600</td></tr>
</table>
To check if an association exists between Age Groups and Soda types, calculate the conditional distributions for any soda type. Since the distributions are not the same, an association exists between the variables. Age group seems to have an effect on what types of soda is consumed.</td><td>Remember that when the conditional distributions are the same in any column, then there is no association/dependence/ relation.</td></tr>
<tr><td>14 B</td><td>Calculate the conditional distribution as shown for one column as shown. Across age groups, the opinions have the same probability – 0.4. This indicates no association.
<table>
<tr><th>Age Group</th><th>Useful</th><th>Not useful</th><th>Total</th></tr>
<tr><td>1-10</td><td>80
80/200=0.4</td><td>120</td><td>200</td></tr>
<tr><td>11-18</td><td>120
120/300=0.4</td><td>180</td><td>300</td></tr>
<tr><td>Total</td><td>200
200/500=0.4</td><td>300</td><td>500</td></tr>
</table>
</td><td>If the conditional probabilities are the same across different groups of the same variable (age group in this case), there is no association between the variables (age group and opinion)</td></tr>
</table>

15 B	You are asked to compare the standard deviation of two sets of data. In Test-1, several data values are at 60 and 61 and a few values are at 55. So the average is likely to be between 60 and 62. Since the values of 9 guinea pigs are clustered around the mean, the standard deviation is likely to be very less. In Test-2, the mean is likely to be about 59 since the values are distributed around 59. But the values are also dispersed widely. So, the standard deviation of Lab Test-2 is likely to be significantly greater than the standard deviation of Lab Test-1.	
16 D	Note that this question does not show you a two-way table of data but instead summarizes it and shows the percentages in a stacked bar chart. The categorical variables are Professions and Opinions. The groups within Professions are Engineers and Doctors and the groups within Opinions are Yes-Tax and No-Tax. The Engineers bar shows that 20% of them voted Yes and 80% voted No. The Doctors bar shows that 30% voted Yes and 70% voted No. Recognize that these percentages are the same as conditional probabilities of these groups with respect to the other groups. For example, 20% of Engineers say Yes to tax. This means that the probability that a randomly selected Engineer will say Yes to tax is 20% or 0.2. For an association (relation) to exist between professions and opinions, the conditional probabilities must be the same. Since the conditional probabilities for Yes-Tax are 0.2 for Engineers and 0.3 for Doctors, there seems to be a relation between professions and taxes in that the doctors seems to be more inclined to accept more taxes than engineers.	In questions that ask if relations exist, first recognize the two categories and the groups within their categories. Then identify the conditional probabilities of one group across other groups. In this problem, find the conditional probability of Yes-Tax across Engineers and Doctors. If they are the same, there is no relation between the categories. If they are different, there is a relation between the categories.
17 D	Choice A is incorrect since an observational study is not going to tell you how effective the drug is. Choice B is incorrect, since the 50 warehouse workers from New York city alone is not an unbiased sample. Choice C is incorrect, since the 50 warehouse workers from across the country may not have back pain before the drug was administered on them. Choice D is correct, since a controlled experiment on 50 workers with back pain, is likely to give reliable results about the efficiency of the drug.	Expect questions like this that give you the goal of the study and ask you which of the given choices is the best study design that will yield reliable results. Remember that surveys should be unbiased, and samples must be taken at random to yield best results. Polls and Surveys are observational studies. Experimental studies apply treatment on the subjects to find if there is a cause and effect relationship. They also have a control group on which treatment is not applied.

FOCUSPREP CHECKLIST

- What are the different ways of counting?
- What are the Addition and Multiplication principles of counting?
- What is the Permutation formula and when do I use it?
- What is the Combination formula and when do I use it?
- Workout practice problems in Counting

Q1 What are the different ways of counting?

A1 There are several different ways to count - making up a list, using the multiplication or addition counting principles, placing the numbers in a Venn Diagram, using the Permutations formula $n\text{P}r$ and using the Combinations formula $n\text{C}r$.

Q2 What are the types of counting problems?

A2 Examples of counting problems include finding the number of ways in which officers can be selected from available candidates, finding the number of ways in which a team can be formed, problems involving Venn diagrams, license plate problems, phone number problems, etc.

Q3 What is the Multiplication Principle of Counting?

A3 The Multiplication Principle of Counting states that when one task can be done in m ways and another task can be done in n ways, both tasks can be done in $m \cdot n$ ways.

Example: There are 5 ways to go from New York to London. There are 3 ways to go from London to Beijing. How many ways are there to go from New York to Beijing?

Solution: For each of the 5 ways from New York to London, you can take one of the 3 ways to go from London to Beijing. Using the multiplication principle of counting, there are $5 \cdot 3 = 15$ ways to go from New York to Beijing.

Q4 What is the Addition Principle of Counting?

A4 The Addition principle of counting states that when one task can be done in m ways and another task can be done in n ways, and both tasks can be done in k ways, then there are $m + n - k$ ways of doing both tasks.

Problem: From a standard deck of playing cards, if you pick one card only, in how many ways can you pick a Diamond or a card with an odd number?

Solution: There are 4 suits of cards – each suit has 13 cards. So, the Diamond suit has 13 cards. In each of the 4 suits, there are 4 odd numbered cards (3,5,7,9). So, totally there are $4 \cdot 4 = 16$ odd numbered cards. The number of cards that are both odd numbered and Diamond is 4. So, by the addition counting principle, there are $13 + 16 - 4 = 25$ ways to pick a card that is either a Diamond or an odd numbered card.

Q5 How do I use Venn diagrams to solve counting problems?

A5 Venn diagram problems will describe two sets or three sets of information. Pay very careful attention while placing numbers inside the diagrams. For example, in the 2-set Venn diagram below, the number of English speakers is 3+2=5 and this includes the number of English only speakers(3) and the number of English speakers that speak Spanish(2). Also note that some speakers may speak neither English nor Spanish and they also have to be accounted for. In this 2-set example, 2 people speak neither English nor Spanish and are placed outside the circles.

2-set Venn Diagrams

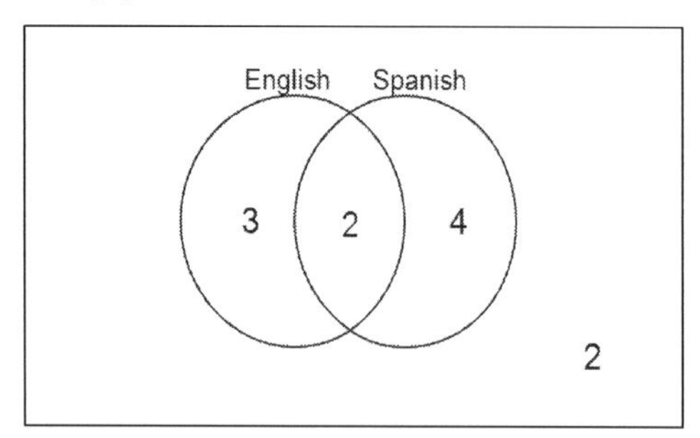

3-set Venn Diagrams

The 3-set Venn Diagram below shows three sets of data and how they are related. Note the meaning of each area of the Venn Diagram carefully. For example, there are 13 people who speak English(4+2+3+4), 4 people who speak English only, 2 people who speak English and Spanish but not French, 3 people who speak English, Spanish, and French, and 4 people who speak English and French but not Spanish.

40

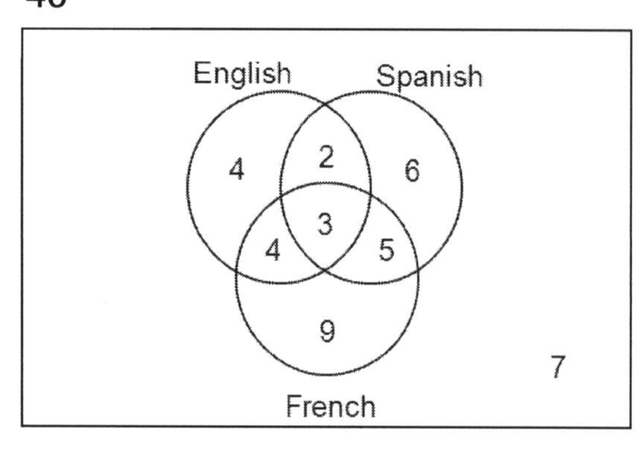

Q6 What is the factorial of a number n?

A6 Factorial of a number n is represented by $n!$ and is defined as $n! = n \cdot (n-1) \cdot (n-2) \cdot (n-3) \cdot \ldots 3 \cdot 2 \cdot 1$ Note that $n! = n \cdot (n-1)! = n(n-1)(n-2)!$ and so on.

Examples:

$4! = 4 \cdot 3 \cdot 2 \cdot 1 = 24.$

$6! = 6 \cdot 5! = 6 \cdot 5 \cdot 4!$

Q7 What is the Permutation formula? When do I use it?

A7 The Permutation formula helps you to find out the number of ways you can select r items from the available n items, where the order of items selected matters. It is represented as $n\mathrm{P}r$ and is calculated as $n\mathrm{P}r = \frac{n!}{(n-r)!}$

Problem: From five letters A,B,C,D,E in how many ways can two letters be selected if the order of selection matters?

Solution:: Using the permutation formula, $n = 5, r = 2,\ n\mathrm{P}r = 5P2 = \frac{5!}{(5-2)!} = \frac{5!}{3!} = \frac{5 \cdot 4 \cdot 3!}{3!} = 20$ ways. Note that since ordering matters in permutation problems, AB and BA are separate selections and are counted as two separate selections. See below for the same problem where the order of selection does not matter. You can work out more Permutation problems in the practice section.

Q8 What is the Combination formula? When do I use it?

A8 The Combination formula helps you to find out the number of ways you can select r items from n available items, where the order of items selected does not matter. It is represented as $n\mathrm{C}r$ and is calculated as $n\mathrm{C}r = \frac{n!}{r!(n-r)!}$

Problem: From five letters A,B,C,D,E in how many ways can two letters be selected if the order of selection is not important.

Solution: Using the Combination formula, $n = 5, r = 2, n\mathrm{C}r = \binom{5}{2} = \frac{5!}{2!(5-2)!} = \frac{5!}{2!3!} = \frac{5 \cdot 4 \cdot 3!}{2!3!} = \frac{20}{2} = 10$ ways. As you can see, in this answer using Combination formula, AB and BA are considered one selection and are counted only once. You can work out more Combination problems in the practice section.

PROBLEM SOLVING AND DATA ANALYSIS		
Lesson 12	Counting	Practice

CALCULATOR SECTION

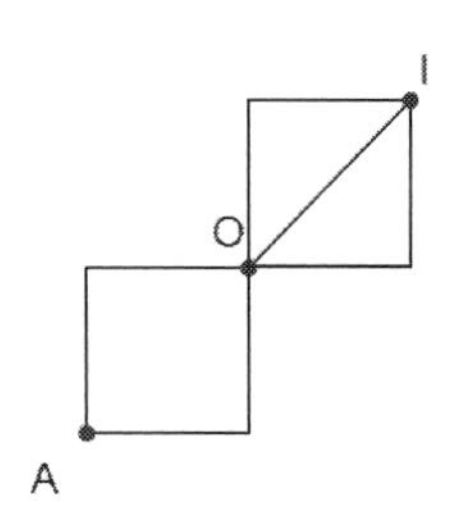

1. In the figure above, how many ways are there to go from A to I?
(A) 2
(B) 3
(C) 5
(D) 6

2. There are 6 highways from A to B, 3 train routes from A to B, and 4 ferry routes from B to C. In how many ways can you go from A to C?
(A) 12
(B) 24
(C) 36
(D) 48

3. There are 5 pencils and 6 crayons in a box. If you pick one item only, in how many ways can you choose a pencil or a crayon?
(A) 5
(B) 6
(C) 11
(D) 30

CALCULATOR SECTION

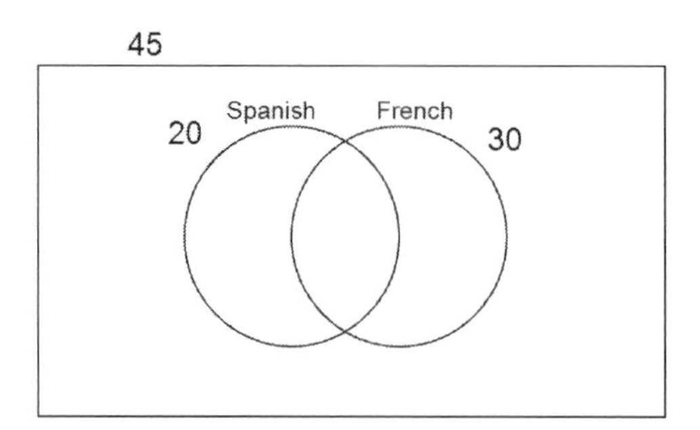

20 students in a class learn Spanish and 30 students learn French. There are 45 students in the class as shown in the Venn diagram.

Questions 4, 5 and 6 refer to the above diagram

4. How many students learn both Spanish and French?
(A) 5
(B) 6
(C) 20
(D) 30

5. How many students learn French but not Spanish?
(A) 10
(B) 20
(C) 25
(D) 30

6. How many students learn neither French nor Spanish?
(A) 0
(B) 5
(C) 10
(D) 20

CALCULATOR SECTION

In a housing community, 15 people play Tennis, 20 people play Soccer, and 25 people play Baseball. 5 People play Tennis and Soccer but not baseball. 4 people play Tennis and Baseball but not Soccer. 6 people play Soccer and Baseball but not Tennis. There are 35 people in the housing community.

Questions 7-10 refer to the problem above.

7. How many people play all three games?
(A) 3
(B) 4
(C) 5
(D) 9

8. How many people play Soccer and Baseball?
(A) 4
(B) 9
(C) 10
(D) 11

9. How many people play only one game?
(A) 1
(B) 4
(C) 10
(D) 15

CALCULATOR SECTION

10. A student council plans to fill three positions, namely the President, Vice President, and Treasurer. Eight students stand for elections to these three positions. In how many ways can the positions be filled?
(A) 256
(B) 336
(C) 408
(D) 512

11. The license plate for a special vehicle will consist of three letters, picked from A to Z. Letters can be repeated. How many license plates can be given out for this special vehicle?
(A) 15,600
(B) 17,576
(C) 18,200
(D) 18,576

12. The license plate for a special vehicle will consist of three letters, picked from A to Z. Letters cannot be repeated. How many license plates can be given out for this special vehicle?
(A) 10,630
(B) 12,200
(C) 15,600
(D) 16,500

Student ID

0				

13. A student ID will be created with 5 digits chosen from 0 to 9. The first number must be 0 and the second number must be less than 4. The numbers cannot be repeated. What is the maximum number of students that can be issued an ID under this scheme?
GRID IN

14. From a class of 15 boys and 8 girls, in how many ways can a team of 5 students be selected?
(A) 22,500
(B) 33,250
(C) 33,649
(D) 41,249

15. From pool of 10 Robotic Engineers and 7 Biotechnology Engineers, a team needs to be created that has 3 Robotic Engineers and 2 Biotechnology Engineers. How many teams can be created?
GRID IN

CALCULATOR SECTION

16. The picture above needs to be shaded such that each of the four sections is shaded with a different color that is picked from a 5 color palette set. In how many ways can the above picture be colored?
GRID IN

17. XXX-XXX

A cell phone company wants to issue phone numbers to its customers in the format above where X stands for any number from 0-9. The last digit must always be 0 and numbers cannot be repeated. How many customers can be issued a number in the above format?
(A) 10,250
(B) 12,150
(C) 15,020
(D) 15,120

PROBLEM SOLVING AND DATA ANALYSIS

Lesson 12	Counting	Answers

#	Explanation	Comments
1 D	In this figure, you can go from A to O in 2 ways and O to I in 3 ways – so you can go from A to I in $2 \cdot 3 = 6$ ways.	An easy way to solve these type of problems is to count the ways from the starting point to a mid point and from midpoint to the destination and then multiply.
2 C	6 highways from A to B 3 train routes from A to B 4 ferry routes from B to C Totally 6+3=9 ways to go from A to B; 4 ways to go from B to C – so 9 · 4=36 ways to go from A to C.	Use the multiplication principle of counting. Be careful not to do 6 ·3·4=72; read the question carefully.
3 C	5 pencils, 6 crayons, only one item is picked 1 pencil can be picked in 5 ways (one of the 5 pencils) 1 crayon can be picked in 6 ways(one of the 5 crayons) 0 ways to choose both a pencil and a crayon, since only one item is picked. Totally 5+6-0=11 ways to choose 1 pencil or 1 crayon.	Use the addition principle of counting.
4 A	Let x be the number of students who learn both. $20 - x$ learn Spanish; x learn both, $30 - x$ learn French; 45 total; So $20 - x + x + 3 - x = 45$; $50 - x = 45$; $x = 50 - 45 = 5$.	
5 C	The question is "how many students learn French but not Spanish" – this is the same as asking "how many learn French only" – see the diagram – the answer is $30 - x = 30 - 5 = 25$	
6 A	How many learn neither French nor Spanish? All the areas of the Venn diagram add up to 45. 15+5+25=45. So, all 45 students learn either French or Spanish or both. Nobody learns anything other than French and Spanish. So, the answer is 0.	
7 C	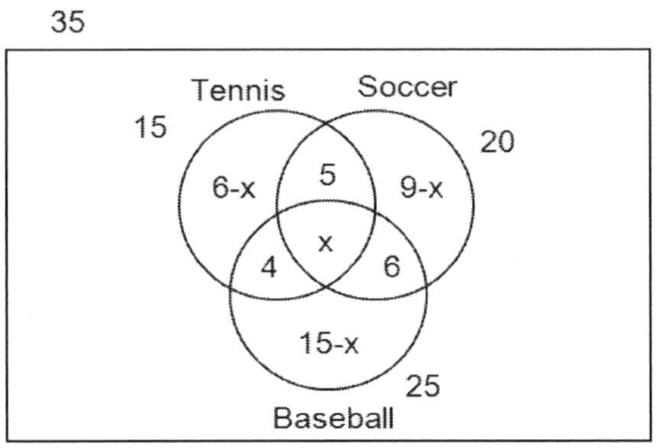 35 Tennis Soccer 15 20 6-x 5 9-x x 4 6 15-x 25 Baseball	Place the numbers accurately in the Venn diagram. Understand the meaning of each area of the Venn diagram.

	Let x be the number of people who play all the games. Place the numbers from the problem in the Venn diagram. Those who play tennis only is $15 - 5 - 4 - x = 6 - x$. Those who play soccer only is $20 - 5 - 6 - x = 9 - x$. Those who play baseball only is $25 - 4 - x - 6 = 15 - x$. There are totally 35 people. Set up an equation. $6 - x + 5 + x + 4 + 9 - x + 6 + 15 - x = 35$ $45 - 2x = 35$ $2x = 10$ $x = 5$; So 5 people play all the games.	
8 D	Soccer + Baseball = $x + 6$=$5 + 6 = 11$.	
9 D	People who play only one game= those who play tennis only+ those who play soccer only + those who play baseball only = 1+4+10=15.	
10 B	8 students want to stand for 3 positions; So, the number of ways these positions can be filled is $8\text{P}3 = \frac{8!}{(8-3)!} = \frac{8!}{5!} = \frac{8 \cdot 7 \cdot 6 \cdot 5!}{5!} = 8 \cdot 7 \cdot 6 = 336$ ways.	Note that you need to figure out if this is a permutation or combination problem. In this problem, 3 positions are filled – so it matters who is in what position – when position matters, it is a Permutation problem. Remember the "P" in Permutation as "Position Matters".
11 B	Three letters are picked from A to Z. So, that is 26 letters to pick from. Problem says that the letters can be repeated – so you can have AAA, AAB, or ABA, etc . The first letter can be picked in 26 ways; second letter in 26 ways, and the third letter in 26 ways. So, totally 26 · 26 · 26 =17,576 3-letter plates can be given out for this vehicle.	
12 C	This is similar to the previous problem but the letters cannot be repeated – that is you cannot have AAB, ABB etc. So, this is a pure permutation problem – of selecting 3 letters from 26 letters – so the answer is $26\text{P}3$ =15,600	Learn how to calculate nPr and nCr using your calculator.
13 1008	There are 10 numbers available form 0-9 1st number = 0 2nd number - must be less than 4 = 0,1,2,3 – but numbers cannot be repeated and 0 has been taken – so 3 numbers are allowed in 2nd spot – numbers 1,2,3 3rd number – so far 2 numbers are taken – so you have 10-2=8 numbers available for 3rd spot 4th number – 8-1=7 numbers available for 4th spot 5th number = 7-1=6 numbers available for 5th sport Totally, you have $1 \cdot 3 \cdot 8 \cdot 7 \cdot 6 = 1008$ numbers available.	This is a permutation problem with constraints; find the possibilities for each spot and then multiply. When you count the available numbers from 0-9, don't forget to count 0.

14 C	15 boys 8 girls = 23 students 5 students can be selected in 23C5 ways=33,649	Note that the problem says there are 15 boys and 8 girls but the team can have boys and girls in any numbers such that the team has exactly 5 students ; do the next problem to see a variation of this problem.
15 2520	10 robotic and 7 biotech engineers available 3 robotic and 2 biotech engineer team 3 robotic engineers can be selected in 10C3 ways – note that order does not matter – this is a combination problem – 2 biotech engineers can be selected in 7C2 ways So the total number of teams is 10C3 · 7C2= 120·21=2520 teams.	
16 120	4 areas in the figure – when you color the first area, 5 colors are available; when you color the second area 4 colors are available, and so on. Only one color can be used in each area. So, for the 4 areas, there are $5 \cdot 4 \cdot 3 \cdot 2 = 120$ ways to color	
17 D	Six spots in the phone number. Available numbers =0-9 = 10 numbers; Last digit is 0 and numbers cannot be repeated – so 10-1=9 numbers available for each of the 5 spots. 1st spot – 9 ways; 2nd spot – 8 ways etc.; last spot is 0. Totally $9 \cdot 8 \cdot 7 \cdot 6 \cdot 5 \cdot 1$=15,120	

PROBLEM SOLVING AND DATA ANALYSIS		
Lesson 13	Probability	Review

FOCUSPREP CHECKLIST

- How do I calculate the probability of an event?
- What are dependent and independent events?
- While selecting objects, what does "with replacement" mean?
- What does conditional probability mean? How do I calculate it?
- How do I calculate the Geometric probability?

Q1 What is a sample space?

A1 The set of all possible outcomes of an experiment is called Sample space.
<u>Example</u>: A coin is tossed. The sample space = {Heads, Tails}
<u>Example</u>: A student is selected and gender is noted. The sample space = {Boy, Girl}

Q2 How is the probability of an event defined?

A2 The Probability of an event is defined as the ratio of the number of favorable outcomes of the event to the total number of possible outcomes of the event.
If A is an event, then the probability of event A= $P(A) = \frac{favorable\ outcomes\ of\ event\ A}{possible\ outcomes\ of\ event\ A}$

<u>Example</u>: A die is rolled. What is the probability that the number 3 will be on the top?
<u>Solution</u>: Number of favorable outcomes= 1 (there is only one way the number 3 will be on top)
Number of possible outcomes=6 (any one of 1,2,3,4,5,6 could be on top)
So, the probability= $\frac{1}{6}$.

<u>Example</u>: A die is rolled. What is the probability that a number less than 3 will be on the top?
<u>Solution</u>: Number of favorable outcomes= 2 (when the numbers 1 or 2 are on the top)
Number of possible outcomes=6 (any one of 1,2,3,4,5,6 could be on top)
So, the probability= $\frac{2}{6} = \frac{1}{3}$

Q3 How do I find the number of favorable outcomes and number of possible outcomes?

A3 Depending on the problem, you can find this by listing and counting, using the addition and multiplication principles of counting, or by using permutation or combination formulas discussed in the lesson on Counting.

Q4 What are the minimum and maximum values of probability of an event?

A4 Minimum value = 0. This is the case when the number of favorable outcomes is 0 which will be true when the event cannot occur at all.
Maximum value = 1. This is the case when the number of favorable outcomes is equal to the number of possible outcomes. For any event A, $0 \leq P(A) \leq 1$

Q5 What is the complement of an event?

A5 The complement of an event A is the probability of it NOT occurring. If $P(A)$ is the probability of an event A, then the probability that the event will not happen (complement) is $P(A') = 1 - P(A)$. Note that $P(A) + P(A') = 1$.

Q6 How do I calculate the probability when two events are involved?

A6 When two events, event A and event B are possible, then only event A can occur or only event B can occur or both event A and event B can occur.

- The probability that either event will occur is $P(A \cup B) = P(A) + P(B) - P(A \cap B)$.
- The probability that both events will occur is $P(A \cap B) = P(A) \cdot P(B)$ if they are independent events.
- The probability that both events will occur is $P(A \cap B) = P(A) \cdot P(B|A)$ if they are dependent events. $P(B|A)$ is called conditional probability of event B given that event A has occurred.

Q7 What are independent and dependent events?

A7 Two events A and B are independent if one event does not affect the sample space of another event. Two events A and B are dependent if one event affects the sample space of another event.

Example (Independent Events):
Consider a set S={1,2,3,4,5,6,7,8,9}. Pick a number from set S and replace it (put it back into the set). Now, pick another number. What is the probability that the first number picked is even and the second number picked is odd?

Solution: Let event A= the number picked is even and event B= number picked is odd. The probability of picking an even number= $P(A) = \frac{4}{9}$ (4 even numbers and 9 numbers in all). After picking the first number, it is replaced (returned back to the sample space) and so the sample space still has 9 numbers when you go to pick the second number. Picking the first number and picking the second number are independent events – they do not depend on each other. So, $P(B) = \frac{5}{9}$ since there are 5 odd numbers. The probability the first number is even and the second number is odd is

$$P(A \cap B) = P(A) \cdot (B) = \frac{4}{9} \cdot \frac{5}{9} = \frac{20}{81}.$$

Example (Dependent Events):
Consider a set S={1,2,3,4,5,6,7,8,9}. Pick a number from set S. Now, pick another number. What is the probability that the first number picked is even and the second number picked is odd?

Solution: The probability that the number picked is even = $P(A) = \frac{4}{9}$ (4 even numbers and 9 numbers in all). After picking the first number, sample space is reduced by 1 and so it now has 9-1= 8 numbers available for picking when you go to pick the second number. Picking the first number and picking the second number are dependent events – one affects the sample space of the other. So, The probability

that the second number picked is odd is = $p(B) = \frac{5}{8}$ since there are 5 odd numbers. The probability the first number is even and the second number is odd is $P(A \cap B) = P(A) \cdot P(B|A) = \frac{4}{9} \cdot \frac{5}{8} = \frac{20}{72} = \frac{5}{18}$.
P(B|A) means the probability of event B given that event A has occurred. P(B|A) is referred to as the conditional probability. For independent events, $P(A \cap B) = P(A) \cdot P(B)$. For dependent events, $P(A \cap B) = P(A) \cdot P(B|A)$. Pay attention to the sample space available when you calculate the probability. Sample space is the list of all possible outcomes.

Q8 What are mutually exclusive events?

A8 Two events A and B are mutually exclusive if they cannot occur at the same time. In this case, $P(A \cap B)$=0.

<u>**Example**</u>: Toss a coin. Event A= you get a Head Event B= you get a Tail. What is the probability of getting a head and a tail?

<u>**Solution**</u>: Sample space(outcome) of event A ={Head} and sample space (outcome) of event B={Tail}. You cannot get a head and tail at the same time. The two events are mutually exclusive. So, the number of favorable outcomes=0. Hence P(Head and Tail) = P(A∩B)=0.

Q9 What does selection with replacement mean?

A9 After you select a specific item from a larger set, if you return it back to the set, then it is called "replacement". For example, say you have 3 balls and you select 1 ball first and then another ball. After selecting the first ball, if you put it back, then it is called "replacement". In that case, the first ball that you selected is available for selecting again when you go to pick the second ball. This is important to note and will affect the probability calculations. Problem statements will indicate if the items are selected <u>with replacement</u>. If they don't then you can assume that the items selected are NOT available for selection again. This will affect the sample space available and you will need to use conditional probability in your calculation.

Q10 What does Geometric probability mean? Where is it used?

A19 Geometric probability is used when you have to calculate probability with respect to an area. For example, what is the probability that a dart thrown on a dart board will fall on the inner ring?

Geometric Probability = $\frac{\text{Favorable Target Area}}{\text{Total Possible Area}}$

Q11 What is a deck of cards made of?

A11 A deck (full set) of cards has a total of 52 cards split into 4 suits – Club ♣, Diamond ♦, Heart ♥ and Spade ♠. Each suite has 13 cards. So, totally there are $4 \cdot 13 = 52$ cards. The 13 cards in each suit consist of one King, one Queen, one Jack, one Ace and 9 cards that are numbered 2,3,4,5,6,7,8,9,10. The cards in Diamond and Heart suites are red in color. The cards in Spade and Club suites are black in color. Remembering this information will help you solve probability problems involving playing cards.

PROBLEM SOLVING AND DATA ANALYSIS		
Lesson 13	Probability	Practice

CALCULATOR SECTION

1. A box has 3 red balls, 4 green balls, and 5 blue balls. What is the probability that a ball picked at random will be a green ball?

(A) $\frac{1}{4}$

(B) $\frac{1}{3}$

(C) $\frac{1}{2}$

(D) 1

2. A box has 3 red balls and 4 green balls. What is the probability that two balls picked randomly one after the other are both red in color?

(A) $\frac{1}{8}$

(B) $\frac{1}{7}$

(C) $\frac{1}{2}$

(D) 1

3. A box has 3 red balls and 4 green balls. What is the probability that two balls picked randomly are both of the same color?

(A) $\frac{1}{7}$

(B) $\frac{2}{7}$

(C) $\frac{3}{7}$

(D) $\frac{4}{7}$

CALCULATOR SECTION

4. In a college, the probability that students will chose a science major is $\frac{3}{5}$ and the probability that they will choose an arts major is $\frac{2}{5}$. If a student can choose only one major, what is the probability of choosing a science major or an arts major?

(A) $\frac{6}{25}$

(B) $\frac{2}{5}$

(C) $\frac{3}{5}$

(D) 1

The Panthers Music team has 6 bassoon players Andrea, Betty, Cindy, Darlene, Emma, and Frank. The coach wants to pick 2 players for a statewide competition.

Questions 5-7 refer to the information above

5. What is the probability that Andrea will be selected for the competition?
GRID IN

6. What is the probability that Andrea and Betty will be selected for the competition?
GRID IN

7. What is the probability that Andrea will go with Betty or Cindy will go with Darlene to the competition?
GRID IN

A,G,L,O

8. If the set of letters above are rearranged to create new sets, then what is the probability that a set will have letters in the following order: G,O,A,L

(A) $\frac{1}{72}$

(B) $\frac{1}{60}$

(C) $\frac{1}{25}$

(D) $\frac{1}{24}$

9. If the letters O,D,G are placed randomly in the three cells in the table above, what is the probability that the cells will read G,O,D from left to right?

(A) $\frac{1}{6}$

(B) $\frac{1}{3}$

(C) $\frac{1}{4}$

(D) $\frac{1}{2}$

CALCULATOR SECTION

Set M = {30,40,50}
Set N= {5,10,15}

10. Two numbers m and n are chosen randomly, one from each set M and N shown above. What is the probability that $\frac{m}{n}$ is an integer?
GRID IN

Set N = {1,2,3,4,5,6,7,8,9,10}

11. What is the probability that a number selected randomly from the set above is a perfect square?

(A) $\frac{1}{6}$

(B) $\frac{1}{5}$

(C) $\frac{1}{4}$

(D) $\frac{3}{10}$

12. Alex has 6 red toys and 8 green toys in a box. He picks one toy at random, notes the color and puts it back in the box. He then picks another toy at random again. What is the probability that the second toy is green?
GRID IN

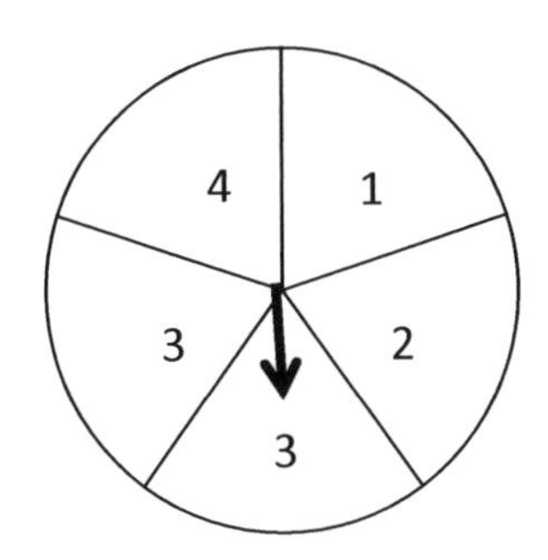

13. If the spinner above is spun twice, what is the probability that you will get a 3 in one spin and a number that is not 3 in the other spin?

(A) $\frac{3}{25}$

(B) $\frac{4}{25}$

(C) $\frac{6}{25}$

(D) $\frac{8}{25}$

14. If a coin is tossed once, the probability of getting Heads is $\frac{1}{2}$. If the coin is tossed twice, what is the probability of getting a Heads both times?
GRID IN

CALCULATOR SECTION

15. A piggy bank has 2 quarters and 3 dimes. If two coins are picked at random one after the other, what is the probability that they add up to more than 35 cents?

(A) $\frac{1}{20}$

(B) $\frac{1}{10}$

(C) $\frac{1}{4}$

(D) $\frac{1}{2}$

16. The probability of seeing a lion at the zoo is $\frac{1}{6}$. How many animals cannot be in the zoo?

(A) 6
(B) 12
(C) 20
(D) 24

17. Two cards are selected from a deck of cards. What is the probability that you will select a 3 in the Hearts suit and a 5 in the Spades suit?

A) $\frac{1}{2704}$

B) $\frac{1}{2652}$

C) $\frac{1}{15}$

D) $\frac{1}{8}$

CALCULATOR SECTION

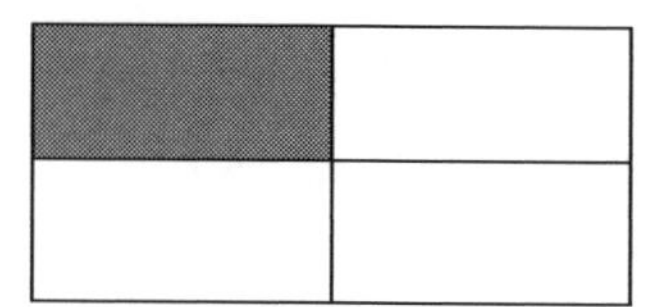

18. In the figure above, a rectangle is divided into 4 equal parts. If a stone is thrown randomly on the rectangle, what is the probability that it will land on the shaded portion?

(A) 0.2
(B) 0.25
(C) 0.5
(D) 0.75

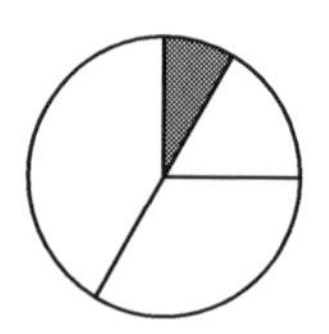

19. In the figure of a circular swimming pool shown above, the arc of shaded portion makes $30°$ at the center of the circle. If a bird falls into the pool, what is the probability that it will fall into the shaded region of the pool?

(A) $\frac{1}{12}$

(B) $\frac{1}{10}$

(C) $\frac{1}{4}$

(D) $\frac{1}{2}$

CALCULATOR SECTION

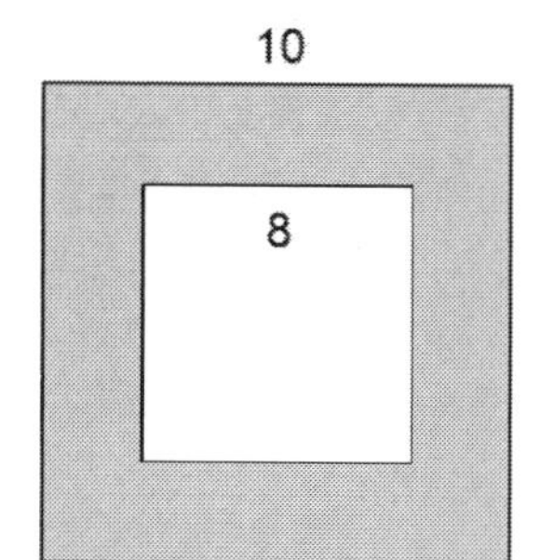

20. The figure above shows a dart board. The outer square is 10 inches wide and the inner square is 8 inches wide. If a dart is thrown at the board, what is the probability that it will fall on the shaded area between the outer and the inner square?

(A) $\frac{8}{25}$

(B) $\frac{9}{25}$

(C) $\frac{2}{5}$

(D) $\frac{3}{5}$

PROBLEM SOLVING AND DATA ANALYSIS		
Lesson 13	Probability	Answers

#	Explanation	Comments
1 B	Favorable outcomes for green=4 Total outcomes=12 P(green) = $\frac{4}{12} = \frac{1}{3}$	If a problem like this is confusing, think what the probability will be if all the balls were green – obviously it will be 1 – since all the balls are not green, the probability is going to be a fraction less than 1 – so it is the number of green balls that helps you to get to the answer.
2 B	First note that the problem does not state that the first ball was replaced(put back). So you have to assume that it was not replaced. P(first is red and second is red)= P(first is red) · P(second is red|first is red). (this is conditional probability) P(first is red)= $\frac{3}{7}$ After first red ball is picked, you have only 2 red balls and 4 green balls left. P(second is red)= $\frac{2}{6} = \frac{1}{3}$ So P(first is red and second is red)= $\frac{3}{7} \cdot \frac{1}{3} = \frac{1}{7}$	Review how conditional probability is calculated.
3 C	3 red and 4 green; pick 2 balls P(2 balls are of same color)=? 2 balls will be of same color if they are Red,Red OR Green,Green P(red,red)= $\frac{3}{7} \cdot \frac{2}{6} = \frac{1}{7}$ P(green,green)= $\frac{4}{7} \cdot \frac{3}{6} = \frac{2}{7}$ P(red,red) or P(green,green)= $\frac{1}{7} + \frac{2}{7} = \frac{3}{7}$	
4 D	P(science)= $\frac{3}{5}$ P(arts)= $\frac{2}{5}$ It is given that a student cannot choose both majors – so P(arts and science)=0. P(science or arts)= P(science) + P(arts)-P(arts and science) = $\frac{3}{5} + \frac{2}{5} - 0 = 1.$	
5 $\frac{1}{3}$	From 6 players – pick 2 for team Total possibilities = $6C2 = \frac{6!}{4!2!}$=15 teams Out of these, Andrea will be in 5 teams (one with each of the other players). So, the probability of Andrea getting selected = $\frac{5}{15} = \frac{1}{3}$.	
6 $\frac{1}{15}$	From 6 players – pick 2 for team Total possibilities = $6C2 = \frac{6!}{4!2!}$=15 teams	

	Out of these, Andrea and Betty will be in 1 team only. So, the probability of Andrea getting selected = $\frac{1}{15}$.	
7 $\frac{2}{15}$	From 6 players – pick 2 for team Total possibilities = $6C2 = \frac{6!}{4!2!}$=15 teams Out of these, Andrea and Betty will be selected in 1 way and Cindy and Darlene can be selected in 1 way – total of 2 ways So, the probability is $\frac{2}{15}$.	
8 D	Note that there are 4 letters – Only one way to get G,O,A,L (that is when G is in 1st spot, O is in 2nd spot, A is in 3rd spot, L is in 4th spot). Possible ways to rearrange the letters = 4·3·2·1=24 ways. So, the P(getting GOAL)=$\frac{1}{24}$.	
9 A	Possible ways=$3 \cdot 2 \cdot 1 = 6$ ways Favorable ways=1 when the word GOD is in the cells. Probability= $\frac{1}{6}$	
10 $\frac{7}{9}$	Favorable ways to have $\frac{m}{n}$ as integer= (30,5), (30,10), (30,15), (40,5), (40,10), (50,5), (50,10) = 7 ways Possible ways to pick 1 from M and 1 from N=3·3=9. So, probability that $\frac{m}{n}$ is an integer = $\frac{7}{9}$.	List out the possibilities to get the favorable outcomes.
11 D	Favorable outcome= 1,4,9 as these are the only three perfect squares; possible outcomes=10. So, the probability=$\frac{3}{10}$	
12 $\frac{4}{7}$	This is a problem of replacement – that is, the sample space is not affected. When he goes to pick the second toy, he has 6+8=14 toys available. There are 8 green toys. So, probability the second toy is green is =$\frac{8}{14} = \frac{4}{7}$	In probability problems, read carefully to see if there is replacement of items picked or not.
13 C	What is the probability that you will get a 3 in one spin and a number that is not 3 in the other – note the "and" in the question. P(3 in first spin) = $\frac{2}{5}$ (since there are two 3s and 5 numbers in total) P(not 3 in second spin) =P(1,2,4)=$\frac{3}{5}$ P(3 in first spin and not 3 in second spin)=$\frac{2}{5} \cdot \frac{3}{5} = \frac{6}{25}$	
14 $\frac{1}{4}$	P(Heads in toss 1 and heads in toss 2)= $\frac{1}{2} \cdot \frac{1}{2} = \frac{1}{4}$	
15 B	Two coins will add up to more than 35 if both of them are quarters. The probability of picking 2 quarters is $\frac{2}{5} \cdot \frac{1}{4} = \frac{1}{10}$.	
16 C	P(lions in the zoo)=$\frac{1}{6}$. If there are 6 animals, you can find 1 lion, if there are 12 animals, you can find 2 lions, etc. If there are 20 animals, then the number of lions=1/6 ·20 – and this is not possible since the number of lions cannot be in	

	fractions. So, the number of animals has to be in multiples of 6. Only choice C is not a multiple of 6.	
17 B	There are 52 cards in the deck with 13 of each suite. To select a 3 of Hearts, the probability is $\frac{1}{52}$ since there is only one 3 of Hearts. After selecting this card, there will be only 51 cards left (the first card is not replaced). The probability of selecting 5 of Spades is $\frac{1}{51}$. So the answer is $\frac{1}{52}\cdot\frac{1}{51}=\frac{1}{2652}$.	Figure out carefully if it is a problem of selection with replacement or not.
18 B	Since the rectangle is divided into equal parts, the shaded area is one fourth of the rectangle. So the geometric probability = target area/total area = $\frac{0.25A}{A}=0.25.$	
19 A	Arc of shaded portion = $30°$ of the circle; since the entire circle is $360°$, the shaded portion is $\frac{30}{360}=\frac{1}{12}$ of the total area. So, the probability= target area/total area = $\frac{\frac{1}{12}A}{A}=\frac{1}{12}$	A $30°$ piece of a circle is not equal to 30% of the area of a circle. Since $360°$ corresponds to the full area of a circle, a $30°$ sector is equal to $\frac{30}{360}=\frac{1}{12}$ of the area of a circle.
20 B	Outer square=10 inches; Inner square=8 inches P(dart will fall in shaded area) =shaded area/total area= $\frac{10^2-8^2}{10^2}=\frac{100-64}{100}=\frac{36}{100}=\frac{9}{25}$.	

CHAPTER 2 HEART OF ALGEBRA	
Lesson	**Title**
Lesson 14	Linear Equations
Lesson 15	System of Linear Equations
Lesson 16	Linear Inequalities
Lesson 17	System of Linear Inequalities
Lesson 18	Linear Models and Graphs
Lesson 19	Absolute Equalities and Inequalities

HEART OF ALGEBRA		
Lesson 14	Linear Equations	Review

FOCUSPREP CHECKLIST

- What is a Linear Equation?
- How do I solve a Linear Equation?
- Can I use PEMDAS to simplify a Linear Equation?
- Workout practice problems in Linear Equations

Q1 What is a Linear Equation?

A1 A Linear Equation of first degree is an equation where the exponent (or power) of the variable is 1. Linear equations can have one or more variables.

A Linear Equation with <u>one variable</u> is an equation typically of the form $ax + b = c$ where x is the variable and a, b, and c are constants and $a \neq 0$. Example: $3x + 5 = 30$.

A Linear equation can have more than one variable. For example, $x + y = 4$ is a linear equation with <u>two variables</u>. Linear equations with two variables are reviewed in the lesson on "Systems of Linear Equations".

<u>Examples</u>

$3x + 5 = 2$; $9x - 2 = 4x + 3$; $\frac{x}{5} = 2$; $2 - \frac{x}{5} = 8$; $\frac{x}{4} - \frac{x}{8} = 18$ are examples of linear equations with one variable.

Q2 What is a Linear Inequality ?

A2 Linear Inequalities have $>, <, \geq, \leq$ signs. They do not have an $=$ sign. Example: $2x + 5 > 7$. Linear Inequalities are reviewed in a different lesson.

Q3 How do I solve a linear equation?

A3 Solving a Linear Equation means finding the value of the variable that will make the equation true. Depending on the problem, linear equations are solved by isolating the variable to one side of the equation, by performing operations on both sides of the equation, cross multiplying, and substituting. You can perform addition, subtraction, multiplication, and division operations on both sides of the equation in order to isolate the variable.

<u>Example (isolating by Addition)</u>:

$$x - 15 = 22$$
$$x - 15 + 15 = 22 + 15$$
$$x = 37$$

Example (isolating by Subtraction):

$$x + 2 = 6$$
$$x + 2 - 2 = 6 - 2$$
$$x = 4$$

Example (isolating by Multiplication):

$\frac{x}{3} = 2$ multiply by 3 on both sides to isolate x

$$3 \cdot \frac{x}{3} = 2 \cdot 3$$
$$x = 6$$

Example (isolating by Multiplying by Inverse):

$\frac{7x}{3} = \frac{21}{6}$ multiply by the inverse of $\frac{7}{3}$ on both sides

$$\frac{3}{7} \cdot \frac{7x}{3} = \frac{3}{7} \cdot \frac{21}{6}$$

$$x = \frac{3}{2}$$

Example (isolating by Cross-Multiplication):

$\frac{7x}{3} = \frac{21}{6}$ cross multiply to remove the denominators

$$6 \cdot 7x = 21 \cdot 3$$

$42x = 63;$ divide by 42 on both sides

$$x = \frac{63}{42} = \frac{21}{14}$$

Example (isolating by Cross-Multiplication):

$\frac{x-1}{3} = \frac{x+1}{4}$ cross multiply to remove denominators

$4(x - 1) = 3(x + 1)$ expand using distributive property

$4x - 4 = 3x + 3$ isolate variable x on one side

$$4x - 3x = x = 3 + 4 = 7$$

Example (isolating by Division):

$7x = 21$ divide by 7 on both sides to isolate x

$$\frac{7x}{7} = \frac{21}{7}; \; x = 21$$

Q4 What is PEMDAS and why is it important while solving linear equations?

A4 When a linear equation has several terms, you can apply the PEMDAS rule to decide the order of operations. PEMDAS stands for: Parentheses, Exponents, Multiplication, Division, Addition, and Subtraction. You apply the rule from left to right of the expression.

Example: Solve for x:

$$3^2 \cdot (3 + 4x \div 2 - 1) = 18$$

$9 \cdot \left(3 + \frac{4x}{2} - 1\right) = 18$ within parenthesis do the division first

$9(3 + 2x - 1) = 18$ process the parenthesis

$$9(2 + 2x) = 18$$
$$2 + 2x = \frac{18}{9} = 2$$

$2x = 2 - 2 = 0$; So, $x = 0$

Example:

Solve for c : $5 \cdot (3 - 5c) = 25$; divide by 5 on both sides

$3 - 5c = \frac{25}{5} = 5$; isolate c on one side

$-5c = 5 - 3 = 2$

$c = \frac{2}{-5} = -\frac{2}{5}$

Q5 What does "in terms of" mean?

A5 When a problem asks you to "express y in terms of x", only y should be on the left hand side of the equation (ie, isolate y) ; x and all other constants must be on the right hand side of the equation.

Example: If $2x + y = 4$, then what is y in terms of x?
You want to isolate y, so, add $-2x$ to both sides

$$2x + y = 4$$
$$-2x + 2x + y = -2x + 4;$$
$$y = -2x + 4$$

Example: If $2x + 3y = 4$, express y in terms of x.
You want to isolate y, so add $-2x$ to both sides:

$$2x + 3y = 4$$
$$-2x + 2x + 3y = -2x + 4$$
$$3y = -2x + 4$$
$$y = \frac{-2x + 4}{3}$$
$$y = \frac{-2x}{3} + \frac{4}{3}$$

Q6 What if there are variables on both sides of the equation?

A6 When there are variables on both sides of the equation, bring the variables to the left hand side and move the constants to the right hand side of the equation.

Example:

Solve $2x + 4 = 7x + 9$

$2x - 7x = 9 - 4$ move terms with x to the left hand side and sum up

$-5x = 5$ divide both sides by -5 to isolate x

$-\frac{5x}{-5} = \frac{5}{-5}$; $x = -1$; arrive at the solution

Example:

Solve $3x + 6 = 7x + 9 - 2x$

$3x - 7x + 2x = 9 - 6$ move terms with x to the left hand side and sum up

$-2x = 3$ divide both sides by -2 to isolate x

$-\frac{2x}{-2} = \frac{3}{-2}$

$x = -\frac{3}{2}$; arrive at the solution

Q7 How do I solve word problems involving linear equalities?

A7 You may encounter word problems in which you will construct a linear equation and then solve it. Several problems in the practice section will help you to gain confidence in these types of problems.

HEART OF ALGEBRA		
Lesson 14	Linear Equations	Practice

NO CALCULATOR SECTION

1. If $3x + 5x - 2x = 1$, what is the value of x?

(A) $\frac{1}{8}$

(B) $\frac{1}{6}$

(C) $\frac{1}{4}$

(D) $\frac{1}{2}$

2. If $\frac{k}{3} = \frac{k+2}{4}$ then k =

(A) 3
(B) 4
(C) 6
(D) 12

3. The expression $-3(x + 6 \div 2) + 2^2 \cdot 3$ can be simplified as

(A) $-3(1 - x)$
(B) $-3(1 + x)$
(C) $3(1 - x)$
(D) $3(1 + x)$

4. If $\frac{3}{7}x + \frac{5}{7}x = 1$, what is the value of x?

(A) $\frac{8}{7}$

(B) $\frac{7}{8}$

(C) $\frac{1}{8}$

(D) $\frac{1}{35}$

NO CALCULATOR SECTION

5. For what value of x will the expression $3[x + (x - 3)] + 5x$ equal to 18?

(A) $\frac{9}{11}$

(B) $\frac{11}{27}$

(C) $\frac{27}{11}$

(D) $\frac{38}{11}$

6. Solve for x: $\frac{(x+6\div 2)}{16} = \frac{1}{2}$

(A) 5
(B) 8
(C) 16
(D) 32

7. If $\frac{z}{2} - \frac{z}{3} = 16$, then $z =$

(A) 6
(B) 32
(C) 48
(D) 96

NO CALCULATOR SECTION

8. A bee keeper has several bees inside a big jar. Due to a small hole in the jar, the bees escape at the rate of 3 bees per minute. If he initially had 1000 bees in the jar, after how many minutes will there be 400 bees in the jar?
(A) 100
(B) 200
(C) 300
(D) 400

9. Brian drove 3 hours at the speed of 60 miles/hr trying to reach his destination 350 miles away. If he drives the remaining distance at 85 miles/hr, how many more hours will he take to reach the destination?
(A) 1
(B) 2
(C) 3
(D) 4

10. 1000 is the result when 365 is subtracted from a number that is increased by 5 and then multiplied by 13. What is the number?
(A) 13
(B) 26
(C) 52
(D) 100

NO CALCULATOR SECTION

11. Brandi's bank balance initially was $1600, but she spent money at the rate of 20% of this amount every day. After how many days will she have a balance of $640 in her account?
(A) 10
(B) 20
(C) 30
(D) 40

12. John's salary includes a base salary of $1700 per month plus a commission of 20% of the monthly car sales, in dollars. If his salary in June was $8700, how much sales in dollars did he have in June?
(A) 25,000
(B) 35,000
(C) 70,000
(D) 75,000

13. Limousine rates are $50 flat rate plus an additional 30 cents for every mile. If Melissa paid $200 for a Limousine ride, how many miles did she travel?
GRID IN

CALCULATOR SECTION

14. A movie producer produces two movies, movie-1 and movie-2. He estimates the first day sales for movie-1 to be $3m + 300$ where m is the number of people who will watch movie-1 on the first day. He also estimates the first day sales for movie-2 to be $2n + 800$ where n is the number of people who will watch movie-2 on the first day. After the movies were released, the first day sales were the same for both movies and 350 people watched movie-2. How many people watched movie-1?
GRID IN

15. Joe purchases a phone plan that costs 30 dollars a month fixed charge plus 33 cents per text message. How much will Joe's monthly bill be if he sends 334 text messages in one month?
(A) \$64.00
(B) \$140.22
(C) \$160.30
(D) \$420.32

16. If $x\sqrt{3} + \sqrt{7} = \sqrt{9}$, then x is approximately equal to
(A) 0.20
(B) 0.42
(C) 1.42
(D) 1.68

CALCULATOR SECTION

17. For each of the first six months of a year, a pond gains 5 inches and for each of the last six months of the year, the pond loses six inches to evaporation. If the height of water in the pond after 3 years is 50 inches, how much water was there at the beginning of the first year?
GRID IN

18. The number of tigers left in the wild is declining at a constant rate. At the beginning of year 2000, there were 9000 tigers left. At the end of year 2010, there were 3500 tigers left. If this rate continues, how many years are left until the tigers population becomes zero? (round to the hundredths place)
GRID IN

HEART OF ALGEBRA

Lesson 14	Linear Equations	Answers

#	Explanation	Comments
1 B	The variable x is on one side of the equation; sum up the variables and solve for x $3x + 5x - 2x = 1;$ $6x = 1$ $x = \frac{1}{6}$	Note that all the problems in this lesson are one-variable linear equations.
2 C	The variable k is on both sides with a denominator; cross multiply and isolate k $\frac{k}{3} = \frac{k+2}{4}$ $4k = 3(k+2) = 3k + 6;$ $4k - 3k = 6$; isolate k to one side $k = 6$ Verify the results $\frac{6}{3} = 2 = \frac{6+2}{4} = \frac{8}{4} = 2$	Verify your results by plugging it back into the equation.
3 C	Use PEMDAS , process the parenthesis first, within the parenthesis, process division first $-3(x + 6 \div 2) + 2^2 \cdot 3$ $-3(x + 3) + 2^2 \cdot 3$ $-3x - 9 + 2^2 \cdot 3$ $-3x - 9 + 4 \cdot 3$ $-3x - 9 + 12$ $-3x + 3$ $3(-x + 1)$ $3(1 - x)$	PEMDAS is critical to evaluating an expression correctly; get familiar with it.
4 B	$\frac{3}{7}x + \frac{5}{7}x = 1$ $x\left(\frac{3}{7} + \frac{5}{7}\right) = 1$; factor out the x that is common $x\left(\frac{8}{7}\right) = 1$ $x\frac{8}{7} \cdot \frac{7}{8} = 1 \cdot \frac{7}{8}$; multiply by reciprocal of $\frac{8}{7}$ to isolate x $x = \frac{7}{8}$	
5 C	$3\left(x + (x - 3)\right) + 5x = 18$ $3(x + x - 3) + 5x = 18$ $3(2x - 3) + 5x = 18$ $6x - 9 + 5x = 18$ $11x - 9 = 18$ $11x - 9 + 9 = 18 + 9 = 27$	Do not forget to add the 9 to both sides.

	$11x = 27$ $x = \frac{27}{11}$	
6 A	$\frac{(x + 6 \div 2)}{16} = \frac{1}{2}$ $\frac{(x+3)}{16} = \frac{1}{2}$; resolve the parenthesis first $2x + 6 = 16$; cross multiply $2x = 16 - 6 = 10$ $x = 5$	Resolve the parenthesis first.
7 D	$\frac{z}{2} - \frac{z}{3} = 16$ $z\left(\frac{1}{2} - \frac{1}{3}\right) = 16$; separate the common factor $z \cdot \frac{3-2}{6} = 16$; simplify using LCM of the denominator. $z \cdot \frac{1}{6} = 16$ $z = 16 \cdot 6 = 96$; cross multiply to get z	
8 B	Initially he has 1000 bees; bees escape at the rate of 3 bees/minute; after some time there are 400 bees; Let m be the number of minutes for the bees in the jar to go from 1000 to 400. In this m minutes, $3m$ bees escape. Initial + net change = final Set the linear equation and solve for m; $1000 - 3m = 400$ $3m = 1000 - 400 = 600$ $m = 200$ minutes	Write the given facts and pause for a few seconds to get a clue about how to set up the equation. 1 minute → 3 bees escape m minutes → 3m bees escape remember that Initial + net change = final Net change can be positive or negative; be careful with the positive/negative sign.
9 B	Total distance = 350 miles 3 hours @ 60 miles/hr = 180 miles Remaining distance is covered at 85 miles/hour Let t be the time taken to cover the remaining distance. Set up the linear equation. $180 + 85\,t = 350$ $85t = 350 - 180 = 170$ $t = 2\ hours$	In some problems involving speed and distances, you may have to use the formula Speed= distance/time to set up the equation. Pay attention to the unit of time – seconds, minutes, or hours.
10 D	$13(5 + x) - 365 = 1000.$ $65 + 13x - 365 = 1000$ $13x - 300 = 1000$ $13x = 1300$ $x = 100$	This is a word problem involving linear equations; translate the words to math carefully. Review the lesson on Word Problems.

11 C	Initial balance = 1600 Spent 20% **everyday** 20/100 · 600=32 everyday Final balance = 640 Let d be the number of days for the balance to drop from 1600 to 640; in 1 day, she spends \$32, so in d days, she would have spent $32d$ dollars; set up the linear equation Initial – amount spent = final $1600 - 32d = 640$ $32d = 1600 - 640 = 960$ $d = \frac{960}{32} = 30$ days	In problems of this type, you will be asked to setup an equation connecting the initial amount and final amount. Note that the final amount may be more than or less than the initial amount depending on whether there is a net deposit or net withdrawal; set up the equation carefully.
12 B	Salary is base salary of1700 /month plus commission of 20% of sales June salary= 8700; how much sales? Let s be the sales for June Base salary + 20% of s = 8700 $1700 + 0.2s = 8700$ $0.2s = 8700 - 1700 = 7000$ $s = \frac{7000}{0.2} = \frac{70000}{2} = 35000$	Note that 20% of sales = $\frac{20}{100} \cdot s = 0.2\ s;$ When dividing $7000/0.2$, multiply numerator and denominator by 10 and then divide.
13 500	\$50 flat rate plus 30 cents per mile Melissa paid \$200 – how many miles? Set up the equation – convert dollars to cents $5000 + 30m = 20000$ $30m = 20000 - 5000 = 15000$ $m = \frac{15000}{30} = 500$ miles	Get familiar with problems involving a flat rate/ fixed charge plus a variable charge based on the miles traveled. Phone companies charge in a similar way; they will have fixed charges plus variable charges based on how long you speak.
14 400	Movie-1 first day sales=$3m + 300$ Movie-2 first day sales= $2n + 800$ First days sales is same for both movies; 350 watched movie-2 on day one. So n=350 $3m + 300 = 2n + 800$ $3m + 300 = 2 \cdot 350 + 800$ $3m + 300 = 700 + 800 = 1500$ $3m = 1500 - 300 = 1200$ $m = \frac{1200}{3} = 400$	In this problem, two linear equations are equated; even though there are two variables m and n, since n is given as 350, this problem becomes a one-variable linear equation problem. Though you can use a calculator for this problem, it is clearly not necessary.
15 B	30 dollars fixed charge Text – 33 cents/text; 334 text messages sent $30 + 0.33 \cdot 334 = 140.22$; Remember to convert cents to dollars.	In this problem, you should use the calculator to get results quickly.

16 A	$x\sqrt{3}+\sqrt{7}=\sqrt{9}$ $x\sqrt{3}=\sqrt{9}-\sqrt{7}=3-\sqrt{7}$ $x=\frac{3-\sqrt{7}}{\sqrt{3}}$ $x=\frac{0.3542....}{\sqrt{3}}$ = approximately 0.20	Learn to calculate square roots and divide numbers by square roots. Note that the problem asks "x is approximately".
17 68	Let the water level at the beginning of the year be h inches. Pond gains 5 feet for 6 months and loses 6 feet for the next six months – so the net gain is $5\cdot6-6\cdot6=-6$ inches/year. After 3 years, the height is 50 inches; so setup the equation as follows: beginning height + net change = final height h + (-6 inches/year· 3years) = 50 $h-18=50$ $h=50+18=68$ inches	Think of this problem as initial + net change=final. Note that the net change is negative in this problem, but it could be positive in some other problem, depending on the data.
18 6.36	Note that data is given for years 2000 and 2010 and the question asks "how many years are left" – this means you need to count from year 2010. You need to find the rate at which tiger population is declining. Over 10 years, it declined by $3500-9000=-5500$. This is a rate of $-\frac{5500}{10}=-500$/year. The problem states that the tiger population is declining at a constant rate and that this rate continues. The question is – how long will it take for the tiger population to go from 3500 to 0. Initial + net change=final $3500\ -550\,t\ =\ 0$ $550t=3500$ t$=\frac{3500}{550}=6.36$ years	Initial + net change=final Note the negative net change in this problem; be careful with the sign for net change – it can be positive or negative.

HEART OF ALGEBRA		
Lesson 15	System of Linear Equations	Review

FOCUSPREP CHECKLIST

- How does a System of linear equations look?
- How do I solve a System of linear equations?
- How many solutions can a system of linear equations have?
- Workout practice problems in System of Linear Equations

Q1 What is a "system" of linear equations?

A1 A System of Linear Equations is a set of linear equations that can be solved together to find the values of the variables. A system can have 2 equations and 2 variables, 3 equation and 3 variables, etc.

Example: The following is a set of linear equations with two variables $x\ and\ y$.

$$x + y = 4$$
$$x - y = 2$$

Q2 How do I solve a system of linear equations involving two variables?

A2 A system of linear equations can be solved by using graphs, tables, or algebraically by substitution. The solution to a system with two variables is the ordered pair (x, y) that satisfies both equations of the system.

Q3 How do I solve a system of linear equations using tables?

A3 Create a table showing x and y values for both equations of the system. Then, see if there is one x value for which the y values of both equations are the same. This (x, y) pair is the solution to the system.

Example: Solve $x + y = 4$; $x - y = 2$
Prepare a table with different x values and y values from each of the two equations. Look for a x-value where the y values are the same. In this case, for $x = 3$, both equations have a y value of 1. So, the solution to the system of equations is $x = 3, y = 1$.

x	0	1	2	3	4
$y = 4 - x$	4	3	2	1	0
$y = x - 2$	-2	-1	0	1	2

Q4 How do I solve a system of linear equations by substitution?

A4 Substitution is the process of using one equation to get one variable in terms of the other, and then plugging this variable into the second equation as shown in the example below.

Example: Solve the system of equations:

$$x + 2 = y$$
$$2x = y$$

Write x in terms of y.

$$x = y - 2$$
$$2x = y$$

Now substitute x into the second equation.

$$2x = y$$
$$2(y - 2) = y \text{ ; substitute } x$$
$$2y - 4 = y$$
$$2y - y = 4 \text{ ; isolate } y$$
$$y = 4$$
$$\text{So, } x = y - 2 = 4 - 2 = 2$$

The solution to this system is $(x, y) = (2,4)$

Q5 How do I solve a system of linear equations by elimination?

A5 You can solve for one variable by adding or subtracting the two equations together or by performing a multiplication or division operation on one or both equations. These equations can then be manipulated to get rid of one variable as shown in the example below.

Example: Solve the following system of linear equations.

$$2x + 3y = 4$$
$$2x + 6y = 7 \text{ ; multiply by -1 on both sides}$$

$$2x + 3y = 4$$
$$-1 \cdot (2x + 6y) = -1 \cdot 7$$

$$2x + 3y = 4$$
$$-2x - 6y = -7$$

$$0 - 3y = -3 \text{ ; add the corresponding terms}$$
$$-3y = -3 \text{ ; divide by } -3 \text{ on both sides}$$
$$y = 1 \text{ ; using } y = 1, \text{ find } x$$
$$2x + 6y = 7 \text{ substitute } y \text{ back into this equation to solve for x}$$
$$x = \frac{7-6y}{2} = \frac{7-6\cdot1}{2} = \frac{1}{2}$$

So, the solution to the system of equations is $x = \frac{1}{2}, y = 1$; Verify this by substituting these values back into the equations. $2x + 3y = 4$; $2\left(\frac{1}{2}\right) + 3 \cdot 1 = 1 + 3 = 4$. So the solution is correct.

Q6 How do I find the solution to a system of linear equations graphically?

A6 Each linear equation in the system can be expressed as $y = mx + b$ and therefore they are straight lines when plotted on a graph. The solution of the system is the point (x, y) in the graph where the two lines meet.

Q7 How many solutions can a system of linear equations have? How do I find this out?

A7 A system of linear equations can have no solution, one solution, or infinitely many solutions. You can find this algebraically or graphically. See the table below for a summary. It is easy to remember this.

No Solution: Example: $y = 2x - 7$ and $y = 2x + 5$
Algebraic: When you solve this system algebraically, you get $2x - 7 = 2x + 5,\ -7 = 5$. Since this is never true, this system has no solution.
Graphic: The slopes of the lines are the same but the intercepts are different. This means that they are parallel (the intercepts separate them) and so the system has no solution.

If the graphs of the equations have the same slope but different y intercept, then the graphs of these equations/lines are parallel lines that do not meet.

Only one solution: Example: $y = 2x - 7$ and $y = 3x + 5$
Algebraic: Substitute y from one equation into the other; $2x - 7 = 3x + 5;\ x = -12; y = 3 \cdot -12 + 5 = -31$. The solution is$(-12,31)$.
Graphic: Slopes of these two lines are 2 and 3 respectively; since they are different, there is only one solution. If the graphs of the equations have different slopes, then they will intersect at one point only and the system will have only one solution.

Infinitely many solutions: Example: $y = 2x - 7$ and $2y = 4x - 14$.
Algebraic: When you solve this system algebraically, you get $y = 2x - 7$ and $y = \frac{4x-14}{2} = 2x - 7$; so, $2x - 7 = 2x - 7; 0 = 0$. Since 0=0 is true, this means both the equations are same – that is, they overlap and so have infinite solutions.

Graphic: If the graphs of the equations have the same slope and y intercept, then the graphs coincide with each other and the system has infinitely many solutions.

System of Linear Equations		
Different slopes	(intersecting lines sketch)	Only one solution
Same slope, different y intercept (parallel)	(parallel lines sketch)	No solution
Same slope and same y –intercept	(single line sketch)	Infinitely many solutions

HEART OF ALGEBRA		
Lesson 15	System of Linear Equations	Practice

NO CALCULATOR SECTION

1. Which of the following is the solution to the system shown below?

$$y = 3$$
$$3x + 2y = 0$$

(A) $(3, -2)$
(B) $(2,3)$
(C) $(-3,2)$
(D) $(-2,3)$

2. Which of the following is the solution to the following system?

$$x - 4 = 3y$$
$$3x + 4y = 38$$

(A) $(10,2)$
(B) $(2,10)$
(C) $(-2,10)$
(D) $(-10,2)$

3. Given the linear equations $2(y + x) = 2.5$, and $x - y = 0.25$. which of the following ordered pairs satisfy the equation?
(A) (1,1)
(B) (0.5, 0.5)
(C) (0.75, 0.5)
(D) (0.25, 0.25)

NO CALCULATOR SECTION

4.What value of c makes the following system have infinite solutions?

$$2x + 2y = 4$$
$$cx + 3y = 6$$

(A) 1
(B) 3
(C) 4
(D) 6

5 5 apples and 3 oranges cost 18 dollars. 7 apples and 4 oranges cost 25 dollars. What is the cost of 12 apples?
(A) 12
(B) 24
(C) 36
(D) 48

6 How many solutions does the following system have?

$$5x + 6y = 7$$
$$-5x - 6y = -7$$

(A) 0
(B) 1
(C) 2
(D) ∞

NO CALCULATOR SECTION

7. A team of 60 boys and girls are to be chosen for a singing competition with the condition that there should be twice as many girls as there are boys in the selection. If b boys and g girls were chosen, then the system of equations that models this scenario is

(A) $b = 50,\ \ g = 60$
(B) $b + g = 60;\ \ 2g = b$
(C) $b + g = 60;\ \ 2b = g$
(D) $b - g = 60;\ \ 2b = g$

8. The two equations $y = 3x + 4$ and $y = 6x + 10$ have a solution in which of the following choices?

(A) $(-2, -4)$
(B) $(-2, -2)$
(C) $(-4, -2)$
(D) $(4, -2)$

9. $\frac{2}{3}$ cups of vanilla ice cream and $\frac{4}{3}$ cup of strawberry ice cream cost \$10. $\frac{1}{3}$ cups of vanilla ice cream and $2\frac{2}{3}$ cups of strawberry ice cream cost \$17. How much does one cup of vanilla ice cream cost?

(A) \$1
(B) \$2
(C) \$3
(D) \$6

NO CALCULATOR SECTION

10.

$$a + 3c = 4$$
$$3b + a = 7$$
$$3c + 3b = 9$$

Which of the following answer choices expresses the values of a, b and c as an ordered triplet(a, b, c) that satisfies all the three equations?

(A) $(2,1,1)$
(B) $(1,2,1)$
(C) $(1,1,2)$
(D) $(2,1,2)$

CALCULATOR SECTION

11. At a party store, 3 balloons and 4 hats cost \$6.50. Also, 4 balloons and 3 hats cost \$7.50. How much do 17 balloons and 10 hats cost? GRID IN

CALCULATOR SECTION

12. A publisher sells two books – a Physics book and a Chemistry book. The Physics book weighs 2 lbs and the Chemistry book weighs 3 lbs. How many Physics books are there in a 150 lb box containing Physics and Chemistry books if there are six times as many physics books as there are chemistry books in it?
GRID IN

CALCULATOR SECTION

13. A department store sells two types of pillows- a soft one and a hard one. The soft pillow costs $5 each and the hard pillow costs $13 each. If the store sells a special bundle made up of 10 pillows for $66 per bundle, how many soft pillows are there in the bundle if the cost of the bundle is the cost of all the pillows that make up the bundle?
GRID IN

HEART OF ALGEBRA		
Lesson 15	System of Linear Equations	Answers

#	Explanation	Comments
1 D	substitute $y = 3$ into the second equation. $3x + 2(3) = 0$ $3x + 6 = 0$ $3x = -6$ $x = -2$ So, the solution to the system is $(-2,3)$	In this problem, y is given to be 3; if it is not given, then substitute x in one of the equations to find y.
2 A	Isolate x from one equation and substitute x into the second equation: $x - 4 = 3y; so\ x = 3y + 4$ $3(3y + 4) + 4y = 38$; substitute x from above $9y + 12 + 4y = 38$ $13y = 38 - 12$ $y = 2$ Plug $y = 2$ into the first equation: $x - 4 = 3(2); so\ x = 4 + 6 = 10$ $x = 10\ , y = 2$; The solution is $(10,2)$	From one equation, write one variable in terms of other and then substitute it into the other equation.
3 C	$2(y + x) = 2.5$. So, $(y + x) = 1.25$. The other equation is $x - y = 0.25$. Choice C satisfies both equations.	
4 B	For a system to have infinitely many solutions, the slope of the lines must be the same and the y-intercept must be the same; slope of a line of the form $y = mx + b$ is m. Convert the first equation into $y = mx + b$ format: $2x + 2y = 4$ $2y = -2x + 4$ $y = -x + 2;$ so the slope is -1, and y-intercept is 2. Convert the second equation into $y = mx + b$ format $cx + 3y = 6$ $3y = -cx + 6$ $y = -\frac{c}{3}x + \frac{6}{2} = -\frac{c}{3}x + 2;$ so the slope is $-\frac{c}{3}$ and intercept is 2. For the system to have infinite solutions, the slope and intercept must be the same. $\text{so}, -\frac{c}{3} = -1; => c = 3$	Review this lesson and learn when a system will have 1 solution, no solution, or infinite solutions. Remember that the solution for a 2-variable Linear system is an ordered pair (x, y) that satisfies the equations in the system.

5 C	Setting this up as a system, using a for apples and o for oranges gives: $5a + 3o = 18$ $7a + 4o = 25$ Eliminate a; LCM of 5 and 7 is 35. Multiply the first equation by 7 and the second equation by 5 so that the coefficient of a will sum up to 0 after subtraction, thereby eliminating it. $7(5a + 3o) = 7(18)$ $5(7a + 4o) = 5(25)$ $35a + 21o = 126$ $35a + 20o = 125$ Subtract the second equation from the first $o = 1$ Plug the o value back into the first equation: $5a + 3(1) = 18$ $5a = 15$ $a = 3$ 1 apple is $3, so, 12 apples cost is $36.	This is a classic system of linear equations problem that can be solved using the substitution and elimination methods discussed in this lesson. You can choose to eliminate either a or o. Remember to operate on both sides of the equation. After solving a system of linear equations, pay attention to the question – it may not ask you for the solution itself – it may ask you the sum or the product or the ratio of the variables involved.
6 D	$5x + 6y = 7$ $-5x - 6y = -7$ The equations are Adding up the equations, you get 0=0. Since this is true, the system has infinite solutions.	
7 C	Total of 60 boys and girls; so $b + g = 60$ Twice as many girls as boys; this can be confusing If you try $b = 2g$; when $g = 1, b = 2$ – there are twice as many boys as girls- so this is wrong; Try $g = 2b$, and plug $b = 1$, you get $g = 2$ – there are twice as many girls as boys; so, $b + g = 60$ and $g = 2b$ are the equations that define the system.	Note carefully that "twice as many girls as boys" translates to $g = 2b$. You don't have to memorize this word to math translation – just plug in $b = 1$ and see if it makes sense.
8 B	You can set the equations equal to each other as follows: $3x + 4 = 6x + 10$ Solving gives $3x = -6; x = -2$ Plug in the value of x to get y: $y = 3(-2) + 4$ $y = -2$ so, the solution of the system is $(-2, -2)$	

9 C	Set this up as a system, using v for vanilla and s for strawberry: $$\frac{2}{3}v+\frac{4}{3}s=10$$ $$\frac{1}{3}v+\frac{8}{3}s=17$$ Multiply the second equation by -2 : $$\frac{2}{3}v+\frac{4}{3}s=10$$ $$\frac{-2}{3}v+\frac{-16}{3}s=-34$$ Add the equations together: $$-\frac{12}{3}s=-24$$ $$4s=24$$ $$s=6.$$ Plug $s=6$ into the first equation: $$\frac{2}{3}v+\frac{4}{3}\cdot 6\ =10$$ $$\frac{2}{3}v+8=10$$ $$\frac{2}{3}v=2$$ $$v=3$$ One cup of vanilla ice cream costs $3.	
10 B	Notice that in this system of 3 variables and 3 equations, no two equations has the same set of two variables. To solve this system, you need to find two equations with the same two variables. You can start by subtracting the second equation from the first. $$3c+a=4$$ $$3b+a=7$$ $$3c-3b=-3$$ You also have $3c+3b=9$. Using these two equations and adding them up, you get: $$3c-3b=-3$$ $$3c+3b=9$$ $$6c=6$$ $$c=1$$ Plugging in $c=1$ into the original equations, you get: $$a+3=4;\ a=1$$	You could also plug in the answer choices one by one into each equation.

	$1 + 3b = 7;\ b = 2$ Thus $(a, b, c) = (1,2,1)$	
11 15.7	$3b + 4h = 6.5$ $4b + 3h = 7.5$ Eliminate b by multiplying the first equation by 4 and the second by 3 and then subtracting the result. $12b + 16h = 26$ $12b + 9h = 22.5$ Subtracting the second equation from the first, you get $16h - 9h = 26 - 22.5$ $7h = 3.5$ $h = 0.5$; substitute this into the second equation to get b $b = \frac{7.5 - 3 \cdot 0.5}{4} = 0.63$ So, 17 ballons and 10 hats cost $17 \cdot 0.63 + 10 \cdot 0.5 = 15.71$	Use your calculator accurately.
12 60	Let there be p Physics and c Chemistry books Weight of these books = $2p + 3c$ These books make up the 150 lb box – so $2p + 3c = 150$ There are six times as many physics books as there are chemistry books – to set this up as an equation, try $p = 6c$ and plug $c = 1$ to verify; when $c = 1, p = 6$ – six times as many physics books as chemistry books. So the system is $2p + 3c = 150$ $p = 6c$ solve by substitution; $2(6c) + 3c = 150$ $12c + 3c = 150;$ $15c = 150$ $c = 10;\ so\ p = 6c = 6 \cdot 10 = 60$	One equation involves weight of books and another involves the number of books. Setup the system of linear equations using this information.
13 8	Let there be s and h soft and hard pillows; bundle has 10 pillows, so $s + h = 10$; bundle costs \$66 and soft pillows cost \$5 and hard pillows cost \$13. $s + h = 10$ -first equation $5s + 13h = 66$ -second equation ---------------------- $5s + 5h = 50$ multiply first equation by 5 $5s + 13h = 66$ ---------------------- $8h = 66 - 50 = 16$ $h = \frac{16}{8} = 2$ So $h = 2$ and $s = 10 - h = 10 - 2 = 8$	In this problem, one equation involves the number of pillows in the bundle whereas another equation involves the cost of the pillows. Get used to solving these types of problems by constructing the system of linear equations.

HEART OF ALGEBRA		
Lesson 16	Linear Inequalities	Review

FOCUSPREP CHECKLIST

- What is a Linear Inequality in one variable?
- How do I solve a Linear Inequality?
- When does the Linear Inequality reverse?
- Workout practice problems in Linear Inequalities

Q1 What is a Linear Inequality in one variable?

A1 A Linear Inequality is similar to a Linear Equality but the equal sign (=), is replaced with one of the inequality signs ($<,>,\leq,\geq$). The solution of an inequality falls within a range of values. Linear Inequalities can have one variable(reviewed in this lesson) or more than one variable (reviewed in the lesson on Systems of Linear Inequalities).

__Example__: $x > 5,\ x + 5 > 9;\ x - 8 > 23;\ 22 + x < 99.53;\ 30x + 500 \geq 700$ Note that the degree of a Linear inequality is 1. Inequalities such as $x^2 > 8$ are not linear inequalities. Pay very careful attention to the inequality signs. There is a big difference between $x > 3\ and\ x \geq 3$.

Q2 How do I solve a linear inequality?

A2 Linear Inequalities are solved just like Linear equalities. You can perform addition, subtraction, multiplication, and division operations on both sides of an inequation.

Q3 When does the inequality sign reverse?

A3 When the inequality is multiplied or divided by a negative number, the inequality sign must be reversed. That is, $>$ will be come $<$, $>=$ will become $<=$ etc. Examples are presented below.

__Example__

Solve the inequality $-x < 3$

__Solution__: Convert $-x\ to\ +x$ by multiplying by -1 on both sides $-1 \cdot -x > -1 \cdot 3;$ so, $x > -3;$ multiplying by a negative number on both sides changes the inequality sign. So, the solution is $\{x|x > -3\}$.

__Example__

Solve the inequality: $-x + 3 > 9$

__Solution__:

$-x + 3 > 9$

$-x + 3 - 3 > 9 - 3$; eliminate 3 by adding -3 on both sides

$-x > 6;\ -1 \cdot x < -1 \cdot 6$

$x < -6$; Solution is $\{x|x - 6\}$.

Note that when you have an inequality like $a < -x < b$; when you multiply by -1 throughout, both signs get changed simultaneously. So, you get $-a > x > -b$ which can be rewritten as $-b < x < -a$.

HEART OF ALGEBRA		
Lesson 16	Linear Inequalities	Practice

NO CALCULATOR SECTION

1. The solution to the inequality

$\frac{-3\pi x}{2} < \frac{3}{2}$ is

(A) $x > -\frac{1}{\pi}$

(B) $x < -\frac{1}{\pi}$

(C) $x > \frac{\pi}{-1}$

(D) $x < \frac{\pi}{-1}$

2. The average of one adult movie ticket ($\$a$) and one child movie ticket ($\$c$) is more than 100. Which equation best models this pricing?

(A) $\frac{a}{c} > 200$

(B) $a + c \leq 100$

(C) $a + c > 200$

(D) $a - c > 200$

NO CALCULATOR SECTION

3. Which of the following number lines represents the solution to the inequality $2x > 3$?

(A) -5 -4 -3 -2 -1 0 1 2 3 4 5

(B) -5 -4 -3 -2 -1 0 1 2 3 4 5

(C) -5 -4 -3 -2 -1 0 1 2 3 4 5

(D) -5 -4 -3 -2 -1 0 1 2 3 4 5

4. Solve for x in $-3x + 8 \leq -2x + 4879$

(A) $x \geq -4871$

(B) $x \leq 4871$

(C) $x < 4897$

(D) $x = 4871$

CALCULATOR SECTION

5. Jean scores 97, 88, 56, 91, and 78 on her first five tests. She wants her average to be at least 80 after she takes her sixth test. What must her score x be on the sixth test to achieve her goal?

(A) $x > 480$

(B) $x < 70$

(C) $x \leq 480$

(D) $x \geq 70$

6. If b is a fraction such that $\frac{1}{4} \leq b \leq \frac{3}{4}$, which of the following is a true statement?

(A) $b \geq b^2 \geq b^{-1}$

(B) $b \leq b^2 \geq b^{-8}$

(C) $b \geq b^2 \geq b^{-1}$

(D) $b \geq b^2 \geq b^8$

CALCULATOR SECTION

7. Emily sells flowers. She wants to charge such that twice the cost of each bouquet (b) is at least 12 dollars and at most 52 dollars. Which inequality represents the pricing of a bouquet?

(A) $-12 \leq b > 52$

(B) $12 \leq b < 52$

(C) $6 \leq 2b \leq 26$

(D) $6 \leq b \leq 26$

8. Three times the number of polar bears (p) is more than twice the number of polar bears plus 45. Which of the following could possibly indicate the number of polar bears?

(A) 38

(B) 40

(C) 45

(D) 48

CALCULATOR SECTION

9. Which of the following points (x, y) satisfies the inequality $x < 3y - 7.5$?

(A) (10, 6)
(B) (7.5, 5)
(C) (5, 2)
(D) (-1, 1)

10. What is the smallest integer for which the following inequality $137 - 7x < -3$ holds true?
GRID IN

CALCULATOR SECTION

11. Pablo the gardener has 20 feet of fencing to enclose a rectangular garden. Which of the following inequalities represents the possible area A of the rectangular garden?

(A) $9 < A < 20$
(B) $10 \leq A \leq 25$
(C) $25 \leq A \leq 9$
(D) $9 \leq A \leq 25$

12. If $-350 \leq 15x + 25 < 650$, then which of the following CANNOT be a solution of this inequality?

(A) -25
(B) 35
(C) 41
(D) 45

HEART OF ALGEBRA

Lesson 16 — Linear Inequalities — Answers

#	Explanation	Comments
1 A	$\frac{-3\pi x}{2} < \frac{3}{2}$; multiply both sides by -2 ; $<$ becomes $>$ $3\pi x > -3$; divide by 3 on both sides $\pi x > -1$ $x > -\frac{1}{\pi}$; divide by π on both sides	Note carefully that the sign is reversed after multiplication by a negative number. If you don't reverse the sign, you will get a wrong answer!
2 C	The average of an adult ticket and a child ticket can be expressed as $\frac{a+c}{2}$. You know that this amount is more than 100, so $\frac{a+c}{2} > 100$. Multiply by 2 on both sides to get $a + c > 200$.	Keep a careful eye on the inequality sign. In this problem, you multiply both sides by a positive number and so the sign does NOT get reversed.
3 C	$2x > 3$; multiply by 2 on both sides $x > \frac{3}{2}$ This means that the number line will have an open circle and will consist of all values greater than 1.5.	An open circle at 1.5 means that the value of 1.5 is not included in the solution.
4 A	$-3x + 8 \le -2x + 4879$ $-3x + 2x \le 4879 - 8 = 4871$; isolate x to one side $-x \le 4871$; multiply by -1 on both sides and reverse sign $x \ge -4871$	
5 D	Set up the inequality using her scores from all the six tests; at least 80 translates to $>= 80$ $\frac{97 + 88 + 56 + 91 + 78 + x}{6} \ge 80$ $410 + x \ge 480$ $x \ge 480 - 410 = 70$ $x \ge 70$	Inequalities can be setup in a variety of real life scenarios. This problem highlights one such scenario. Note that the solution indicates that she has to score at least 70 in her sixth test to average at least 80.
6 D	Use the fact that multiplying a fraction by itself will make the result smaller each time. Thus b will be greater than b^n where $n > 1$. Using this fact, you can conclude that the correct choice is choice D.	You can also plug in a value for b, say ¼ and test the inequalities. This may be an easy way to solve these kinds of problems. Number lines are very helpful to visualize abstract problems like this. In this problem, b^3, b^2, b appear in this order in the number line. Mark them on a number line to help you visualize quickly. So, $b \ge b^2 \ge b^3$

7 D	Since twice the cost of each bouquet costs at least 10 dollars, you know that $2b \geq 12$. Since twice the cost of each bouquet is at most 50 dollars, $2b \leq 52$. Combining these inequalities together, you get $12 \leq 2b \leq 52$; Dividing by 2 throughout, you get $6 \leq b \leq 26$.	Note $12 \leq 2b$ *and* $2b \geq 12$ both mean the same. Sometimes, like in this problem, you will need to combine inequalities.
8 D	"more than" translates to $>$ sign. $3p > 2p + 45$; pay attention to the $\geq$ sign. $3p - 2p > 45$ $p > 45$ Look for an answer choice that is more than 45. 48 in choice D is the correct answer	Note that the answer choices are such that only one falls in the solution range and others do not. Solutions to Inequality problems fall in a range of values.
9 A	Plugging in $x = 10$ *and* $y = 6$ from choice A, you get $10 < 18 - 7.5$, which holds to be true.	In problems like these, you will have to check each choice and see if the inequality holds true.
10 21	$137 - 7x < -3$; add -137 to both sides $-7x < -140$; divide by -7 and reverse sign $x > 20$; So, the smallest integer that will hold the inequality true is 21.	Reverse the sign of inequality if multiplying or dividing by a negative number.
11 D	Find the minimum and maximum values for the area of the garden keeping the perimeter to 20 ft. $2(l + w) = 20$ $l + w = 10$ Try combinations of l and w such that $l + w = 10$. When $l = 9$ and $w = 1, l + w = 10$, $A = lw = 9$. This is the smallest area. When $l = 5$ and $w = 5, l + w = 10, lw = 25$. This is the largest area possible. So, $9 \leq A \leq 25$.	
12 D	$-350 \leq 15x + 25 < 650$; subtract 25 throughout $-350 - 25 \leq 15x + 25 - 25 < 650 - 25$ $-375 \leq 15x < 625$; divide by 15 $-25 \leq x < 41.66$ $x = 45$ falls outside this range and CANNOT be a solution to this inequality.	Note that when you have an inequality like $a < x - k < b$, you have to add k in all three terms for the inequality to hold true. $a < x - k < b$ $a + k < x - k + k < b + k$ $a + k < x < b + k$

HEART OF ALGEBRA

Lesson 17	System of Linear Inequalities	Review

FOCUSPREP CHECKLIST

- What is a System of Linear Inequalities?
- How do I solve a system of Linear Inequalities?
- Workout practice problems in System of Linear Inequalities

Q1 What is a System of Linear Inequalities?

A1 A System of Linear Inequalities is a set of two or more linear inequalities. The solution to the system lies in a region where all the inequalities hold true. For example, the two inequalities $y > x + 1$ and $y < -2x$ form a set of linear inequalities.

Q2 How is the solution region of a system of linear inequalities expressed?

A2 The solution is expressed as a shaded region formed by the overlapping of the regions that represent each of the inequalities. Since the solution is a region, it can have infinite points that satisfy the inequalities. It is also possible that there is no overlapping region in which case the system does not have any solution.

Q3 Can a system of linear inequalities have more than two equations?

A3 Yes. The system can have two, three, four, or more equations that bound the solution region.

Q4 How do I find out if a given answer choice is in the solution region of a system of linear inequalities?

A4 Plug the answer choice into each of the inequalities. A solution for a system of inequalities must satisfy all inequalities.

Q5 How do I solve a system of Linear Inequalities graphically?

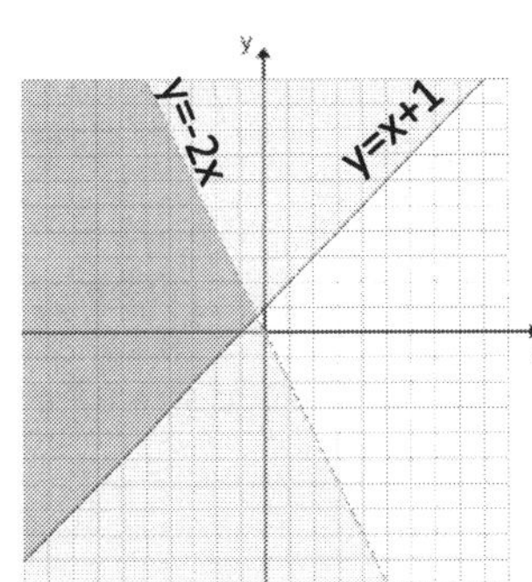

A5 Each inequality in the system is graphed and the region that overlaps all the inequalities is the solution region.

Example: Which area of the graph shown indicates the solution to the system of linear inequalities defined as follows?

$y > x + 1$

$y < -2x$

Solution: Shade the areas defined by the inequalities – the intersecting area is the solution region for the system. In this set, the area above the line $y = x + 1$ is the solution region of the inequality $y > x + 1$ and the area below the line $y = -2x$ is the solution region of the inequality $y < -2x$. The intersecting regions are shown in a darker shade.

NO CALCULATOR SECTION

$x \leq 6$
$x > 4$
$y < x$
$y < 3$

1. For the system of inequalities shown above, one possible solution could be
   (A) (4,6)
   (B) (5,2)
   (C) (5,6)
   (D) (5,3)

$y \leq 3$
$y > -2$
$y < -x + 6$
$y \leq 3x + 5$

2. A system of inequalities is shown above. Which of the following is one possible solution for this system?
   (A) (0,1)
   (B) (0,4)
   (C) (5,1)
   (D) (5,3)

NO CALCULATOR SECTION

A manufacturing company pays interns according to the table below.

Hours Worked Per week	Pay Per Hour
≤ 20	\$15/hr
> 20 and ≤ 40	\$20/hr

3. Sara and Tara were the only two interns who worked during summer. Sara earned \$15/hr and Tara earned \$20/hr. If Sara worked s hours per week and Tara worked t hours per week, and the total budget for intern pay is \$1600 per week, which of the following system of inequalities model their pay during one week of their internship?

(A) $15s + 20t < 1600$
$s > 0$
$s < 20$
$t > 20$
$t < 40$

(B) $15s + 20t \leq 1600$
$0 \leq s$
$s \leq 20$
$20 < t$
$t \leq 40$

(C) $15s + 20t \leq 1600$
$s > 0$
$s \leq 20$
$t > 20$
$t < 41$

(D) $15s + 20t \leq 1600$
$s > 0$
$s < 20$
$t > 20$
$t < 41$

CALCULATOR SECTION

4. Sanjay decides to apply to colleges in north and south of the country only but not those in east and west. He plans to apply to at most 10 colleges. The application fee for northern colleges is $100 each and that for southern colleges is $90 each. Which of the following pairs of northern and southern colleges can he apply to if his total application fee must be below $950?

(A) 5,10
(B) 5,5
(C) 6,5
(D) 4,5

5. At Sing&Dance, customers can rent singing and dancing rooms in increments of 1 minute with a minimum total of 30 minutes. The cost for renting the singing room is $10 per minute and the cost for renting the dancing room is $20 per minute. If the minimum total must be $500, then which of the following choices indicate a possible combination of singing and dancing minutes that can be rented?

(A) (15,15)
(B) (15,16)
(C) (15,17)
(D) (15,18)

NO CALCULATOR SECTION

6. A system of inequalities is shown below. Which regions marked in the graph represent the solution to the system?

$y < 3x$
$y \geq 3x - 5$

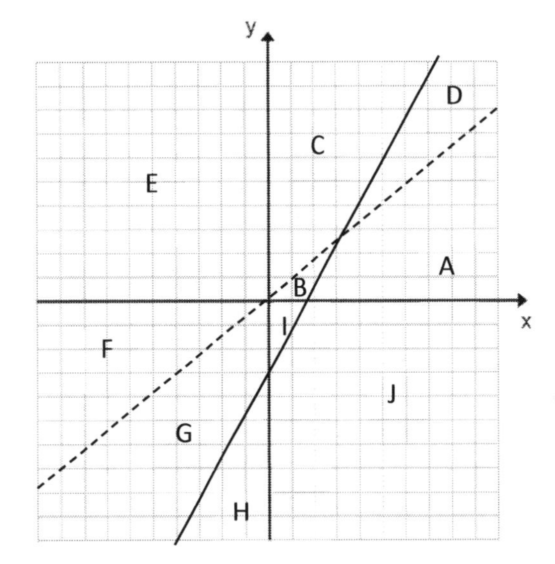

(A) B,I
(B) G,I
(C) B,G,I
(D) B

HEART OF ALGEBRA		
Lesson 17	System of Linear Inequalities	Answers

#	Explanation	Comments
1 B	$x \leq 6$; $x > 4$; $y < x$; $y < 3$ (5,2) satisfies all the inequalities $5 \leq 6$; $5 > 4$; $2 < 5$; $2 < 3$	A solution for a linear inequality must satisfy all the inequalities.
2 A	$y \leq 3$; $y > -2$; $y < -x + 6$; $y \leq 3x + 5$ (0,1) satisfies all inequalities $1 \leq 3$; $1 > -2, 1 < 6; 1 < 5$	
3 B	Sara worked s hours and earned $15/hour. Tara worked t hours and earned $20/hour. So, the total intern pay per week is $15s + 20t$; since the budget is 1600, $15s + 20t < 1600$. From the table, you can infer that since Sara earned $15/hour, she worked $\leq$ 20 hours; so $s \leq 20$. Similarly, Tara earned $20/hour, so she worked $>$ 20 hours and less than or equal to 40 hours. So $t > 20$ and $t \leq 40$.	Check the inequations against the facts given; pay close attention to $>, \geq, <, \leq$ signs.
4 D	Let N be the number of colleges he applies to in the north and S be the number in the south. N+S <=10. Total cost of applications = $100N + 90S < 950$. So, the system of inequalities is : $N + S <= 10$ $100N + 90S < 950$ Plug in the answer choices to see which one fits ALL inequalities; For $N = 4, S = 5$, you have $N + S = 9 \leq 10$ and $100 \cdot 4 + 90 \cdot 5 = 400 + 450 = 850 < 950$.	When plugging the answer choices to a system of inequalities, be careful not to mix up the first and second numbers in the ordered pair.
5 D	Let S be the number of minutes rented from the song room and D be the number of minutes rented from the dance room. Minimum total is 30 minutes – so $S + D \geq 30$ Minimum total cost of dancing = $10S + 20D \geq 500$. Plug in the choices – for $S = 15$ and $D = 18$, both inequalities are satisfied. $S + D = 15 + 18 = 33 > 30$ and $10 \cdot 15 + 20 \cdot 18 = 510 > 500$.	
6 C	Identify the lines corresponding to $y = 3x$ and $y = 3x - 5$. They both have positive slopes but one has a negative intercept and the other line passes thru the origin. Note the solution region for each inequality. For $y < 3x$, the solution region is G,H,B,A,I,J. For $y >= 3x - 5$, the solution region is G,F,E,B,C,I. The region common to both is G,B,I	The dotted line indicates that the solution does not fall on the line itself. When noting the solution region, go clockwise or anticlockwise, one quadrant at a time to avoid missing any region.

HEART OF ALGEBRA		
Lesson 18	Linear Models and Graphs	Review

FOCUSPREP CHECKLIST

- What is a Linear Model?
- How do I create a linear model – from a table, and from a graph?
- Workout practice problems in Linear Models and Graphs

Q1 What is a Linear model? How does it look?

A1 A Linear model is an algebraic equation that connects the dependent variable y and the independent variable x in such a way that when the data is graphed, the model is a straight line of the form $y = mx + b$ where m is the slope of the line and b is the y-intercept.

<u>Examples</u>:
$s = 5.85\,t$; where s = revenue for a movie, and t=number of tickets sold
$b = 0.03\,p + 200$; where b=bank balance, p is the principal amount

Q2 In a Linear model, what is the dependent variable and what is the independent variable?

A2 The dependent variable derives its value based on the values of the independent variable. It is the "y" variable in the model. The independent variable is plotted along the x-axis and the dependent variable is plotted along the y-axis.

<u>Example</u>:
In the linear relationship model, $s = 40\,t$; where s is the distance traveled by a car after driving for time t, s is the dependent variable and t is the independent variable. As time t increases, the distance traveled also increases linearly.

Q3 How do I create a Linear model?

A3 Depending on how the data is available, a Linear model can be created in different ways.

<u>Data is in a report/text format:</u> If the data is in a textual format, identify the independent and dependent variables , tabulate them in two rows, one for independent variable x and one for dependent variable y, and use trial and error of $\Delta y/\Delta x$ to see if there is a linear relationship of the form $y = mx + b$.

<u>Data is in a table:</u> If the data is already in a tabular form, identify the independent and dependent variables and use trial and error of $\Delta y/\Delta x$ to see if there is a linear relationship of the form $y = mx + b$.

<u>Data is in a graph:</u> If the data is in the form of a scatterplot, identify the independent and dependent variables, draw a line of best fit through the data, and use the slope intercept formula $y = mx + b$ to create the linear model.

<table>
<tr><td colspan="3">HEART OF ALGEBRA</td></tr>
<tr><td>Lesson 18</td><td>Linear Models and Graphs</td><td>Practice</td></tr>
</table>

NO CALCULATOR SECTION

S	N
1	200
2	180
3	160
4	140
5	120

Questions 1 and 2 refer to the table shown above.

1. Shoe sales at a store are shown in the table where S is the size of the shoe and N is the number of shoes sold at that size. Which one of the following choices models the number of shoes sold in terms of the size of shoes?

(A) $N = -10S + 200$
(B) $N = 10S + 220$
(C) $N = -20S + 220$
(D) $N = -20S + 200$

2. Using the data shown above, what is the best estimate of the number of shoes that will be sold for a shoe size of 10?

(A) 0
(B) 20
(C) 40
(D) 200

NO CALCULATOR SECTION

More rain means more grasshoppers. That was the conclusion made by Karla, the zoo keeper responsible for grasshoppers, after she recorded the growth in grasshopper population over time as shown below.

Year (Y)	2008	2010	2012	2014
Grasshopper count (C)	0	300	600	900

Questions 3 and 4 refer to the table shown above.

3. Which of the following equations can be used by Karla to model the grasshopper count (C) as a function of the time elapsed (t) in years since 2008?

(A) $C = 300\,t$
(B) $C = 300 + t$
(C) $C = 150\,t$
(D) $C = 150 - t$

4. Using the table above, what is the best estimate of the number of grasshoppers in the zoo in 2013?

(A) 700
(B) 750
(C) 800
(D) 900

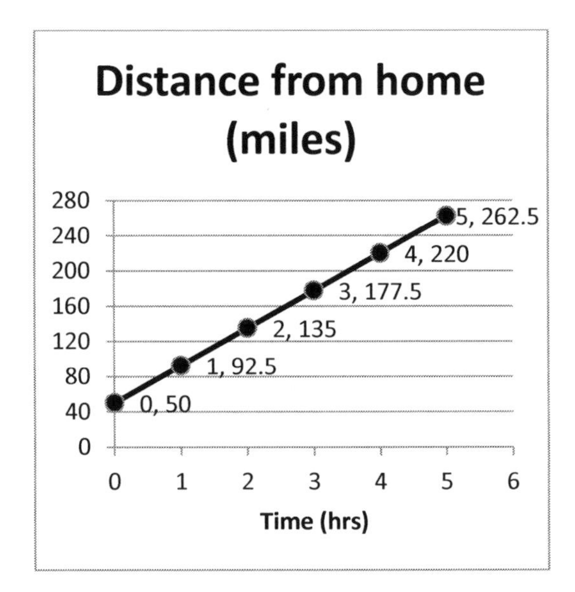

Questions 5 to 7 refer to the graph above.

5. Jane visited her friend and then drove to the beach several hundred miles away from home. The graph above shows her location over time. Which of the models below describes her distance from home d at time t after she left for the beach?

(A) $d = 40 + t$
(B) $d = 40 + 40t$
(C) $d = 50 + 42.5t$
(D) $d = 50 - 40t$

6. Approximately how far was she from home after driving for 3.25 hours?

(A) 168 miles
(B) 178 miles
(C) 188 miles
(D) 288 miles

7. Which model describes Jane's distance from her friend's house?

(A) $d = 50 + 42.5t$
(B) $d = 50 - 40t$
(C) $d = 45t$
(D) $d = 42.5t$

NO CALCULATOR SECTION

8. An eagle sitting on top of a 50 foot tall building starts flying and gains altitude at a constant speed of 30 miles/hour. Which of the following graphs shows its altitude at time t after it starts flying?

(A)

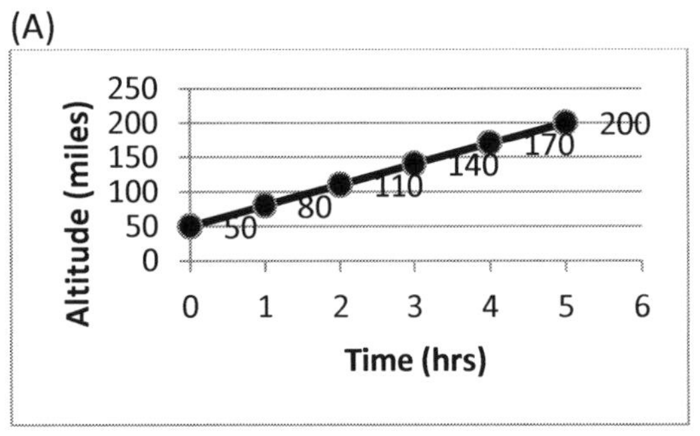

(B)

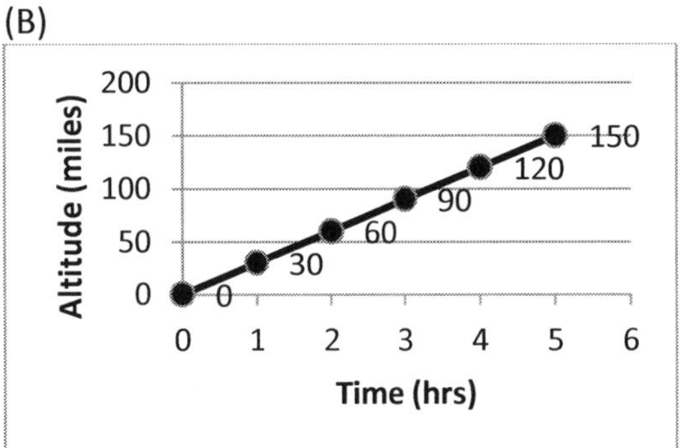

(C)

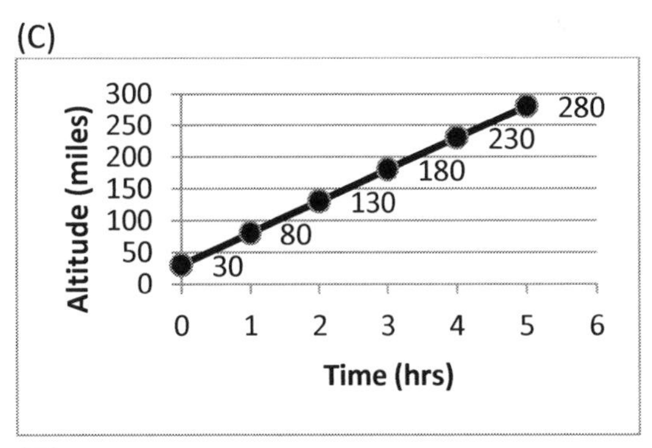

(D)

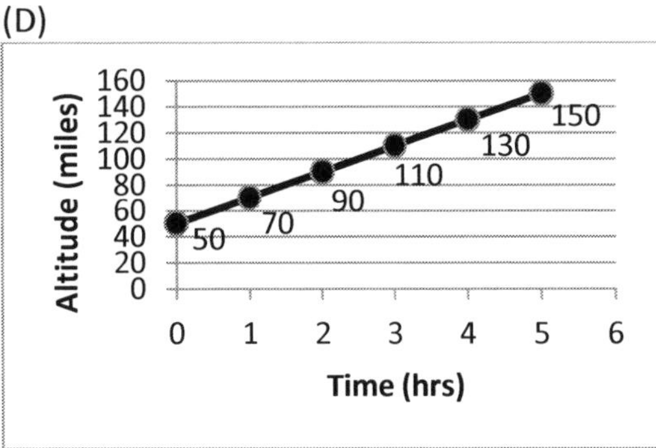

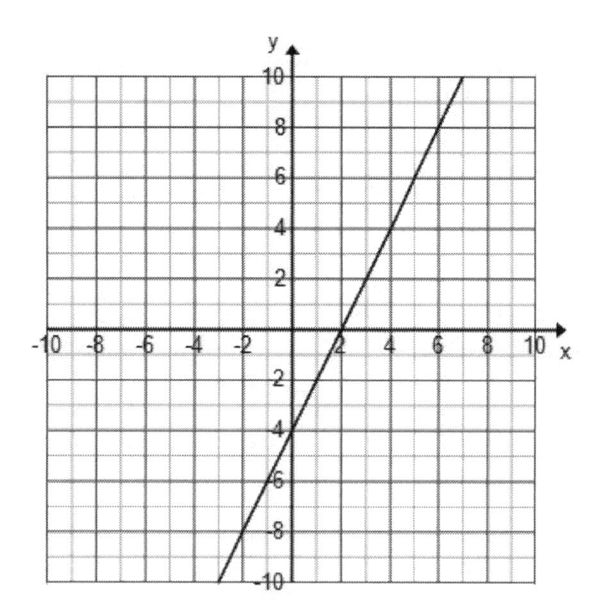

9. Which of the linear models below represents the graph shown above?

(A) $y = 2x + 4$
(B) $y = 2x - 4$
(C) $y = x - 4$
(D) $y = -x + 4$

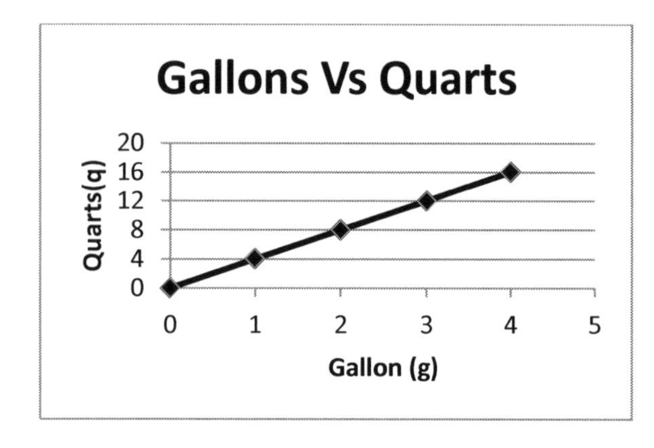

10. The graphical relationship between gallons (g) and quarts (q) is shown above. Which of the choices below represents the algebraic relation between gallons and quarts?

(A) $g = 4q$
(B) $g = 2q$
(C) $q = 4g$
(D) $q = 2g$

NO CALCULATOR SECTION

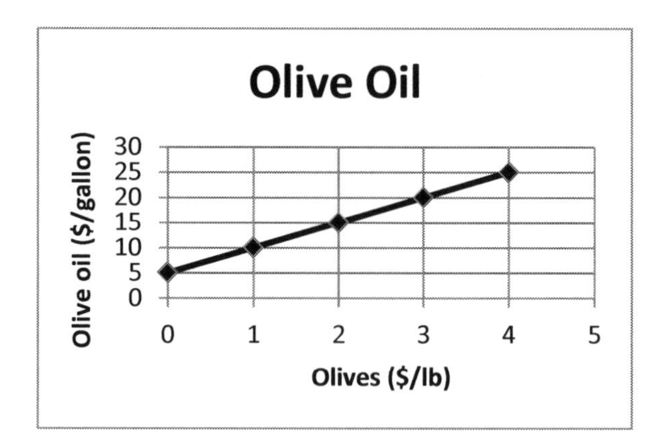

11. The relation between the cost of olives per pound and the sale price of olive oil per gallon includes a surcharge of $5 as shown above. If the surcharge is increased by $2, which of the following graphs will show the modified price of olive oil per gallon?

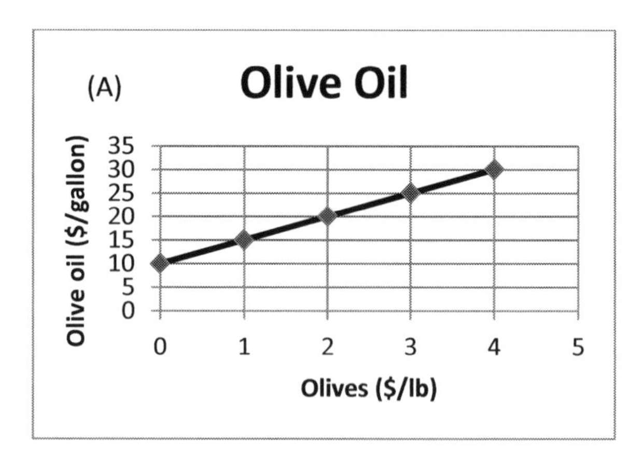

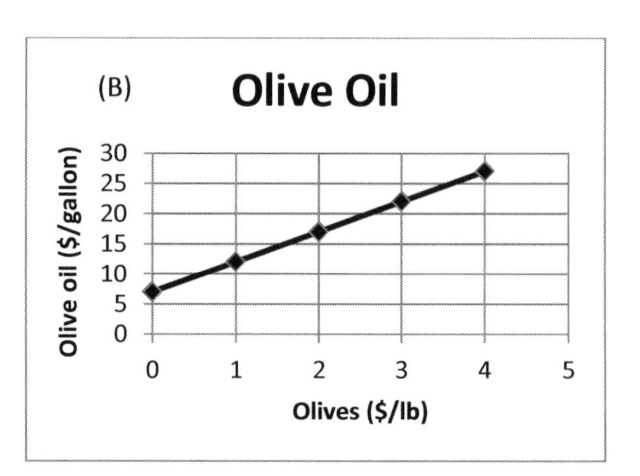

NO CALCULATOR SECTION

12 If 1 mile (mi) is equal to 1760 yards (yd) and 1 yard (yd) is equal to 3 feet (ft) and 1 foot (ft) is equal to 12 inches(in) then, which of the following graphs represents the relation between miles and inches?

(A)

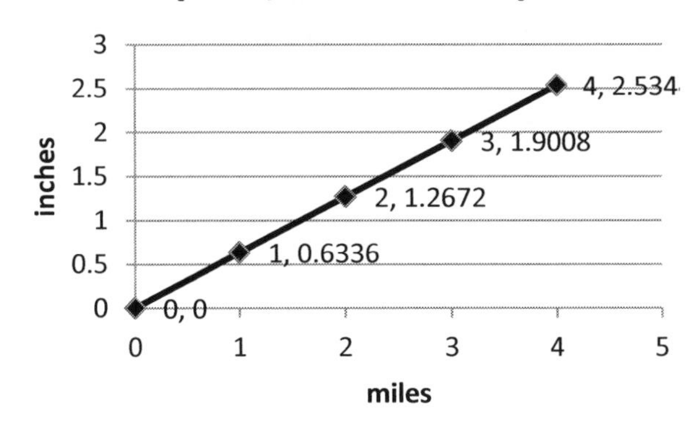

(B)

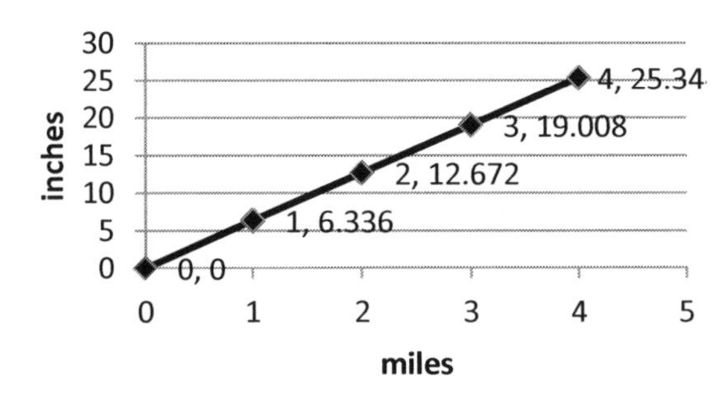

(C)

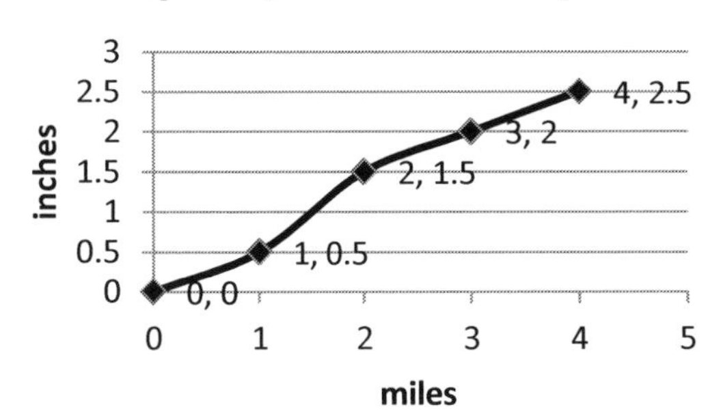

(D)

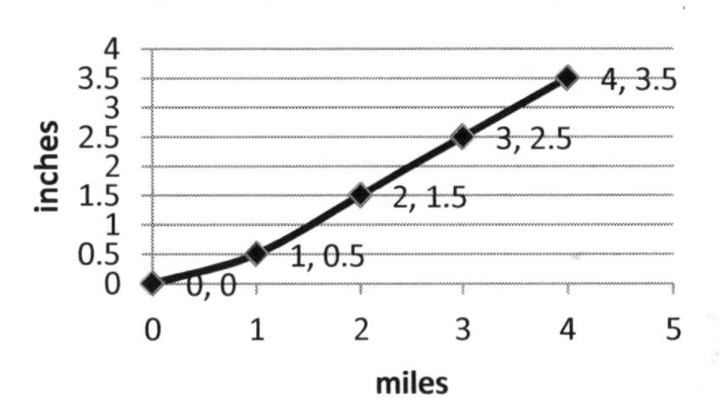

HEART OF ALGEBRA		
Lesson 18	Linear Models and Graphs	Answers

#	Explanation	Comments
1 C	Data is given in tabular form. Answer choices present several linear models. Take one choice and see if it models the data. Substitute s=1,2,3, etc., and see if the model gives the value of N correctly. The model $N = -20S + 220$ fits all the data points.	
2 B	Using the data in the table, the model that best fits this data was found to be $N = -20S + 220$; So, for a shoe size of 10, $S = 10, N = -20 \cdot 10 + 220 = -200 + 220 = 20$	Models can be used to estimate future values.
3 C	Note that the relationship expected is the elapsed time in years since 2008 – so, create another independent variable t which has a value of 0 when data collection began- that is t=0 in 2008, t=2 in 2010,etc. Year Y / Elapsed Time t: 2008 / 0; 2010 / 2; 2012 / 4; 2014 / 6 Grasshopper count C: 0; 300; 600; 900 Every 2 years, the grasshopper count C increases by 300 – so per year growth is 300/2=150. C=150 t is the linear model that fits the data.	
4 B	In year 2013, t=5, that is, 2013 would be 2013-2008=5 years since the data collection began. So C=150 · 5=750 grasshoppers.	Be careful while plugging in the value of the independent variable. In this problem, it was indexed from 2008 with a different variable- t.
5 C	Note that the graph is given and you are asked to pick a model. The graph is linear. So, it can be modeled using the slope intercept formula $y = mx + b$, where b is the y-intercept. It is clear from the graph that the y-intercept is 50. So, the model will be, partially, $y = mx + 50$. So, it has to be choices C or D. To find m, the slope, pick any two points and find Δy/Δx. For example, pick (1,92.5) and (2,135). Δy/Δx=(135-92.5)/(2-1)=42.5/1=42.5. So, the linear model is $d = 42.5t + 50$	Note that the value of d at $t = 0$ is 50, as labeled in the graph.
6 C	After 3.25 hours, she was 42.5·3.25+50=188.12=188	
7 D	Note that this question is about her distance from her friend's house – not her distance from home. At t=0, she was at her friend's house and then her distance is described by the graph with a slope of 42.5 and a y-intercept of 0. The model for this is $d = 42.5$t	In this problem, the model's point of reference has changed from her home to her friend's home. So, the y-intercept is 0.

8 A	This problem describes the model in verbal format. It says an eagle is at top of a 50 feet building. So, this is its starting height. Then it gains altitude at the rate of 30 miles/hour. So its altitude at any time is $50 + 30t$ *or* $30t + 50$. This corresponds to a line that has a y-intercept of 50 and that has a slope of 30. Choice A and D are the only choices that have a y-intercept of 50. To eliminate one of these choices, you have to find which graph has a slope of 30. Choice A has a $\Delta y/\Delta x$ of 30 since each data point is 30 more than the previous one. Choice D has a $\Delta y/\Delta x$ of 20.	Read the graph carefully. To calculate slope of a line, pick any 2 points, and calculate $\Delta y/\Delta x$.
9 B	Note that the graph is a straight line – so the algebraic model is $y = mx + b$; The line has an intercept of -4 and answers B and C have an y-intercept of -4. So, you need to look at the slope. Pick 2 points on the line (2,0) and (4,4). The slope is $\Delta y/\Delta x = (4\text{-}0)/(4\text{-}2)=2$. So, the equation of the model is $y = 2x - 4$.	Pay attention to the labels in the x and y axes. The major units increase by 2 on both axes.
10 C	Note carefully that g is on the x-axis and q is on the y-axis. For $g = 1, q = 4$, for $g = 2, q = 8$ – for every 1 gallon, the quarts increases 4 times. So $q = 4g$ describes the graph correctly.	
11 B	The surcharge was initially $5 and it increased by $2 to $7. So, the y-intercept must be shifted up to 7. But the slope of the graph must still be the same since only the surcharge has increased. Choice B shows an y-intercept of 7 and the same slope of 5.	
12 A	1 mile=1760 yards · 3 feet/yard · 12 inches/ feet = 63360 inches. Since the graph is in 100,000 units, 1 mile= 63360/100000=0.6336.	Read the graph carefully and note the units on the title.

HEART OF ALGEBRA

Lesson 19	Absolute Equalities and Inequalities	Review

FOCUSPREP CHECKLIST

- What is the Absolute value of a number?
- How do I solve an Absolute equality problem?
- How do I solve an Absolute inequality problem?
- Workout practice problems in absolute equalities and inequalities.

Q1 What is the absolute value of a number?

A1 The absolute value of a number x is represented as $|x|$ and is defined as follows:
$|x| = x$ when $x > 0$
$-x$ when $x < 0$

Example:
$|3| = 3$; $|-4| = 4$; $|4-7| = |-3| = 3$; $|7-4| = |3| = 3$
Note that $|x-y| = |y-x|$ for any two numbers x and y.

Q2 What is an absolute equality? How do I solve it?

A2 An absolute equality is an equality involving an absolute variable. You can solve an absolute equality for the variable by using the fact that if $|x| = k$, then $x = +k$ *or* $x = -k$. Thinking of numbers as being placed in a number line will help in visualizing and solving problems involving absolute numbers.

Example: Solve for x: $|x| = 43$
Solution $\{x|x = -43 \text{ or } x = 43\}$.

Example: Solve for x: $|x+3| = 43$
Solution: $x + 3 = -43$ *or* $x + 3 = 43$
If $x + 3 = -43$, then $x = -46$; If $x + 3 = 43$, then $x = 40$.
So the solution to $|x+3| = 43$ is $x = -46$ or $x = 40$. Substitute and verify.

Q3 What is an Absolute value Inequality? How do I solve it?

A3 The absolute value inequality is an inequality involving an absolute variable.

$|x| \leq k$ implies that $-k \leq x \leq k$

$|x| \geq k$ implies that $x \leq -k$ *or* $x \geq k$

Examples
$|x| < 3$ implies that $-3 < x < 3$

$|x-4| \leq 3$ implies $-3 \leq x - 4 \leq 3$; $-3 + 4 \leq x \leq 3 + 4$; so the solution is $1 \leq x \leq 7$

$|x-4| > 3$, so $x - 4 > 3$ *or* $x - 4 < -3$; so the solution is $x > 7$ or $x < 1$

HEART OF ALGEBRA		
Lesson 19	Absolute Equalities and Inequalities	Practice

NO CALCULATOR SECTION

1. If $|4m + 8| = 40$, then which of the following is one possible solution?
   (A) -8
   (B) 12
   (C) -12
   (D) 14

2. If $|3v - 4| = 20$ then one possible value of v is:

   (A) $-\frac{3}{16}$
   (B) -8
   (C) $\frac{3}{16}$
   (D) None of the above

3. If $|3x + 4| = 3$, then which of the following is one possible solution?
   (A) $+\frac{7}{3}$
   (B) -8
   (C) $-\frac{1}{3}$
   (D) No Solution

NO CALCULATOR SECTION

4. How many integer solutions does the inequality $\frac{|3x+6|}{3} < 5$ have?
   (A) 0
   (B) 8
   (C) 9
   (D) 11

5. Which of the following is <u>not</u> a solution of the inequality $\left|\frac{2x+4}{6}\right| \leq 12$?
   (A) -40
   (B) -38
   (C) 16
   (D) 34

6. Mondays' high temperature is $x°$. Tuesday's high temperature is $y°$. The high temperature on Wednesday is the absolute difference between Monday's and Tuesday's high temperatures. Which of the following represents the temperature on Wednesday?
(A) $|y - x|$
(B) $|xy|$
(C) $|x + y|$
(D) None

7. If $|2x + 3| < -|2x + 5|$, what is a possible value for x?
(A) -2
(B) -1.5
(C) 2
(D) No solution

NO CALCULATOR SECTION

8. How many points of intersection do the graphs of $y = |2x - 3|$ and $y = 15$ have?
(A) 0
(B) 1
(C) 2
(D) No Solution

9. The Mariana trench has a depth of 11 kilometers below sea level. Mount Kilimanjaro has a height of 6 kilometers above sea level. What is the absolute difference between the two heights?
GRID IN

10. What value of x satisfies both absolute equations shown below?

$$|4x - 6| = 4$$
$$|8x + 3| = 7$$

GRID IN

HEART OF ALGEBRA		
Lesson 19	Absolute Equalities and Inequalities	Answers

#	Explanation	Comments
1 C	$4m + 8 = 40$, or $4m + 8 = -40$. $m = \frac{32}{4} = 8$ or $m = -\frac{48}{4} = -12$.	Note that only one solution will be in the choices.
2 D	$3v - 4 = 20$, or $3v - 4 = -20$. $v = 8$ or $v = -\frac{16}{3}$. Since neither of these answers are choices, the answer is none of the above.	The solution does not always have to appear in the choices.
3 A	$\|3x + 4\| = 3$ $3x + 4 = 3$, or $3x + 4 = -3$ $x = -\frac{1}{3}$ or $x = -\frac{7}{3}$.	Remember that if $\|x\| = k$ then $x = -k$ or k
4 C	$\frac{\|3x+6\|}{3} < 5$ $\|3x + 6\| < 15$ $-15 < 3x + 6 < 15$ add -6 to all terms $-21 < 3x < 9$; divide by 3 throughout $-7 < x < 3$ The possible values of x are $-6, -5, -4, -3, -2, -1, 0, 1, 2$, a total of nine possibilities. Remember that 0 is an integer and must be counted.	Simplify the inequality. Remember that if $\|x\| \leq k$ $then$ $x \geq -k$ or $x \leq k$. Remember that less than signs are not inclusive. That is, if $x < 3$, then $x = 3$ is not valid.
5 B	$-12 \leq \frac{2x+4}{6} \leq 12$. Multiply by 6 throughout $-72 \leq 2x + 4 \leq 72$; subtract 4 throughout $-76 \leq 2x \leq 68$; divide by 2 throughout $-38 \leq x \leq 34$. -40 does not satisfy the range of values of for x.	Note that the question has a <u>not</u> in it.
6 A	The difference in temperatures between Monday and Tuesday is $\|x - y\|$. This is not an answer choice. Note that $\|x - y\| = \|y - x\|$, since the difference is absolute.	Remember that $\|x - y\| = \|y - x\|$. For example |4-6|=|6-4|=2
7 D	Pause and think for a second before proceeding. The absolute value $\|2x + 3\|$ is always positive, and $-\|2x + 5\|$ is always negative. Since a positive number cannot be less than a negative number, the inequality does not have a solution.	Lookout for tricky problems; positive values are always greater than negative values.
8 C	When two graphs intersect, their values are the same at the point of intersection. So, you can set the equation $\|2x - 3\| = 15$. You know that solving this absolute equality will give us 2 solutions. $2x - 3 = +15$ giving $x = 9$ and $2x - 3 = -15$ giving $x = -6$.. At $x = 9$ and $x = -6, y = \|2x - 3\| = 15$ and this graph intersects with $y = 15$ at	

	these two points.	
9 17	Since one is a depth and the other is a height, you need to sign the numbers correctly before calculating the difference. Measurements above the ground are positive and below the ground are negative. Mariana trench has a height of -11, Mount Kilimanjaro has a height of +6. The absolute value $\|11-(-6)\|=17$.	Depth is negative.
10 $\frac{1}{2}$	Solve the first equation first $\|4x-6\|=4$ $4x-6=4 \; or \; 4x-6=-4$ $x=\frac{5}{2}$ or $x=\frac{1}{2}$. Plugging $x=\frac{5}{2}$ into the second equation gives $\left\|8\cdot\frac{5}{2}+3\right\|=9<>7$. This means that $x=\frac{5}{2}$ is not a solution. Plugging $x=\frac{1}{2}$ into the second equation gives $\left\|8\cdot\frac{1}{2}+3\right\|=7$. This means that $x=\frac{1}{2}$ satisfies both equations and therefore is a solution.	This problem is an example of a system of absolute equalities in one variable. Solve one equation and check which one of the two solutions will fit the second equation.

CHAPTER 3 PASSPORT TO ADVANCED MATH	
Lesson	**Title**
Lesson 20	Polynomials and Quadratic Equations
Lesson 21	Linear- Quadratic Systems
Lesson 22	Functions and Transformations
Lesson 23	Radicals and Fractional Exponents

FOCUSPREP CHECKLIST

- How do I add, subtract, multiply, and divide polynomial expressions?
- How do I factorize polynomial expressions?
- How do I solve polynomial equations?
- How do I complete the square to solve quadratic equations?
- Workout practice problems in Polynomials and Quadratic equations

Q1 What is a Polynomial?

A1 A Polynomial is an expression of one or more terms. If there is only one term, it is a monomial. If it has two terms, it is called a binomial. If it has three terms, it is called a trinomial. It can have any number of terms.

Examples:

Monomial: $x,\ 2x, -4xy\ , x^2$ – these polynomials have only one term
Binomials: $x^2 + 3x, xy + 4,\ x^3 - 3$ – these polynomials have two terms
Trinomials: $2x^9 + 3x^5 + 2x^2,\ x^4 - x^2 + x$ – these polynomials have three terms

Q2 What is the degree of a polynomial?

A2 The degree of a term is the sum of the exponents of all variables in the term. The degree of a polynomial is the degree of the term with the highest degree. To find the degree of a polynomial, first find the degree of all the terms. The highest degree you have is the degree of the polynomial.

Example: $2x^{11} + 3x^2 + 1$ The first term has a degree of 11, the second term has a degree of 2 and the third term has a degree of 0. The highest degree is 11. So this polynomial has a degree of 11.

Example: $2x^2y^2 + 3xy + 1$ The first term has a degree of $4\ (2 + 2)$, the second term has a degree of $2(1 + 1)$ and the third term has a degree of 0. The highest degree is 4. So, this polynomial has a degree of 4.

Q3 What are polynomials used for?

A3 Polynomials are used to model a variety of scenarios in the real world. Linear and Quadratic functions are special types of polynomial functions that are used to model physical, chemical, biological, and economic observations, to name a few. For example, the value of a property can be modeled with a quadratic polynomial. The altitude gained by an aircraft can be modeled with a linear polynomial. Using data gathered in experiments, you can model the relationship between dependent and independent variables using polynomial functions.

Q4 What operations can I do on a polynomial?

A4 You can add, subtract, multiply, or divide polynomials.

Add Polynomials: Add two polynomials by adding the like terms. For example, a term that has x^2 term must be added to another term that also has x^2.

Example: $(2x^3 + 2x^2 + 2x) + (3x^3 + 5x^2 + 3x + 1)$

$= 2x^3 + 3x^3 + 2x^2 + 5x^2 + 2x + 3x + 1$; gather like terms and add them

$= 5x^3 + 7x^2 + 5x + 1$

You can also place the polynomials one below the other and line up the like terms and add them up.

Subtract Polynomials: Subtracting polynomials is similar to subtracting two numbers – just remember to negate the second polynomial.

Example:

$(2x^3 + 2x^2 + 2x) - (3x^3 + 3x^2 + 3x + 1)$

$= 2x^3 + 2x^2 + 2x - 3x^3 - 3x^2 - 3x - 1$; negate the second polynomial

$= 2x^3 - 3x^3 + 2x^2 - 3x^2 + 2x - 3x - 1$; gather like terms

$= -x^3 - x^2 - x - 1$; add like terms

Multiply Polynomials: Use distributive property of multiplication ; $a(b + c) = ab + ac$

Example: (multiply a monomial(one term) and trinomial(three terms))

$2x(x^5 + 3x^4 + 2x)$;

$= 2x \cdot x^5 + 2x \cdot 3x^4 + 2x \cdot 2x$; use $a(b + c + d) = ab + ac + ad$

$= 2x^6 + 6x^5 + 4x^2$; simplify

Example: (multiply a binomial and another binomial)

Use the FOIL method (First, Outer, Inner, Last) to multiply the two binomials.

$(2x + 4)(x + 3)$

$= 2x.x + 2x.3 + 4.x + 4 \cdot 3$;use FOIL method

$= 2x^2 + 6x + 4x + 12$; simplify

$= 2x^2 + 10x + 12$; add like terms

Divide Polynomials: (divide a polynomial by a monomial). Divide each term of the polynomial by the denominator separately as shown:

Example:

$$\frac{16x^4 + 4x^2 + 8}{4}$$

$$= \frac{16x^4}{4} + \frac{4x^2}{4} + \frac{8}{4}$$

$$= 4x^4 + x^2 + 2$$

Example: (divide a polynomial by another polynomial)

There are two ways to divide a polynomial by another polynomial: Factoring and Long Division.

Divide two polynomials by factoring: Factor normally, and then cancel out the numerator and denominator as shown below: Factoring is discussed in detail later in this lesson.

Example: (division by factoring)

$\frac{x^2+9x+14}{x+7}$; factor the numerator

$= \frac{(x+2)\cancel{(x+7)}}{\cancel{(x+7)}}$

$= (x+2)$

Example: (division by long division – no remainder)

$$x+7|\overline{x^2+9x+14}$$

$$\begin{array}{r} x+2 \\ x+7|\overline{x^2+9x+14} \\ -\underline{(x^2+7x)} \\ 0+2x+14 \\ \underline{2x+14} \\ 0 \end{array}$$

When the polynomial cannot be divided into the divisor anymore, the extra part is left as the remainder.
Example: (Division by long division – with remainder)

$$\begin{array}{r} x^2-2x+4 \\ 3x+1|\overline{3x^3-5x^2+10x-6} \\ \underline{-(3x^3+x^2)} \\ -6x^2+10x-6 \\ \underline{-(-6x^2-2x)} \\ 12x-6 \\ \underline{-(12x+4)} \\ -10 \end{array}$$

In this case, the answer to the division is $x^2-2x+4-\frac{10}{3x+1}$. This is similar to how division works with real numbers. For example, when you divide 7 by 4, you get a quotient of 1 and a remainder of 3. You can write this as $\frac{7}{4}=1+\frac{3}{4}$. The result of the above polynomial division is also written in this way.

Q5 What does <u>factoring</u> a polynomial mean? Why do I need to factorize a polynomial?

A5 When you say that 9 and 4 are factors of 36, you know that 9·4=36. Factoring a polynomial is also similar in meaning. Factoring a polynomial is the process of breaking down the polynomial into other polynomials(factors) such the product of the factors is equal to the original polynomial.

Factoring a polynomial is useful when finding the zeros of a polynomial function and while solving polynomial equations. Zeros of a function is covered in the lesson on Functions.

Q6 What are some special factorizations to remember?

A6 Remembering the following formulas will help you in factoring the polynomials quickly. See the examples column to learn how they are used.

Special Factorizations	Examples
$a^2+b^2+2ab=(a+b)^2$ Perfect Square Formula	$x^2+4x+4=(x+2)^2$
$a^2+b^2-2ab=(a-b)^2$ Perfect Square Formula	$x^2-6x+9=(x-3)^2$
$a^2-b^2=(a+b)(a-b)$ Difference of Squares Formula	$x^2-81=(x+9)(x-9)$
$(a^3-b^3)=(a-b)(a^2+ab+b^2)$ Cubic Formula	$x^3-27=(x-3)(x^2+6x+9)$
$(a^3+b^3)=(a+b)(a^2-ab+b^2)$ Cubic Formula	$x^3+27=(x+3)(x^2-6x+9)$

Q7 How do I factor a polynomial?

A7 There are a several methods available to factor polynomials. Be familiar with all the methods since some factoring problems can be tricky. Note that these methods apply to factoring any type of polynomial-binomials, trinomials, quadratics etc. As you solve problems, these methods will come naturally to you. Polynomials in SAT are not difficult to factorize, but you have to be careful to handle all the terms correctly. Always remember the special factorizations listed above.

<u>Method 1: Factoring using GCF</u>: If the terms of a polynomial has factors that appear to be common, then use the GCF(Greatest Common Factor) and extract out the common factors. This method can be used as part of other methods. GCF has been reviewed in a different lesson.

<u>Example</u>: Factor $4x^3-2x^2$

The GCF OF 2 and 4 is 2 and the GCF of x^2 *and* x^3 is x^2. So, factor out $2x^2$.

$4x^3-2x^2$

$=2x^2(2x-1)$

<u>Method 2: Factoring by Grouping</u>: Often, all the terms may not contain a common factor, but a pair of terms may. In that case, group the terms in pairs and factor out the common factors using GCF method.

<u>Example</u>: Factor x^3+x^2-x-1

Solution: All the terms do not contain a common factor other than 1. So, try the grouping method. Pause a few seconds to observe if a pair of terms can be factored out and which terms would best form the pair.

$x^3 + x^2 - x - 1$
$= (x^3 + x^2) - x - 1$; group the terms that have a common factor
$= x^2(x + 1) - 1(x + 1)$; $x + 1$ is the common factor
$= (x + 1)\ (x^2 - 1)\ = (x + 1)\ (x\ + 1)(x - 1)$; use the difference of squares factorization

Method 3A Factoring $x^2 + bx + c$ by Reverse FOIL method:
If you have a quadratic expression $ax^2 + bx + c$, where the coefficient of $x^2 = a = 1$, then find two numbers p and q such that their product is c and their sum is b. If you can find p and q, then $(x + p)(x + q)$ are the factors of the quadratic.

Example: Factorize (or, what are the factors of) $x^2 - 4x + 3$

Solution: GCF method will not work since there is no common factor in all the three terms. Grouping method will not work since you have only 3 terms and you need 4 terms to group. Using Reverse FOIL method, you have to find two numbers p and q such that $p.q = 3$ and $p + q = -4$. If $p = -1$ and $q = -3$, then $pq = 3$ and $p + q = -4$. So $x - 1$ and $x - 3$ are factors. So, $x^2 - 4x + 3 = (x - 1)(x - 3)$. You can expand using FOIL to check whether $(x - 1)(x - 3)$ adds up to $x^2 - 4x + 3$.

Method 3B Factoring $x^2 + bx + c$ by Reverse FOIL method:
Since it is possible to make mistakes while writing the factors correctly as $x + p$ *and* $x + q$ when p and q are negative, you can follow an alternative method shown below.

$x^2 - 4x + 3$
Find p, q such that $pq = 3, p + q = -4.$ Try $p = -3$ *and* $q = -1$; now, rewrite the polynomial using p and q.

$x^2 - 4x + 3$
$= x^2 - 3x - x + 3$; rewrite using p and q to sum up to coefficient of x
$= x(x - 3) - 1(x - 3)$; group and factor out the GCF;
$= (x - 3)(x - 1)$; $(x - 3)$ is common to both terms

Method 4 Factoring $ax^2 + bx + c,\ a \neq 1$ by Reverse FOIL method: If you have a quadratic expression $ax^2 + bx + c$ where the coefficient of x^2 *is* a, *and* $a \neq 1$, then find two numbers p and q such that their product is $a \cdot c$ and their sum is b. Then, rewrite the expression in terms of p and q and group the terms and factorize.

Example: Factor $2x^2 + 11x + 12$
Solution: GCF method will not work since there is no common factor in all the three terms. Grouping method will not work since you have only 3 terms and you need 4 terms to group. So, try the FOIL method with $a \neq 1$. Using FOIL method, you have to find two numbers p and q such that $p.q = a.c = 2 \cdot 12 = 24$ *and and* $p + q = b = 11$. If $p = 8$ *and* $q = 3$, *then* $pq = 24$ *and* $p + q = 11$.

$2x^2 + 11x + 12$
$= 2x^2 + 8x + 3x + 12$; rewrite using p and q; $2x$ and 3 are common factors
$= 2x(x + 4) + 3(x + 4)$; $(x + 4)$ is the common factor
$= (x + 4)(2x + 3)$

Method 5: Using special factorizations: While factorizing some polynomials, it may be easier to use the special factorization formulas discussed earlier to factorize.

Example: Factorize $4x^2 - 4x + 1$

Solution: Pause to observe the terms for a few seconds. You can observe that the first term is $(2x)^2$ and the last term is 1^2. The perfect square formula is $a^2 + b^2 - 2ab = (a-b)^2$. So, you can factorize $4x^2 - 4x + 1$ as $(2x)^2 - 2 \cdot 2x + 1^2 = (2x-1)^2$.

Example: Factorize $27x^3 - 8y^3$

Solution: Pause to observe the terms for a few seconds. You can observe that the terms are in the forms of $a^3 - b^3$. Notice that his polynomial has two variables x and y. Use the special factorization formula for cubes.

$27x^3 - 8y^3$
$=(3x)^3 - (2y)^3$; 27 and 8 are perfect cubes, and the expression is in the cubic form of $a^3 - b^3$
$= (3x-2y)(9x^2 + 6xy + 4y^2)$ – use the special factorization formula for cubes

Q8 What is the Factor Theorem? When is it useful?

A8 The factor theorem states that for any polynomial $P(x)$, $(x-a)$ is a factor if and only if $P(a) = 0$. This theorem does not give you all the factors of a polynomial. It only tells you under what condition $(x-a)$ will be a factor.

Example: Is $(x-4)$ a factor of $x^2 - 16$?

Solution: The value of the polynomial when $x = 4$ is $4^2 - 16 = 16 - 16 = 0$; So, according to Factor theorem, you can conclude that $x - 4$ will be a factor.

Q9 How is polynomial factoring helpful in simplifying rational expressions?

A9 Rational expressions are of the form $\frac{a}{b}$, where a and b are polynomial expressions and b is not 0. To simplify, factorize and cancel out common factors in numerator and denominator.

Example: Simplify $\frac{x+1}{x^2-1}$

Solution:

$$\frac{x+1}{x^2-1}$$

$$= \frac{\cancel{x+1}}{(\cancel{x+1})(x-1)}$$; use difference of squares to factorize the denominator

$$= \frac{1}{(x-1)}$$

Example: Simplify $\frac{x^2+y^2+2xy}{x^2-y^2}$

Solution:

$$= \frac{(x+y)^2}{(x+y)(x-y)}$$; factorize using perfect square formula, and difference of squares

$$= \frac{(x+y)\cdot(x+y)}{(x+y)(x-y)} = \frac{x+y}{x-y}$$

Q10 How do I solve a polynomial/quadratic equation?

A10 Use one or more of the following methods to solve a polynomial/quadratic equation.
Isolate the variable and constants and set the equation to 0.
Factorize and solve for the variable.
Take square root or cube root on both sides of the equation if required.
Use special factorizations if required.
Use the completing the square method explained below if applicable for the problem at hand.

Example Solve for x in $x^2 - 5x + 4 = 18$
$x^2 - 5x + 4 = 18;$
$x^2 - 5x + 4 - 18 = 0;$
$x^2 - 5x - 14 = 0$; find p and q such that $pq = -14$, and $p + q = -5$; try $p = -7,\ q = 2$
$x^2 - 7x + 2x - 14 = 0$; rewrite using p and q
$x(x - 7) + 2(x - 7) = 0$
$(x - 7)(x + 2) = 0$
$x - 7 = 0$ and $x + 2 = 0$
$x = 7$ and $x = -2$
Verify by substituting in the equation; when $x = 7,\ 7^2 - 5 \cdot 7 + 4 = 18$; when $x = -2, (-2)^2 - 5 \cdot -2 + 4 = 18$.
So, the solutions are $x = -2$ and $x = 7$

Example Solve $(x - 3)^2 = 16$
$(x - 3) = \pm\sqrt{16} = \pm 4$; take square root on both sides
$x = 3 \pm 4;\ 3 + 4 = 7$ *or* $3 - 4 = -1$

Example Solve $(x - 3)^3 = 27$
$(x - 3) = \sqrt[3]{27} = 3$; note that $\sqrt[3]{27} <> -3$; it is only $+3$
$x = 3 + 3 = 6$

Q11 How do I complete the square to solve a quadratic equation?

A11 While solving polynomial equations, if you have to factorize $x^2 + bx$ but don't have the remaining term, you can add $\left(\frac{b}{2}\right)^2$ and complete the square. This is called the "completing the square" method.

Example: Solve for x: $4x^2 + 16x = 0$
Solution: Pause to observe the terms for a few seconds. Observe the GCF of 4 in both terms. Factor it out and observe further.

$4x^2 + 16x = 0$
$4(x^2 + 4x) = 0$ factor out 4 from both terms; $x^2 + 4x$ is missing one term that will make it a square
$x^2 + 4x = 0$ divide by 4 on both sides
$(x^2 + 4x + 4 - 4) = 0$; to complete the square, add $\left(\frac{b}{2}\right)^2$ where b=4 ; so add $\left(\frac{4}{2}\right)^2 = 4$ and subtract 4
$(x + 2)^2 - 4 = 0$; use the perfect square formula
$(x + 2)^2 = 4$
$x + 2 = \pm\sqrt{4}$; take square root on both sides
$x = -2 \pm 2;\ x = -2 + 2 = 0$ and $-2 - 2 = -4$
Verify the results: when $x = 0\ 4 \cdot 0^2 + 16 \cdot 0 = 0$; when $x = -4, (-4)^2 + 16(-4) = 64 - 64 = 0$

PASSPORT TO ADVANCED MATH		
Lesson 20	Polynomials and Quadratic Equations	Practice

NO CALCULATOR SECTION

1. Which of the following can be a solution to the quadratic equation below?

$$x^2 - 81 = 0$$

(A) -12
(B) -10
(C) -9
(D) -3

2. The sum of the solutions of $(x-2)^2 = 16$ is
(A) -12
(B) -10
(C) -8
(D) 4

3. If $x^2 + 8x = 0$, then which of the following is true?
I $x = 0$
II $x = 8$
III $x = -8$

(A) I only
(B) II only
(C) I and III
(D)II and III

4. If $z^2 - 4z = 21$, the product of the solutions is
(A) -28
(B) -24
(C) -21
(D) -15

NO CALCULATOR SECTION

5. The largest solution to $(x+4)^2 = (x+4)$ is
(A)-3
(B)-2
(C) 3
(D) 12

6. If $p^2 - 2^2 = 8 \cdot (p+2)$, then p=
(A)2
(B)8
(C)10
(D)12

7. The solution to $(x+2)^2 - (x-2)^2 = 88$ is
(A) less than 11
(B) equal to 11
(C) greater than 11
(D) cannot be determined

8. If $(m+5)(3m-21) = 0$ then $m =$
(A) -5 and -7
(B) 5 and -7
(C) -5 and 7
(D) 5 and 7

9. If $(z-p)^2 = 36$, then z could be
(A) p
(B) $p+6$
(C) $6p$
(D) $\frac{6}{p}$

NO CALCULATOR SECTION

10. If $x^3 + y^3 = 2a(x^3 - y^3)$ then $\frac{x^3}{y^3} =$

(A) $\frac{2a+1}{1-2a}$

(B) $\frac{2a-1}{2a+1}$

(C) $\frac{2a+1}{2a-1}$

(D) $\frac{2a+1}{1-2a}$

11. If $\frac{9x^2}{3x+1} = \frac{1}{3x+1} + A$, what is A in terms of x?

(A) $2x + 1$

(B) $3x + 1$

(C) $2x - 1$

(D) $3x - 1$

NO CALCULATOR SECTION

12. $\frac{100x^3y^3 - 50x^2y^2}{25xy} =$

(A) $\frac{2xy}{2xy-1}$

(B) $\frac{2xy}{xy-1}$

(C) $2xy(2xy - 1)$

(D) $2xy(2xy + 1)$

13. If $\frac{1}{x} + a = \frac{1}{y}$ then what is x in terms of y?

(A) $\frac{y}{1+ay}$

(B) $\frac{y}{1-ay}$

(C) $\frac{1+ay}{y}$

(D) $\frac{1-ay}{y}$

NO CALCULATOR SECTION

14. The factors of $x^2 + 8x + 12$ are
(A) $(x + 6)$ and $(x - 2)$
(B) $(x - 6)$ and $(x - 2)$
(C) $(x - 6)$ and $(x + 2)$
(D) $(x + 6)$ and $(x + 2)$

15. The factors of $x^2 + x - 12$ are
(A) $(x + 4)$ and $(x - 3)$
(B) $(x + 4)$ and $(x + 3)$
(C) $(x - 4)$ and $(x - 3)$
(D) $(x - 6)$ and $(x + 2)$

16. The factors of $x^2 - 8x - 20$ are
(A) $(x + 2)$ and $(x + 10)$
(B) $(x - 2)$ and $(x - 10)$
(C) $(x + 2)$ and $(x - 10)$
(D) $(x - 2)$ and $(x + 10)$

NO CALCULATOR SECTION

17. The factors of $-4p^2 - 16p + 9$ are
(A) $(2p - 1)$ and $(2p + 9)$
(B) $-(2p - 1)$ and $(2p + 9)$
(C) $(2p - 9)$ and $(2p - 1)$
(D) $-(p - 1)$ and $(p + 1)$

18. After using the completing the square method, $x^2 + 16x$ can be simplified as
(A) $(x + 8)^2 - 8$
(B) $(x + 8)^2 + 8$
(C) $(x + 8)^2 + 64$
(D) $(x + 8)^2 - 64$

19. After using the completing the square method, $4x^2 - 16x$ can be simplified as
(A) $4(x - 2)^2 - 4$
(B) $(x - 2)^2 + 16$
(C) $4(x - 2)^2 + 16$
(D) $4((x - 2)^2 - 4)$

20. The area of a rectangle is given by the expression: $x^2 + 9x + 18$. What is the perimeter of the rectangle?

(A) $x + 9$
(B) $2x + 9$
(C) $4x + 9$
(D) $4x + 18$

21. The length of a rectangle of l is three times its width w. If the length is increased by 5 units and width is increased by 2 units, the area of a rectangle is given by which of the following expression?

(A) $3w^2 + 11w + 10$
(B) $3w^2 - 11w + 10$
(C) $11w^2 + 3w + 10$
(D) $11w^2 - 3w - 10$

NO CALCULATOR SECTION

22. When $3x^2 + 4x + 1$ is divided by $3x + 1$, the remainder is

(A) $x + 1$
(B) 0
(C) $2x + 1$
(D) $2x - 1$

#	Explanation	Comments
1 C	$x^2 - 81 = 0$ $x^2 = 81$ $x = \sqrt{81} = \pm 9$ Since only -9 is in the answer choice, C is the correct answer	
2 D	$(x-2)^2 = 16$ $(x-2) = \sqrt{16} = \pm 4$ $x = 2 \pm 4 = 6\ or - 2$ Sum of the solutions=$6 + (-2) = 6 - 2 = 4$	Note that the question asks for the sum of the solutions.
3 C	$x^2 + 8x = 0$ In this expression, $x^2 + 8x$ appears like it is missing a term to complete the square $x^2 + 8x + 16 - 16 = 0$ $(x+4)^2 - 16 = 0$ $(x+4)^2 = 16$ $(x+4) = \sqrt{16} = \pm 4$ $x = -4 \pm 4$ $x = 0\ or - 8$ Choice C indicates these 2 solutions	Completing the square is an important method for solving quadratic equations.
4 C	$z^2 - 4z = 21$ $z^2 - 4z - 21 = 0$; find $p, q\ such\ that\ pq = -21\ and$ $p + q = -4$; try $p = -7\ and\ q = 3$ $z^2 - 7z + 3z - 21 = 0$ $z(z-7) + 3(z-7) = 0$ $(z-7)(z+3) = 0$ $z - 7 = 0; or\ z + 3 = 0$ $z = 7\ or\ z = -3$ Product of the solutions is $7 \cdot -3 = -21$	Note that the quadratic variable is z; it does not have to be x all the time.
5 A	$(x+4)^2 = (x+4)$ $x^2 + 8x + 16 = x + 4$ $x^2 + 8x + 16 - x - 4 = 0$ $x^2 + 7x + 12 = 0$ $x^2 + 4x + 3x + 12 = 0$ $x(x+4) + 3(x+4) = 0$ $(x+4)(x+3) = 0$ $x = -4, or\ x = -3$; verify these by substituting The larger of these is -3.	
6 C	$p^2 - 2^2 = 8 \cdot (p+2)$ $p^2 - 4 = 8p + 16$ $p^2 - 4 - 8p - 16 = 0$ $p^2 - 8p - 20 = 0$	

	$p^2 - 10p + 2p - 20 = 0$ $p(p - 10) + 2(p - 10) = 0$ $(p - 10)(p + 2) = 0$ $so, p = 10 \; or \; p = -2$ Choice C is equal to 10 and is the correct answer.	
7 B	$(x + 2)^2 - (x - 2)^2 = 88$ $x^2 + 4x + 4 - (x^2 - 4x + 4) = 88$ $x^2 + 4x + 4 - x^2 + 4x - 4 = 88$ $8x = 88$ $x = 11$	
8 C	$(m + 5)(3m - 21)$=0; so either or both is 0 $(m + 5) = 0 \;\; m = -5$ $3m - 21 = 0; \; m = 7$	Use zero product rule – if $a \cdot b = 0$ then $a = 0$ or $b = 0$ or both $= 0$.
9 B	$(z - p)^2 = 36$ $z - p = \pm 6$ $z = p \pm 6$ $z = p + 6 \; or \; p - 6$	If you see only one solution of the quadratic in the answer choices, pick that answer choice.
10 C	$x^3 + y^3 = 2a(x^3 - y^3)$ $x^3 + y^3 = 2ax^3 - 2ay^3$ $x^3 - 2ax^3 = -y^3 - 2ay^3$ $x^3(1 - 2a) = -y^3(1 + 2a)$ $\frac{x^3}{y^3} = \frac{-1(1 + 2a)}{(1 - 2a)} = \frac{2a + 1}{2a - 1}$	This is a problem involving simplifying an algebraic fraction; isolate the variables and simplify Do not be intimidated by the problem; pause for a second to see patterns and then proceed.
11 D	$\frac{9x^2}{3x + 1} = \frac{1}{3x + 1} + A$ Notice that the denominator is the same, A can be written in terms of x and simplified $A = \frac{9x^2}{3x + 1} - \frac{1}{3x + 1}$ $A = \frac{(3x)^2 - 1^2}{3x + 1} = \frac{(\cancel{3x + 1})(3x - 1)}{(\cancel{3x + 1})} = 3x - 1$	Isolate A and then use the difference of square formula to simplify this rational expression.
12 C	$\frac{100x^3y^3 - 50x^2y^2}{25xy}$ $= \frac{50x^2y^2(2xy - 1)}{25xy}$ $= 2xy(2xy - 1)$	Factor out the GCF from the two terms in the numerator.

13 B	$\frac{1}{x} + a = \frac{1}{y}$ $\frac{1}{x} = \frac{1}{y} - a = \frac{1 - ay}{y}$ $x = \frac{y}{1 - ay}$	
14 D	Several choices are given for the factors of $x^2 + 8x + 12$. So, without factorizing, you can evaluate the answer choices. In choice D, $6 \cdot 2 = c = 12$ and $6 + 2 = b = 8$, so it is the correct answer.	Remember that for a quadratic $x^2 + bx + c,\ (x + p) and\ (x + q) are\ factors\ if\ pq = c$ and $p + q = b$.
15 A	$x^2 + x - 12$ Find p, q such that $pq = -12\ and\ p + q = 1$, then $(x + p)(x + q)$ are factors. Choice A shows $p = 4\ and\ q = -3, pq = -12$ and $p + q = 1$	
16 C	$x^2 - 8x - 20$ Find p, q such that $pq = -20\ and\ p + q = -8$, then $(x + p)(x + q)$ are factors. Choice C shows $p = 2\ and\ q = -10, pq = -20$ and $p + q = -8$	
17 B	$-4p^2 - 16p + 9$ $= -1(4p^2 + 16p - 9)$ Find p, q such that $pq = 4 \cdot -9 = -36$ and $p + q = 16$. Try $p = 18$ and $q = -2$. $= -1(4p^2 + 18p - 2p - 9)$ $=-1((2p(2p + 9) - 1(2p + 9))$ $=-1\ (2p + 9)(2p - 1)$	Remember that for a quadratic $ax^2 + bx + c$, $find\ p\ and\ q\ such\ that\ pq = ac\ and\ p + q = b$. Then write out the expression using p and q and factorize; a little tedious process but if you take care of the positive and negative signs, you can find the answer confidently.
18 D	$x^2 + 16x$ $x^2 + 16x + 64 - 64$; add $\left(\frac{16}{2}\right)^2$ to complete the square $(x + 8)^2 - 64$	Review the completing the square question in the review section; add $\left(\frac{b}{2}\right)^2 = \left(\frac{16}{2}\right)^2$.
19 D	$4x^2 - 16x$ $= 4(x^2 - 4x)$ $= 4(x^2 - 4x + 4 - 4)$; $= 4((x - 2)^2 - 4)$;	Choice A looks similar to choice D but is different. Choice D has an extra parenthesis.
20 D	Area of rectangle is given as $x^2 + 9x$+18 You know that the area of a rectangle $A = l.w$. So, the length and width are factors of the area. Factorize $x^2 + 9x$+18 $= x^2 + 6x + 3x + 18$ $= (x + 6)(x + 3)$	

	So, the sides of the rectangle are $(x+6)$ and $(x+3)$ Perimeter of rectangle= $2(l+w) = 2(x+6+x+3) =$ $2(2x+9) = 4x+18.$	
21 A	$l = 3w$ $new\ area = (l+5)(w+2)$ $= (3w+5)(w+2)$ $= 3w^2 + 6w + 5w + 10$ $= 3w^2 + 11w + 10$	
22 B	Do the long division $$\begin{array}{r} x+1 \\ 3x+1\overline{)3x^2+4x+1} \\ -(3x^2+x) \\ \hline 0+3x+1 \\ -(3x+1) \\ \hline 0 \end{array}$$	

PASSPORT TO ADVANCED MATH		
Lesson 21	Linear Quadratic Systems	Review

FOCUSPREP CHECKLIST

- What is a Linear Quadratic System?
- How do I solve a Linear Quadratic System?
- How many solutions can a Linear Quadratic System have?
- Workout practice problems in Linear Quadratic Systems

Q1 What is a Linear Quadratic System?

A1 A Linear Quadratic system contains two functions - a linear function and a quadratic function.

Example:

$y = x^2 + 6x + 10$
$y = 3x - 6$

The graph of this system will have a parabola corresponding to the quadratic function and a straight line corresponding to the linear function. The functions may intersect each other at two points (2 solutions) or at one point (one solution) or may not intersect at all (no solution).

At the points of intersection, the values of both functions are the same.

Examples:

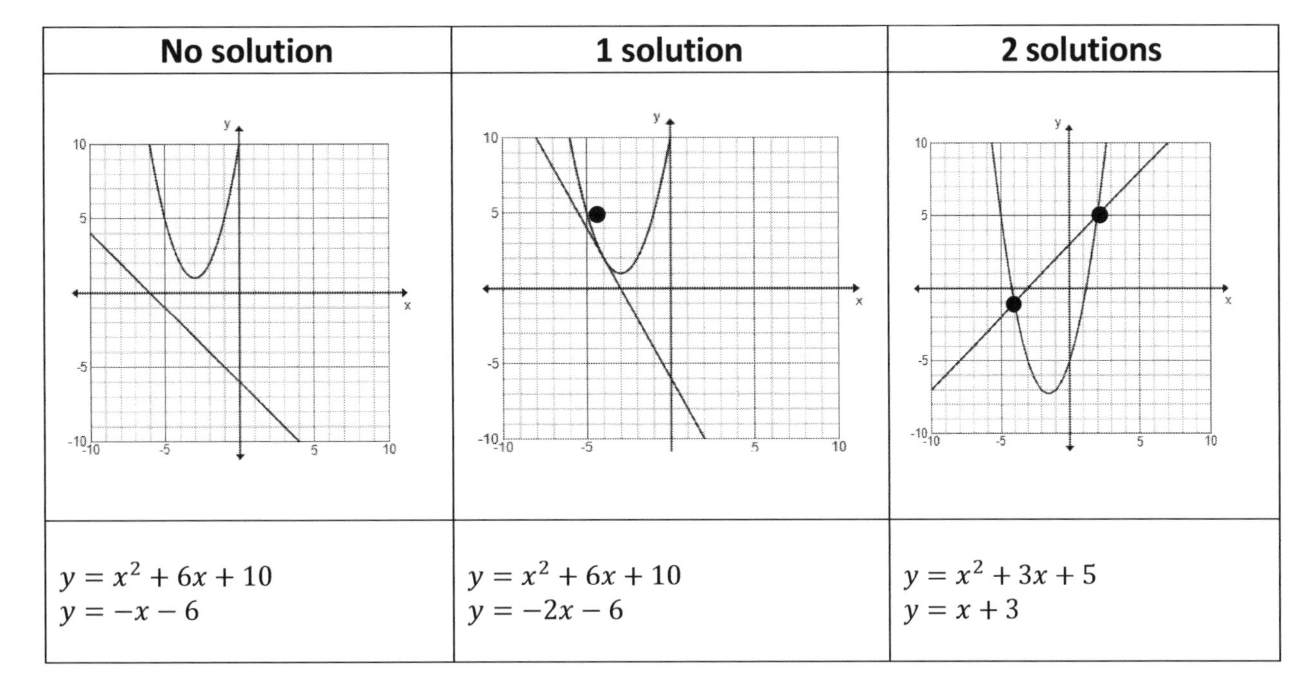

No solution	1 solution	2 solutions
$y = x^2 + 6x + 10$ $y = -x - 6$	$y = x^2 + 6x + 10$ $y = -2x - 6$	$y = x^2 + 3x + 5$ $y = x + 3$

Q2 How do I solve a Linear Quadratic System? How many solutions can be there?

A2 The system can be solved algebraically by equating the two functions and finding the solution. Remember that you may end up with 1 solution, 2 solutions, or no solution.

Example (2 Solutions) : Solve the system of linear and quadratic equations.

$y = -4x - 3$
$y = x^2$

Equate the two functions: $-4x - 3 = x^2$
Write in standard form: $x^2 + 4x + 3 = 0$
$(x + 3)(x + 1) = 0$; factorize
$\text{so}, x = -3, x = -1$
$\text{when } x = -3, y = (-3)^2 = 9$; $\text{when } x = -1, y = (-1)^2 = 1$
So the solutions are $(-3, 9), (-1, 1)$. There are 2 solutions.

Example (1 solution): Solve the system of linear and quadratic equations.

$y = x^2 + 6x + 10$
$y = -2x - 6$

Equate the functions, and simplify:
$x^2 + 6x + 10 = -2x - 6$
$x^2 + 6x + 2x + 10 + 6 = 0$
$x^2 + 8x + 16 = 0$; find p and q such that $pq = 16$ and $p + q = 8$; try
$x^2 + 4x + 4x + 16 = 0$
$x(x + 4) + 4(x + 4) = 0$; factorize
$(x + 4)^2 = 0$
$(x + 4) = 0, so\ x = -4$
when $x = -4, y = -2 \cdot -4 - 6 = 8 - 6 = 2$
This system of linear-quadratic has only one solution at $(-4,2)$. If you draw both functions, you will see that they intersect at only one point $(-4,2)$.

Example: A graph of quadratic function $g(t) = -t^2 + 4t$ intercepts the graph of linear function $h(t) = -t + 4$ at which of the following points?

(A) $(1,3)$ and $(2,0)$
(B) $(2,3)$ and $(3,0)$
(C) $(1,3)$ and $(4,0)$
(D) $(2,3)$ and $(4,0)$

Solution: When they meet, both functions have the same value. Equate the functions and solve for t.
$-t^2 + 4t = -t + 4$
$t^2 - 5t + 4 = 0$; find $p\ and\ q$ such that $pq = 4\ and\ p + q = -5;\ try\ p = -4\ and\ q = -1$
$t^2 - 4t - t + 4 = 0$;
$t(t - 4) - 1(t - 4) = 0$;
$(t - 4)(t - 1) = 0$
$t = 1$ and $t = 4$
when $t = 1$ $h(t) = 3$ and when $t = 4$ $h(t) = 0$;
So, the functions intercept each other at $(1,3)$ and $(4,0)$. The correct answer is (C).

NO CALCULATOR SECTION

1. The solution to the system below that lies in the first quadrant of the Cartesian coordinate system is

$$y = x^2 - 6$$
$$y = x + 6$$

(A) $(4, -10)$
(B) $(-4, 10)$
(C) $(4, 10)$
(D) $(-3, 3)$

2. The distance between the solutions to the following system in the Cartesian plane is

$$y = x^2 - 6$$
$$y = x + 6$$

(A) 7
(B) $\sqrt{2}$
(C) $7\sqrt{2}$
(D) $7\sqrt{7}$

NO CALCULATOR ECTION

3. The solution to the system below that lies in the third quadrant is

$$y = x^2 - 3$$
$$y = x - 1$$

(A) $(-1, 2)$
(B) $(-1, -2)$
(C) $(2, 1)$
(D) $(-2, -1)$

4. A stone is thrown from the ground along a parabolic path defined by the function $y = -x^2 + 4x$. The stone hits the tip of a vertical pole that is 4 feet tall at the vertex of its path. How far is the pole from the point where the stone was thrown?

(A) 1
(B) 2
(C) 4
(D) 16

NO CALCULATOR SECTION

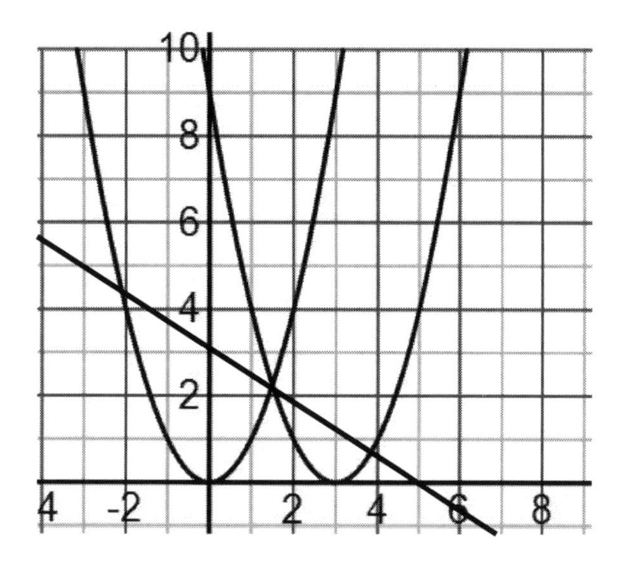

5. The system of functions shown above has a solution at

(A) $(-2, 4.5)$

(B) $(1.5, 2.1)$

(C) $(4, 0.9)$

(D) $(0, 0)$

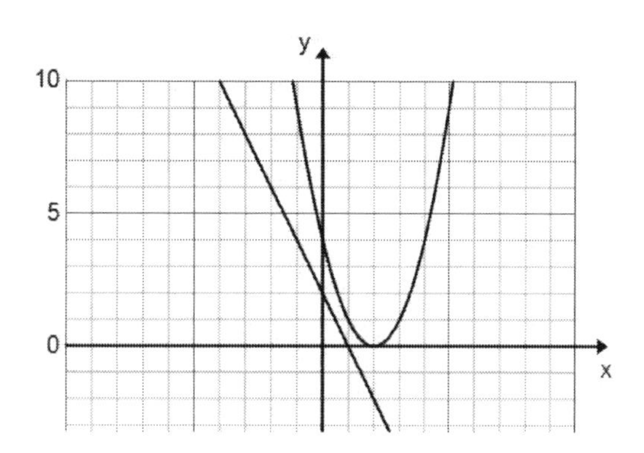

6. How many solutions does the linear quadratic system graphed above have?

(A) 0

(B) 1

(C) 2

(D) 3

CALCULATOR SECTION

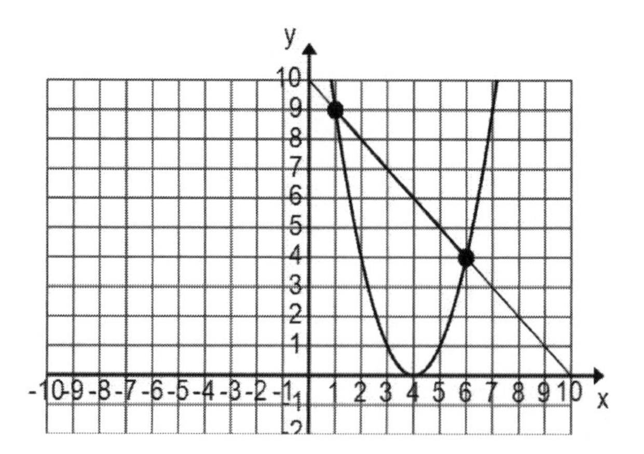

7. A circus clown walks down a straight rope from a point 9 feet above the ground as shown. At the same time, a trapeze artist swings down a parabolic path shown. After crossing the trapeze artist for the first time at 9 feet, approximately how far does the clown walk down the rope before meeting the trapeze artist again?

(A) 3

(B) 5

(C) 6

(D) 7

PASSPORT TO ADVANCED MATH		
Lesson 21	Linear Quadratic Systems	Answers

#	Explanation	Comments
1 C	$x^2 - 6 = x + 6$ $x^2 - 6 - x - 6 = 0$ $x^2 - x - 12 = 0$; find p and q such that $pq = -12$ and $p + q = -1$; try $p = -4, q = 3$; rewrite the equation with p and q $x^2 - 4x + 3x - 12 = 0$ $x(x-4) + 3(x-4) = 0$ $(x-4)(x+3) = 0$ $x - 4 = 0 \; or \; x + 3 = 0$ $x = 4 \; or \; x = -3$ The question asks which solution is in the first quadrant; when $x = 4, y = 4 + 6 = 10$. So, $(4,10)$ is the solution in the first quadrant.	Observe first that this is a Linear Quadratic System, one function is quadratic and another is linear. To find the solution to this system, equate them and solve for x and then find y.
2 C	$x^2 - 6 = x + 6$ $x^2 - 6 - x - 6 = 0$ $x^2 - x - 12 = 0$; find p and q such that $pq = -12$ and $p + q = -1$; try $p = -4, q = 3$; rewrite the equation with p and q. $x^2 - 4x + 3x - 12 = 0$ $x(x-4) + 3(x-4) = 0$ $(x-4)(x+3) = 0$ $x - 4 = 0 \; or \; x + 3 = 0$ $x = 4 \; or \; x = -3$ when $x = 4 \;\; y = 4 + 6 = 10$ when $x = -3 \;\; y = -3 + 6 = 3$ The solutions are $(4,10)$ and $(-3,3)$ The distance between these points= $\sqrt{(3-10)^2 + (-3-4)^2} = \sqrt{49+49} = \sqrt{(2 \cdot 49)} = 7\sqrt{2}$	This is a linear quadratic system; the question asks for the distance between the solutions; find the solutions first and then find the distance.
3 B	$x^2 - 3 = x - 1$ $x^2 - 3 - x + 1 = 0$ $x^2 - x - 2 = 0$; find p and q such that $pq = -2$ and $p + q = -1$; try $p = -2, q = 1$; rewrite the equation with p and q $x^2 - 2x + x - 2 = 0$ $x(x-2) + 1(x-2) = 0$ $(x-2)(x+1) = 0$ $x - 2 = 0 \; or \; x + 1 = 0$ $x = 2 \; or \; x = -1$ when $x = 2 \;\; y = 2 - 1 = 1$ when $x = -1 \;\; y = -1 - 1 = -2$ The solutions are $(2,1)$ and $(-1,-2)$.	Remember that in the third quadrant, both x and y are negative.

4 B	The stone takes a parabolic path which opens downward, since the coefficient of x^2 is -1. The path of the stone intersects the tip of the pole that is 4 feet tall. This can be represented as $y = 4$. Together, you have a linear quadratic system. $y = -x^2 + 4x$ $y = 4$ Equate them and solve for x. $-x^2 + 4x = 4$ $x^2 - 4x = -4$ $x^2 - 4x + 4 = 0$ $x^2 - 2x - 2x + 4 = 0$ $x(x-2) - 2(x-2) = 0$ $(x-2)(x-2) = 0$ $(x-2) = 0; x = 2, y = 4$ The stone touches the pole at $x = 2$.	Read the given facts carefully; one equation is given but only a hint is given for the other equation. The hint is that the stone hits the tip of the pole that is 4 feet tall. Draw a small sketch as shown below to figure out that you need the other function $y = 4$ to solve this system.
5 B	Note that the solution to the system is at the point where all the functions of the system meet. This is at point (1.5,2.1) in the first quadrant.	At the solution point, all the functions must have the same value. Note that there are two quadratics and one linear function in this system.
6 A	For a linear quadratic system to have a solution, the line and the quadratic must meet. From the graph, there is no point of intersection; so there is no solution	
7 D	The first point where they meet is $(1, 9)$. The second point of meeting is $(6,4)$. The distance that the clown walked down the rope is $\sqrt{(4-9)^2 + (6-1)^2} = \sqrt{25+25} = 7.07$ ft. This is approximately equal to 7 feet.	Select the points from the graph; note that the question asks "approximately how far", thereby giving you a clue to round your answer. Use the distance formula and your calculator to find the square root.

FOCUSPREP CHECKLIST

- What are the algebraic forms of linear, quadratic, exponential, and cubic functions?
- What are the graphical forms of linear, quadratic, exponential, and cubic functions?
- How do I find the Zeros of a function?
- What is a Composite function $(fog)(x)$?
- How do I to find $f(g(x))$ algebraically and from a graph?
- What happens to a function when it is transformed (Translated, Reflected, Stretched, and Compressed) ?
- Workout practice problems in functions and transformations

Q1 What is a Function? What are they used for?

A1 A Function is an algebraic expression that models the relation between a dependent variable and an independent variable. Functions are used to make estimates, to find out maximum and minimum values and other properties of the variables that are modeled. The independent variable is plotted on the x axis and dependent variable is plotted on the y axis. The general form of a function is represented as $y = f(x)$.

Q2 What is the domain and range of a function?

A2 The domain of a function is a set of all values for which it is defined. The range is the set of all y-values that correspond to the x-values.

Q3 What are the different types of functions? How do they look?

A3 There are several types of functions – linear functions, quadratic functions, exponential functions, cubic functions, etc. Their graph and their algebraic expressions are shown in the table below.

<table>
<tr><th>Linear Function $y = mx + b$</th><th>Quadratic Function $y = ax^2 + bx + c$</th></tr>
<tr><td>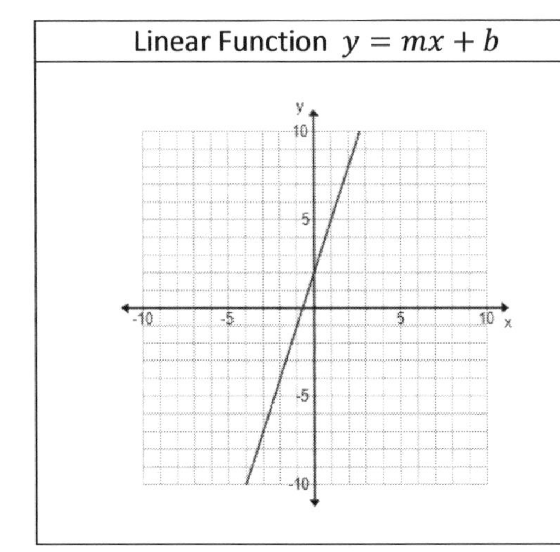
</td><td>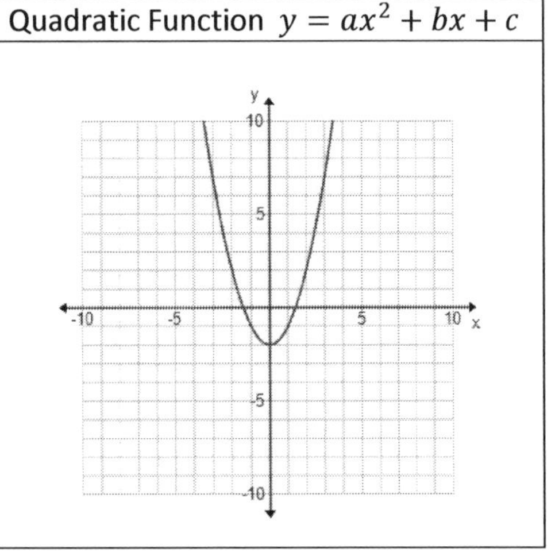
</td></tr>
</table>

Exponential Function $y = ab^x$	Cubic Function $y = x^3$
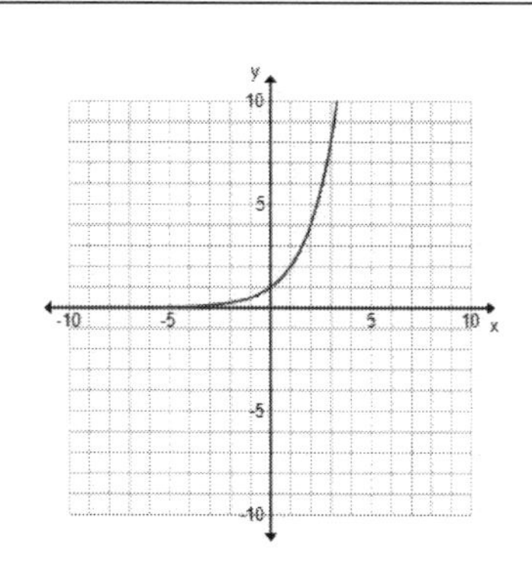	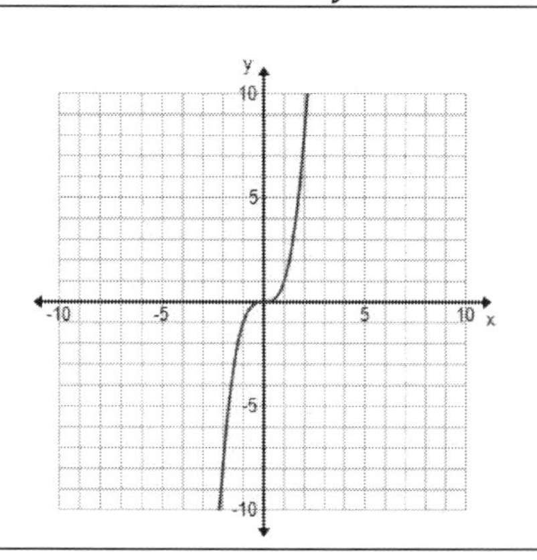

Q4 What are the important things to remember about linear, quadratic, exponential and cubic functions?

A4 The table below summarizes the important facts about linear, quadratic, exponential and cubic functions.

Linear Function $y = mx + b$	**Quadratic Function** $y = ax^2 + bx + c$
slope-intercept formula: $y = mx + b$ where m is the slope and b is the y-intercept. slope $=m=\frac{y2-y1}{x2-x1}$ where $(x1, y1)$ *and* $(x2, y2)$ are two points on the line. point slope formula: $y - y1 = m(x - x1)$ At the y-intercept, $x = 0$; when $x = 0, y = b$ At x-intercept, $y = 0$: when $y = 0, x = -\frac{b}{m}$ **Examples:** $y = 4x + 5$; $y = 8.5x + 33.67$	Quadratic graphs take the form of a parabola. **Standard form** is $y = ax^2 + bx + c$ Axis of symmetry: $x = -\frac{b}{2a}$ Vertex of parabola : $(-\frac{b}{2a}, f(-\frac{b}{2a}))$ If $a > 0$ the parabola opens upward, the minimum point is at $(-\frac{b}{2a}, f\left(-\frac{b}{2a}\right))$ If $a < 0$ the parabola opens downward, the maximum point is at $(-\frac{b}{2a}, f(-\frac{b}{2a}))$ y-intercept = c **Vertex form** is $y = a(x - h)^2 + k$ Vertex is at (h, k) Axis of symmetry: $x = h$ y-intercept: find by substituting $x = 0$ If $a > 0$, parabola opens upward and has minimum point (minima) at the vertex (h, k).

	If $a < 0$, parabola opens downward and has maximum point (maxima) at the vertex (h, k). **Examples:** Standard form: $y = 3x^2 - 2x + 4$; Vertex form: $y = (x - 4)^2 + 5$
Exponential Function $y = ab^x$	**Cubic Function $y = x^3$**
$y = ab^x$ When $b > 1$ then it is exponential growth. When $0 < b < 1$ then it is exponential decay. Another detailed form of exponential function: Exponential Growth: $y = a(1 + r)^t$; where a=initial value, r=percentage rate of growth, t=time period of growth Exponential Decay: $y = a(1 - r)^t$; where a=initial value, r=percentage rate of decay, t=time period of growth **Examples:** $y = 1.5 \cdot 2^t$ $y = 0.7^x$	steeper than quadratic function the ends of the function go in opposite directions. **Examples:** $y = x^3$ $y = 2x^3 + 3x^2 - 77$

Q5 What does Zeros or Roots of a function mean?

A5 The Zeros or Roots of a function $f(x)$ are the x-values where the function has a value of 0. In graphical sense, the zeros are the intercepts on the x-axis. If a function intercepts the x-axis at more than one point, those points are called Zeros of the function. A function has one or more zeros or no zeros.
For example, the quadratic function $x^2 - 1$ has $(x + 1)$ and $(x - 1)$ as factors. To find the Zeros of the function, set it to 0, since its value at the x-intercept is 0. So $(x + 1) \cdot (x - 1) = 0$. So, by the zero product rule, you have $x + 1 = 0 \Rightarrow x = -1$ and $x - 1 = 0 \Rightarrow x = 1$. There are 2 zeros for this function. The figure below shows the graph of this function. Notice that the zeros of the function are the x intercepts at -1 and $+1$. At these zeros, the function has a value of 0.

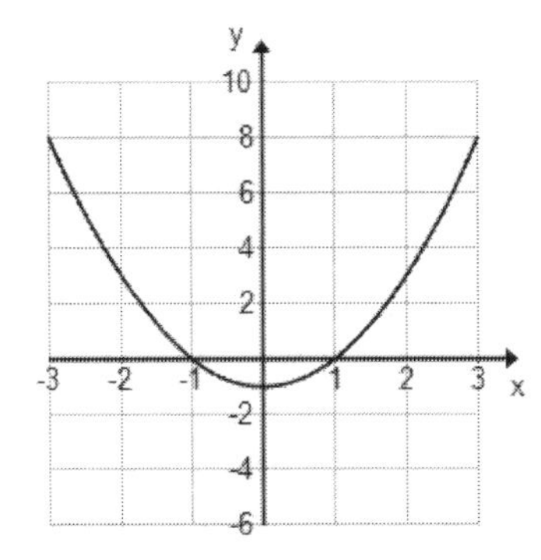

Q6 How do I find the zeros/roots of function? How many zeros (or roots) does a function have?

A6 To find the zeros/roots of a function, follow these steps:

Step 1: set the function to 0

Step 2: solve for x, factorize if necessary

Linear Functions: Since linear functions of the type $y = mx + b$ are graphed as straight lines, they have only one zero/root.

Example: What are the roots of $f(x) = 2x + 3$?

Solution: Set the function to 0: $2x + 3 = 0;\ x = -\frac{3}{2};$

Quadratic functions $f(x) = ax^2 + bx + c$ can have

2 Distinct Real solutions - function intercepts the x axis at two different points

1 Real solution- function intercepts the x axis at one point only

2 Distinct complex number solutions of the form $a + bi$ – function does not intercept the x-axis

You can find the roots of a quadratic function by setting it to 0, and factoring it. You can also use the following quadratic formula:

$$x = \frac{-b \pm \sqrt{b^2 - 4ac}}{2a}$$

Depending on the value of the discriminant $\sqrt{b^2 - 4ac}$ as shown in the table below, there can be 1 or 2 real solutions or 2 complex solutions.

$b^2 - 4ac > 0$	2 distinct real solutions	$\frac{-b+\sqrt{b^2-4ac}}{2a};\ \frac{-b-\sqrt{b^2-4ac}}{2a}$
$b^2 - 4ac = 0$	1 real solution	$-\frac{b}{2a}$
$b^2 - 4ac < 0$	2 distinct complex number solutions	$-\frac{b}{2a} + i\frac{1}{2a}\sqrt{b^2 - 4ac};$ $-\frac{b}{2a} - i\frac{1}{2a}\sqrt{b^2 - 4ac};$

Example: What are the roots of $f(x) = x^2 - 4x + 3$?

Solution:

$x^2 - 4x + 3 = 0;$ Set the function to 0:

$x^2 - 3x - x + 3 = 0$

$x(x - 3) - 1(x - 3) = 0$

$(x - 3)(x - 1) = 0$

$(x = 3) = 0$ and $(x - 1) = 0$

$x = 3$ and $x = 1$ are the roots of the equation.

Q7 What are the parts of a parabola (quadratic function)?

A7 Note carefully, the maxima, minima, vertex, axis of symmetry, and the roots/zeros. Parabolas that open upward have minima at their vertex and parabolas that open downwards have maxima at their vertex.

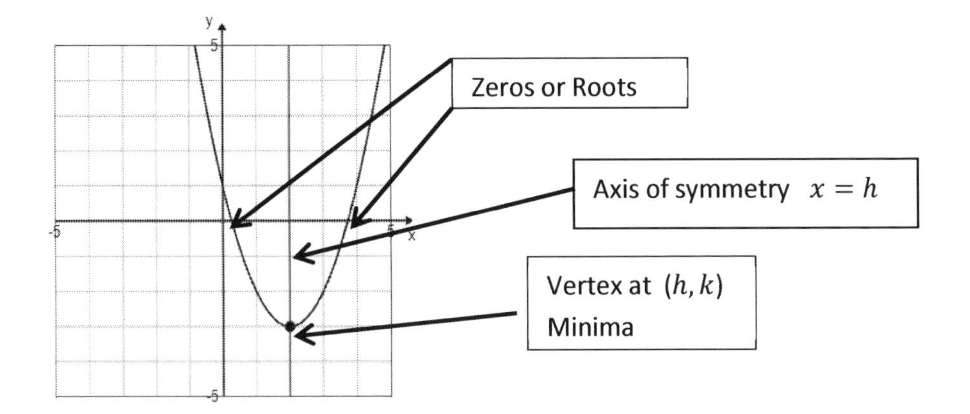

Q8 What operations can be performed on functions?

A8 Functions can be added, subtracted, multiplied, and divided similar to the way these operations are performed on polynomial expressions.

Example:

If $(x) = x^2 + 2x + 2;\ \ g(x) = 3x + 4$, then the following operations can be performed on these functions.

Addition: $(f + g)(x) = f(x) + g(x) = x^2 + 2x + 2 + 3x + 4 = x^2 + 5x + 6$

Subtraction: $(f - g)(x) = f(x) - g(x) = x^2 + 2x + 2 - 3x - 4 = x^2 - x - 2$

Multiplication: $(fg)(x) = f(x)g(x) = (x^2 + 2x + 2)(3x + 4) = 3x^3 + 10x^2 + 8$

Division: $(\frac{f}{g})(x) = \frac{f(x)}{g(x)} = \frac{x^2+2x+2}{3x+4} = \frac{(x+1)^2}{3x+4}$

Q9 How do I find the Zeros of a function from a graph?

A9 Zeros of a function $f(x)$ are the x-values where $f(x) = 0$. If you have the graph of the function, then you can find the Zeros of the function by reading its x-intercepts from the graph.

Q10 How do I find all the points where a function has the same value?

A10 To find all the points where a function has the same value, say k, draw a horizontal line y=k and note the x-value points where this line intercepts the function.

Example: At what values of x does the function shown below have a value of 7?

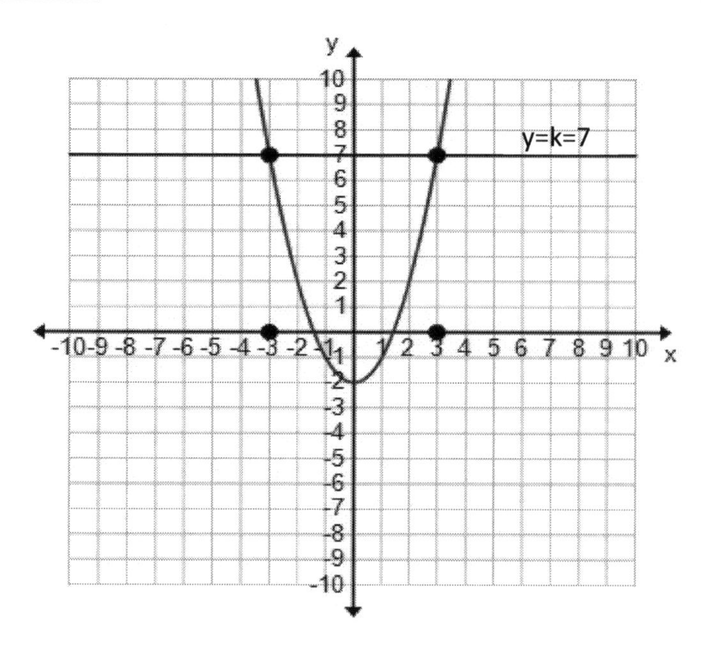

(A) -1 and 1
(B) -2 and 2
(C) -3 and 3
(D) -4 and 4

Solution: Draw a line of y=7 and note the two intercepts – the x values of these points are -3 and +3.

Example: For the function shown in the graph, what are the zeros of the function?

Solution: The Zeros are where the function has a value of 0. These are points where the function intercepts the x-axis. From the graph, the zeros are $x = -1.5$ and $x = 1.5$.

Q11 What is a **composite** function? How is it defined?

A11 A composite function is a function obtained by "composing" two functions. If you have two functions $f(x) and\ g(x)$, the composite function is $f\big(g(x)\big)$. Evaluate the inner function first and then the outer function. Another notation for composite function is $(fog)(x) - pronouced$ "fog" of x.

Example: Let $f(x) = x^2\ and\ g(x) = x + 1$. What is the value of composite function $f\big(g(x)\big)$? What is the value of g$\big(f(x)\big)$?

Solution: $f\big(g(x)\big) = f(x + 1)$; evaluate the inner function first, $g(x) = x + 1$

$= (x + 1)^2$; since $f(x) = x^2, f(x + 1) = (x + 1)^2$

So, the composite function $f\big(g(x)\big) = (x + 1)^2$

$g\big(f(x)\big) = g(x^2)$; evaluate the inner function first, $f(x) = x^2$

$= x^2 + 1;$ since $g(x) = x + 1, g(x^2) = x^2 + 1$

So, the composite function $g(f(x)) = x^2 + 1$

Example: In the functions $f(x)$ *and* $g(x)$, evaluate $f(g(2))$ *and* $g(f(2))$.

Solution: $f(g(2)) = f(2 + 1) = f(3) = 3^2 = 9$

$g(f(2)) = g(2^2) = g(4) = 4 + 1 = 5$

Q12 What happens when a function/graph is moved horizontally or vertically? Stretched or Compressed horizontally or vertically? Reflected over its x-axis or y-axis?

A12 When a function/graph is **transformed** as described in the question, all the points in the graph get moved to new positions and a new graph/function is created. For example if you move the graph of $f(x)$ by 2 units to the right, you have a new graph and the new function corresponding to this graph is $f(x - 2)$. Similarly, you get new functions for other types of transformations. More details are given in the answers to the following questions. Transformations include Translation, Reflection, Stretch, and Compression.

Remember that a function has an algebraic form and a graphical form. When you transform this function, you get a new function with a new algebraic form and a new graph.

Q13 What happens when a graph/function is **translated** (moved) horizontally or vertically?

A13 The table below shows the new function that will be created due to translation.

The graph of $f(x)$ is moved horizontally to the right by k units. The graph of $f(x)$ is moved horizontally to the left by k units.	$f(x)$ becomes $f(x - k)$ $f(x)$ becomes $f(x + k)$
The graph of $f(x)$ is moved vertically up by k units. The graph of $f(x)$ is moved vertically down by k units.	$f(x)$ becomes $f(x) + k$ $f(x)$ becomes $f(x) - k$
Examples in graphical form are shown below. The function can be in linear or quadratic or in any other form.	

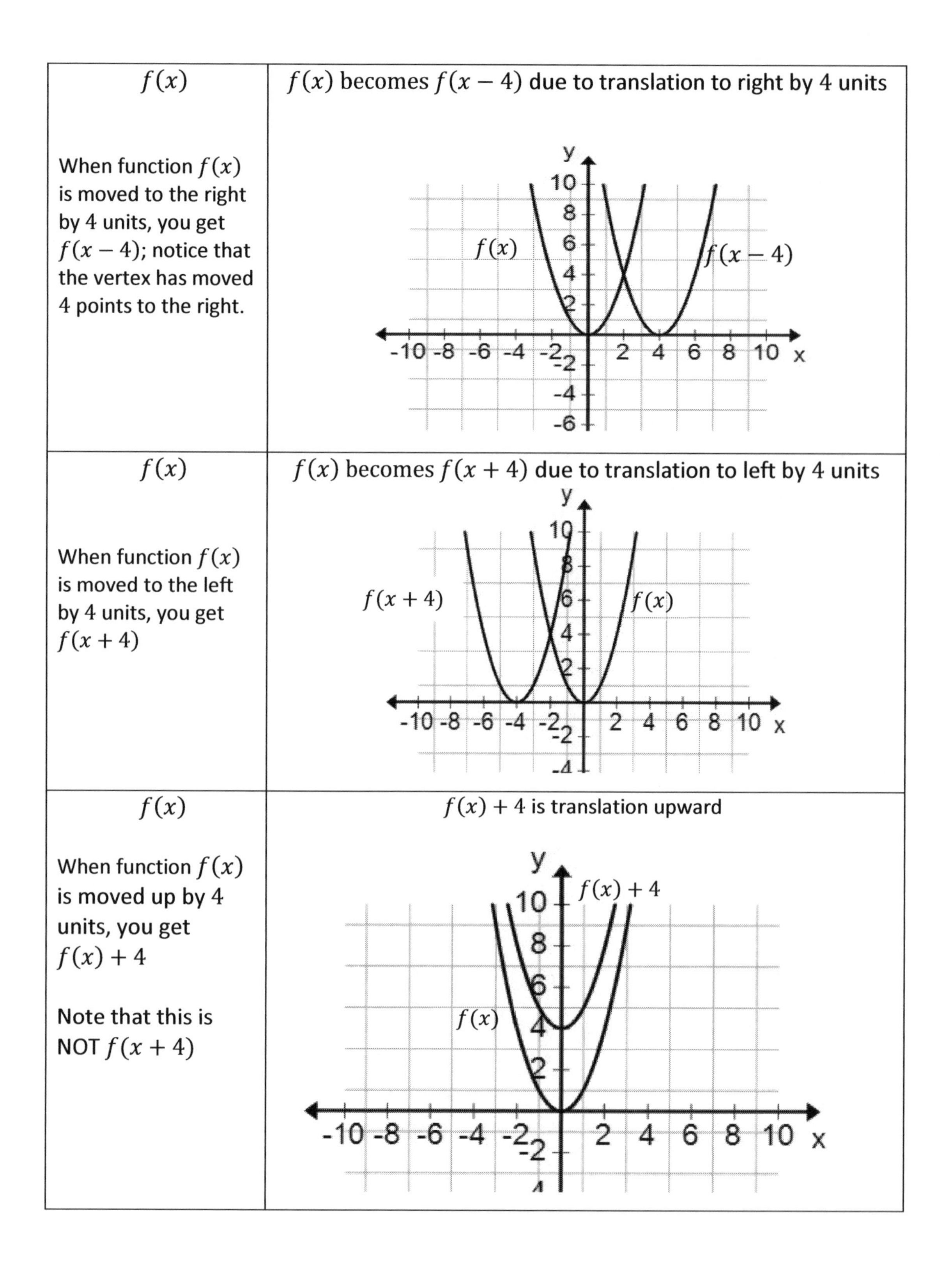

$f(x)$	$f(x)$ becomes $f(x-4)$ due to translation to right by 4 units
When function $f(x)$ is moved to the right by 4 units, you get $f(x-4)$; notice that the vertex has moved 4 points to the right.	
$f(x)$	$f(x)$ becomes $f(x+4)$ due to translation to left by 4 units
When function $f(x)$ is moved to the left by 4 units, you get $f(x+4)$	
$f(x)$	$f(x)+4$ is translation upward
When function $f(x)$ is moved up by 4 units, you get $f(x)+4$ Note that this is NOT $f(x+4)$	

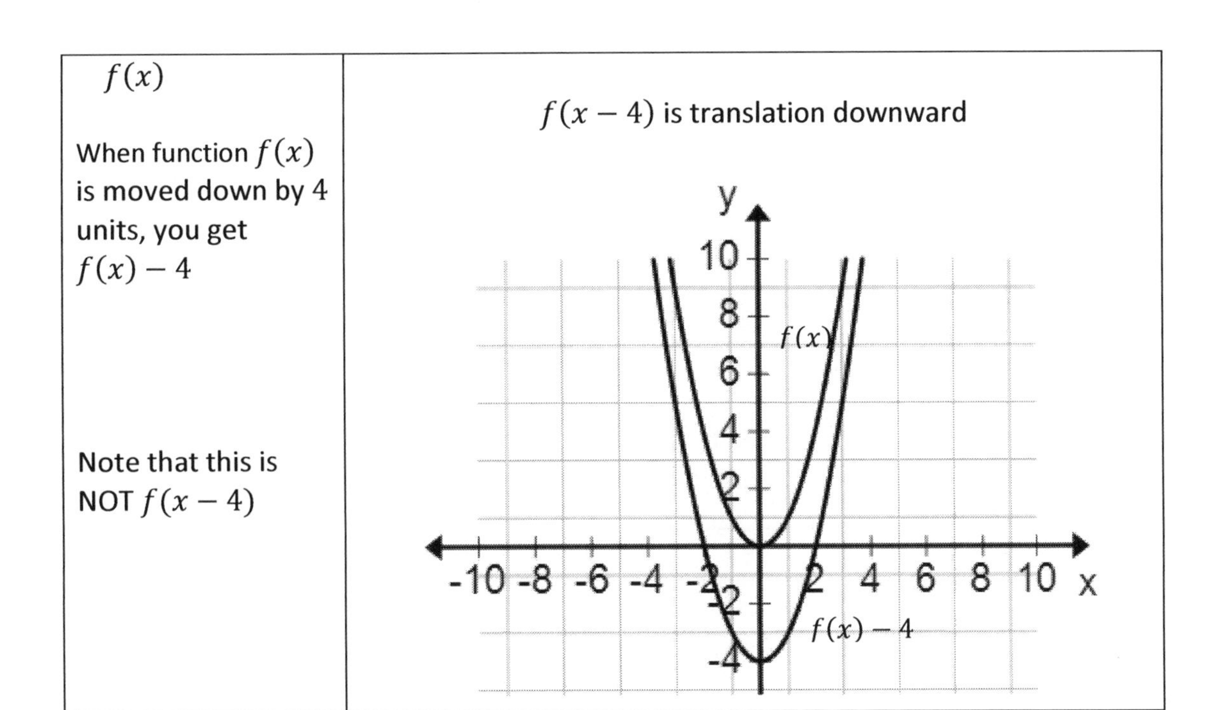

$f(x)$ When function $f(x)$ is moved down by 4 units, you get $f(x) - 4$ Note that this is NOT $f(x-4)$	$f(x-4)$ is translation downward

Q14 What happens when a function is reflected over the x-axis or y-axis?

A14 The table below shows the new function that will be created due to reflection.

The graph of $f(x)$ is reflected over the x-axis	$f(x)$ becomes $-f(x)$
The graph of $f(x)$ is reflected over the y-axis.	$f(x)$ becomes $f(-x)$
Examples in graphical form are shown below. The function can be in linear or quadratic or in any other form.	

Function $f(x)$ is reflected over the x-axis. When a function is reflected over the x axis, all y values become negative y values. So, $f(x)$ becomes $-f(x)$	$-f(x)$ is reflection of $f(x)$ over x-axis 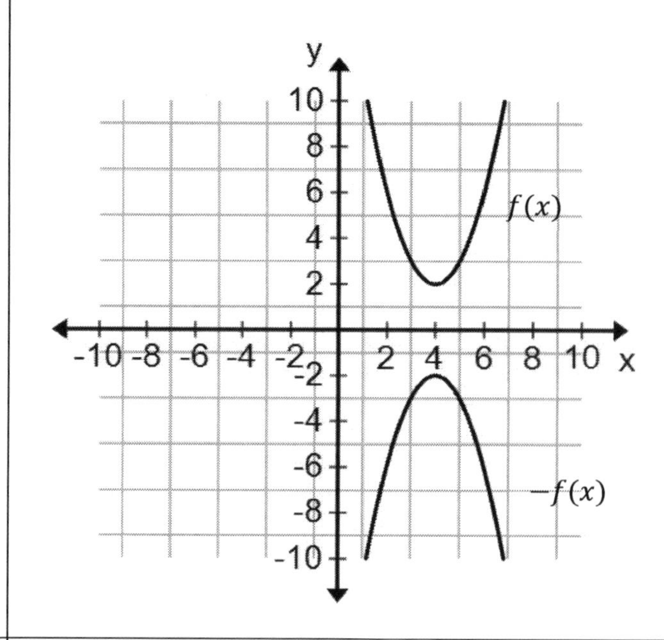
Function $f(x)$ is reflected over the y-axis When a function is reflected over the y axis, all x values become negative x values. So, $f(x)$ becomes $f(-x)$	$f(-x)$ is reflection of $f(x)$ over y-axis 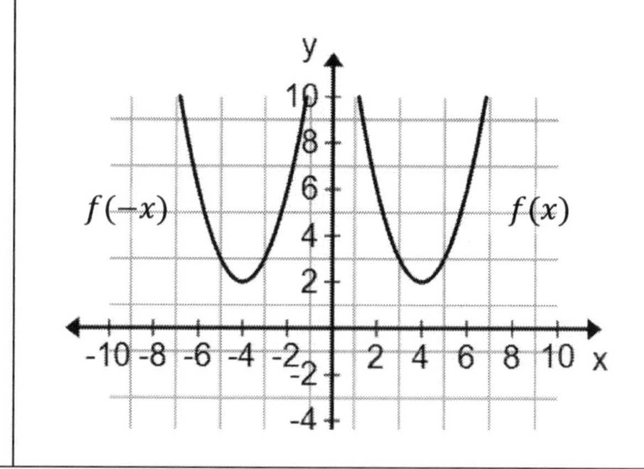

Q15 What happens when a function is **<u>stretched or compressed horizontally or vertically</u>**?

A15 The table below shows the new function that will be created due to stretching and compression.

Horizontal Stretch/Compression General Formula: $f(x)$ *becomes* $f\left(\frac{1}{b}x\right)$	$b > 1$ Horizontal Stretch $0 < b < 1$ Horizontal compression
Vertical Stretch/Compression General Formula: $f(x)$ *becomes* $bf(x)$	$b > 1$ Vertical Stretch $0 < b < 1$ Vertical Compression
Examples in graphical form are shown below. The function can be in linear or quadratic or in any other form.	

Function $f(x)$ is **horizontally stretched/compressed** by a factor of b General formula for horizontal stretch/ compression : $f(x)$ becomes $f(\frac{1}{b}x)$ $b > 1$ is stretch $0 < b < 1$ is compression **Example**: $f(\frac{1}{3}x)$ is horizontal stretch; $b = 3$ $f(3x)$ is horizontal compression; $b = \frac{1}{3}$	Horizontal Stretch $f\left(\frac{1}{b}x\right), b > 1$ $f\left(\frac{1}{3}x\right)$ is a horizontal stretch by a factor of 3. 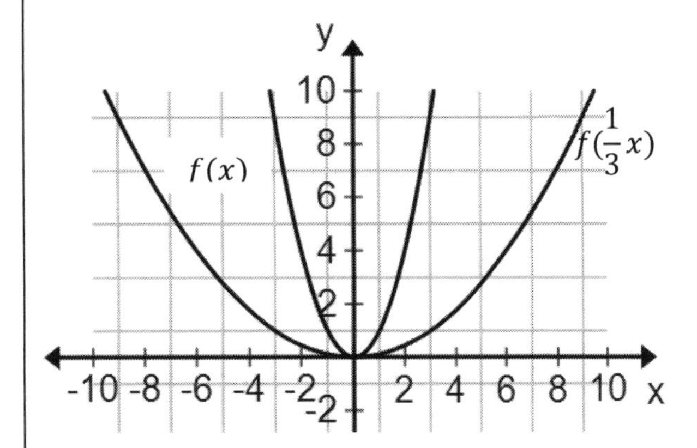 Horizontal Compression $f\left(\frac{1}{b}x\right), 0 < b < 1$ $f(3x)$ is a horizontal compression by a factor of $\frac{1}{3}$. 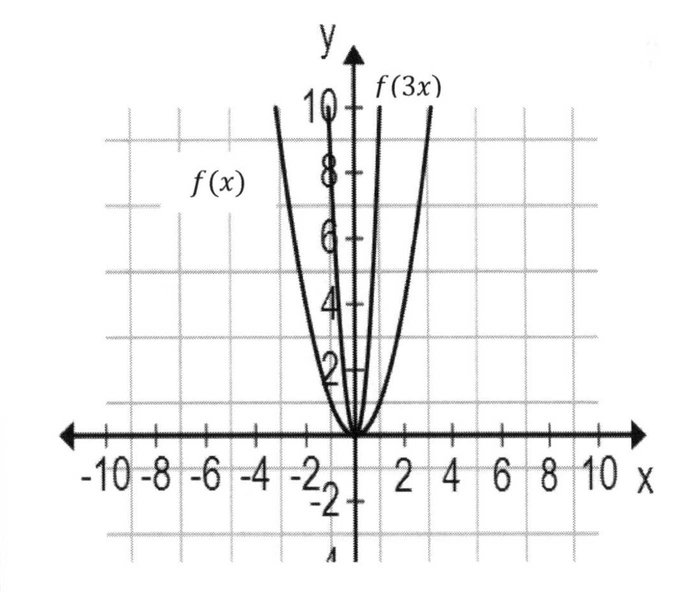

Function $f(x)$ is **vertically stretched/compressed** by a factor of b. General formula for vertical stretch/compression $f(x)$ becomes $bf(x)$ $b > 1$ is stretch $0 < b < 1$ is compression	Vertical Stretch $f(x)$ is vertically stretched to $3f(x)$ by a factor of 3 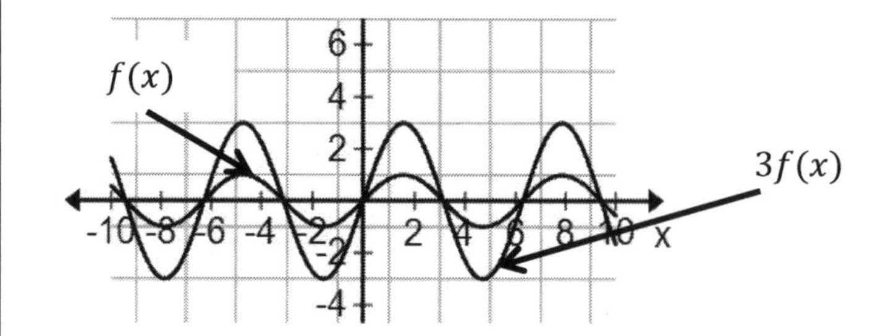 Vertical Compression $f(x)$ is vertically compressed to $\frac{1}{3}f(x)$ by a factor of $\frac{1}{3}$ 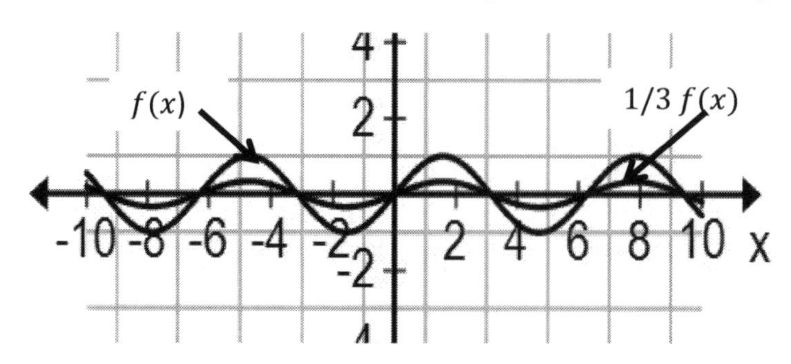

Q16 What happens when a function has more than one transformation – move to the right 5 units and then move down 2 units?

A16 When there are several transformations, apply each transformation one at a time. In this case, $f(x)$ moves to the right 5 units and becomes $f(x-5)$ and then moves down 2 units and becomes $f(x-5)-2$.

Q17 What kind of problems may appear in PSAT regarding functions and transformation of functions?

A17 A few problems and their solutions are presented below. The practice section contains more.

Example: Let $f(x) = x^2 + 2x$. Let $g(x)$ be the function obtained after translating $f(x)$ by 7 units to the left. What is $g(4)$? **Solution**: $g(x) = f(x)$ translated 7 units to the left. So, $g(x) = f(x+7) = (x+7)^2 + 2(x+7)$. So, $g(4) = (4+7)^2 + 2(4+7) = 121 + 22 = 143$.

Example: Let $f(x) = x^2 + 2x$. Let $g(x)$ be the function obtained after translating $f(x)$ 7 units to the left. What is $f(g(4))$? **Solution**: $g(x) = f(x)$ translated 7 units to the left = $f(x+7) = (x+7)^2 + 2(x+7)$. So, $g(4) = (4+7)^2 + 2(4+7) = 121 + 22 = 143$. Now, $f(g(4)) = f(143) = 143^2 + 2 \cdot 143 = 20735$.

Example: Let $f(x-2) = 3x - 5$. What is $f(x)$ and what is $f(4)$? **Solution**: Note that you are given $f(x-2)$ but not $f(x)$. Rewrite it in terms of $(x-2)$ as $f(x-2) = 3(x-2) + 6 - 5 = 3(x-2) + 1$. Since, $3(x-2)$ introduces a -6, you have to cancel it with a $+6$. $f(x-2)$=$3(x-2)+1$ is the same as $f(x) = 3x + 1$. So, $f(4) = 3 \cdot 4 + 1 = 13$. Another method is $f(4) = f(6-2) = 3 \cdot 6 - 5 = 13$.

Example Two functions are shown in the graph below. What is $g(f(2))$?

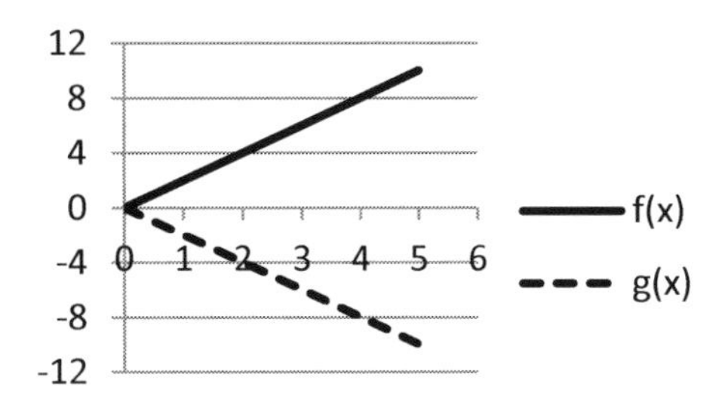

Solution: From the graph, $f(2) = 4$ and so $g(f(2)) = g(4) = -8$

Example: When a function $V(t) = -16t^3 + 21t^2 + 3t - 5$ is stretched horizontally by a factor of 3, what is the value of the new function at t=1?

Solution: $V(t) = -16t^3 + 21t^2 + 3t - 5$. When a function is stretched, the new function is $V(\frac{1}{3}t)$

$V(t) = -16t^3 + 21t^2 + 3t - 5$

$$V\left(\frac{1}{3}t\right) = -16\left(\frac{1}{3}t\right)^3 + 21\left(\frac{1}{3}t\right)^2 + 3\left(\frac{1}{3}t\right) - 5$$

$$= -\frac{16}{27}t^3 + \frac{21}{9}t^2 + t - 5$$

$$= -\frac{16}{27}t^3 + \frac{7}{3}t^2 + t - 5$$

At t=1, the value is $-\frac{16}{27} + \frac{7}{3} - 5 = -3.26$.

Example If the graph of the function shown below is written in the form of $a(x-h)^2 + k$, then $a =$?

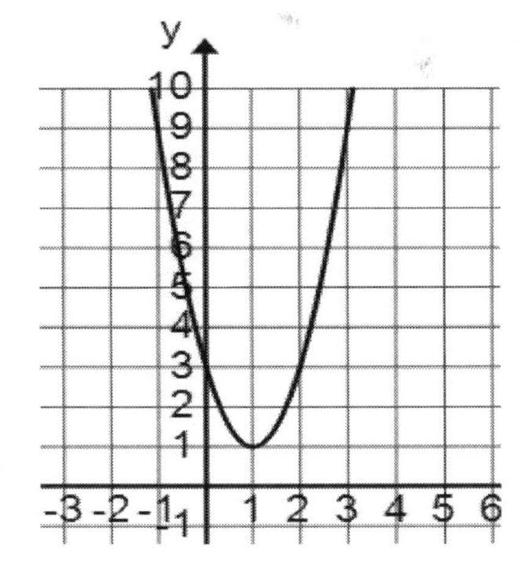

Solution: From the graph, the vertex of the parabola is $(h, k) = (1,1)$. The vertex form of the parabolic function is $y = a(x-h)^2 + k$. Substituting h and k, you get $y = a(x-1)^2 + 1$. Pick any point on the parabola – say (2,3). This point must satisfy the function. So, $3 = a(2-1)^2 + 1$, giving $a = 3 - 1 = 2$. So, the function in the graph is $y = 2(x-1)^2 + 1$ giving us the answer $a = 1$.

Example Express the quadratic $y = 2x^2 - 4x + 3$ in vertex form.

Solution:

The vertex form is $y = a(x-h)^2 + k$

$y = 2x^2 - 4x + 3$

$y = 2(x^2 - 2x) + 3$;

$y = 2(x^2 - 2x + 1) + 3 - 2$; complete the square by adding 2 and subtracting 2

$y = 2(x-1)^2 + 1$; this is in vertex form $a(x-h)^2 + k$

Know how to convert a quadratic in standard form to vertex form and vice versa. To convert from the vertex form to standard form, expand the terms inside the square.

PASSPORT TO ADVANCED MATH		
Lesson 22	Functions and Transformations	Practice

NO CALCULATOR SECTION

1. The table below shows the values of functions $f(x)$ and $g(x)$. What is the value of $f(2) \cdot f(g(2))$?

x	1	2	3	4	5
$f(x)$	1	3	5	7	9
$g(x)$	2	4	8	16	32

(A) 3
(B) 8
(C) 15
(D) 21

2. The table shows the values of functions $f(x)$ and $g(x)$.

x	1	2	3	4	5
$f(x)$	2	3	4	5	6
$g(x)$	6	9	12	15	18

$g(x) =$

(A) $f(x)$
(B) $f(x^2)$
(C) $3f(x)$
(D) $f(3x)$

NO CALCULATOR SECTION

3. If $f(x) = x^2 - 2$ and $g(x) = 2x^2 + 5$ then $(f - g)(x) =$

(A) $-x^2 + 3$
(B) $-x^2 - 7$
(C) $-x^2 - 3$
(D) $-x^2 + 7$

4. If $f(x) = 1 + \frac{1}{x}$ and $g(x) = 1 - \frac{1}{x}$ then what is $(fg)(2)$?

(A) $\frac{1}{4}$

(B) $\frac{1}{2}$

(C) $\frac{3}{5}$

(D) $\frac{3}{4}$

5. If $f(x) = x^2$ and $g(x) = x^4$ then $\left(\frac{f}{g}\right)(3) =$

(A) $\frac{1}{10}$

(B) $\frac{1}{9}$

(C) 3

(D) 9

6. If $f(x) = x^2$ and $g(x) = x + 5$ then what is $g(f(x))$?

(A) $(x + 5)^2$
(B) $x^2 + 5$
(C) $x^2 + x + 5$
(D) $x^3 + 5x$

7. If $f(x) = x^2$ and $g(x) = \frac{1}{x^2}$ then what is $g(f(x))$?

(A) $\frac{1}{x}$

(B) $\frac{1}{x^2}$

(C) $\frac{1}{x^4}$

(D) $\frac{1}{x^3}$

8. If $f(x) = 2^{x-5}$ and $f(b) = 8^3$ then $b =$

(A) 9
(B) 14
(C) 23
(D) 25

NO CALCULATOR SECTION

9. If $f(x) = \sqrt{2x}$ and $g(x) = \frac{1}{\sqrt{3x}}$ then $f(x^2)g(x^2) =$

(A) $\frac{2}{3}$

(B) $\sqrt{\frac{2}{3}}$

(C) $\frac{3}{2}$

(D) $\sqrt{\frac{3}{2}}$

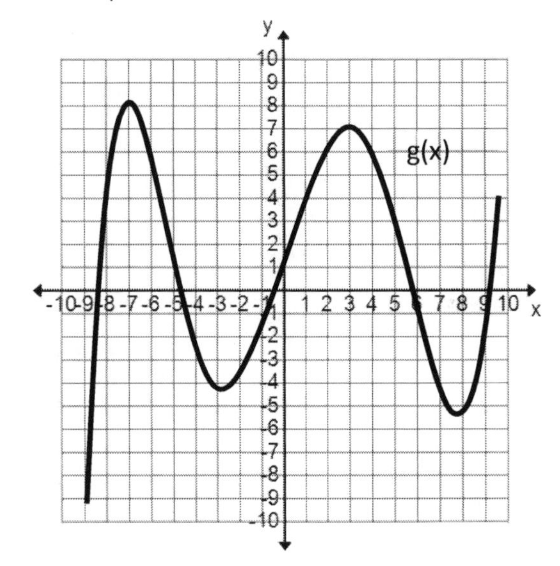

Questions 10-12 relate to the graph shown above.

10. If $g(-7) - g(2) =$

(A) -7
(B) 0
(C) 2
(D) 9

11. The number of turning points in the graph is

(A) 1
(B) 2
(C) 3
(D) 4

12. $h(x)$ is a graph (not shown) obtained by moving $g(x) = x - 3$ to the right by 4 units. What is $h(4)$?

(A) -3
(B) -2
(C) 0
(D) 3

13. If $g(x)$ is a function obtained by moving the function $f(x) = 3x + 5$ by 4 units to the right, then what is $g(6)$?

(A) 11
(B) 27
(C) 30
(D) 33

14. If $g(x)$ is a function obtained by moving the function $f(x) = -2x - 1$ by 2 units to the left, then $f(2) \cdot g(2) =$

(A) 5
(B) 9
(C) 25
(D) 45

15. If $g(x)$ is a function obtained by shifting the function $f(x) = 2x^2 - 3$ by 5 units down, what is $g(x)$?

(A) $g(x) = 2x^2 - 3$
(B) $g(x) = 2x^2 - 2$
(C) $g(x) = 2x^2 - 8$
(D) $g(x) = 2x^2 - 15$

NO CALCULATOR SECTION

16. If $g(x)$ is a function obtained by shifting the function $f(x) = \sqrt{3x + 5}$ by 4 units to the right, then what is $g(6)$?

(A) $\sqrt{11}$
(B) $\sqrt{17}$
(C) $\sqrt{35}$
(D) $\sqrt{39}$

17. If h(x) is a function obtained by moving the function $f(x) = 5x^2 + 12$ to the right by 4 units, and then moving 3 units vertically down, then what is $h(2)$?

(A) 10
(B) 15
(C) 20
(D) 29

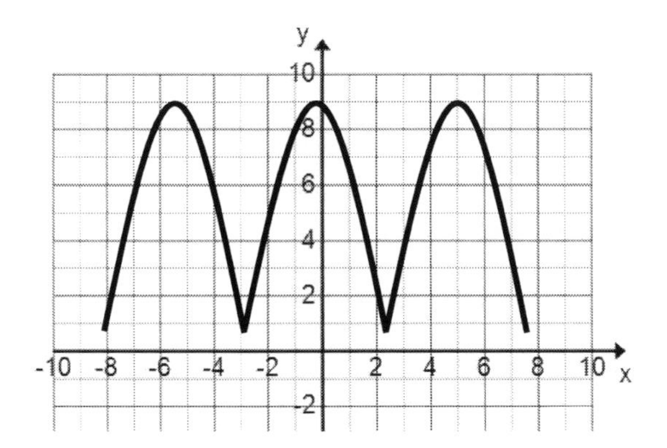

18. The line $y = 4$ intercepts the function shown at how many points?
(A) 3
(B) 4
(C) 5
(D) 6

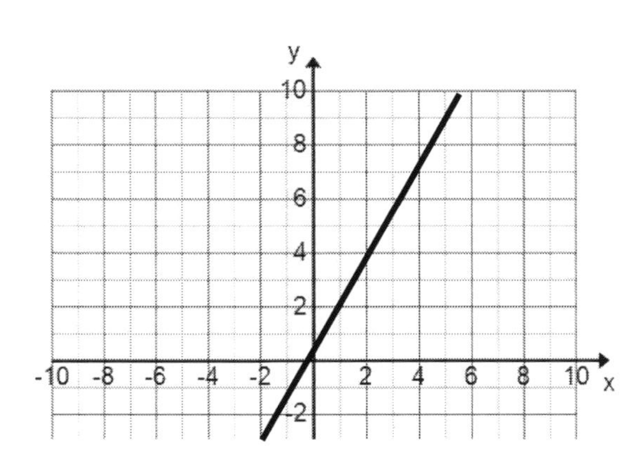

19. The slope of the line shown above, after it is reflected over the y-axis is
(A) -3
(B) -2
(C) 1
(D) 2

NO CALCULATOR SECTION

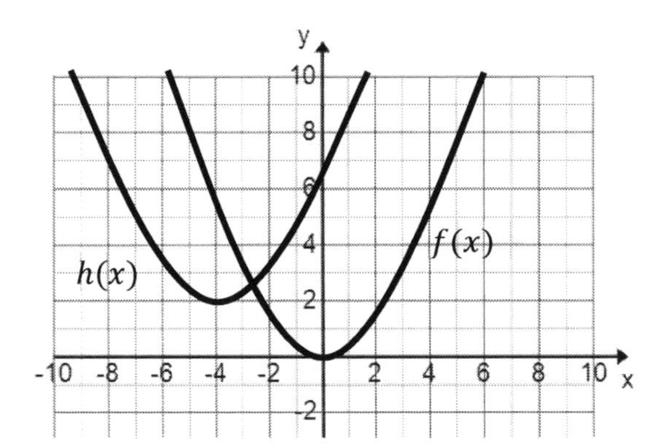

20. The graph of $f(x)$ is shifted to coincide with the graph of $h(x)$. Which of the following is true?
(A) $h(x) = f(x-4) + 2$
(B) $h(x) = f(x+4) - 2$
(C) $h(x) = f(x+4) + 2$
(D) $h(x) = f(x-4) - 2$

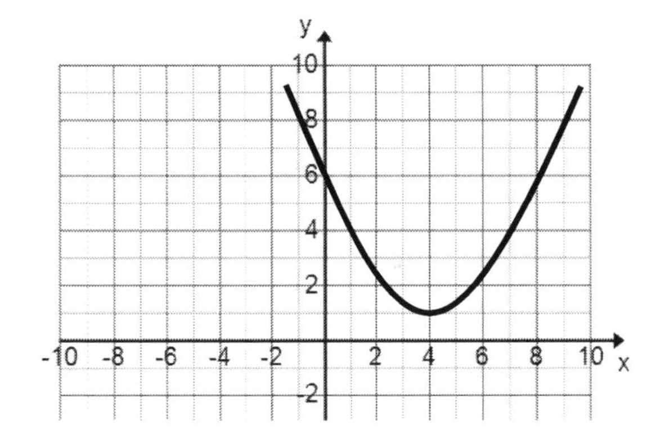

21. If the parabola shown above is moved to the left by 6 units and moved up 4 units, the vertex will be at
(A) $(-4,5)$
(B) $(-2,-5)$
(C) $(-2,5)$
(D) $(4,-5)$

22. If a function $p(x) = 8x^2 + 24$ is stretched horizontally by a factor of 2, the resulting function will be

(A) $h(x) = 4x^2 + 12$
(B) $h(x) = 2x^2 + 12$
(C) $h(x) = 2x^2 - 24$
(D) $h(x) = 2x^2 + 24$

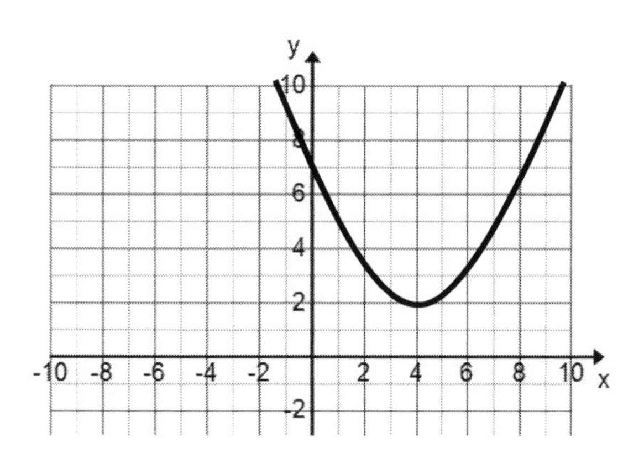

23. If the graph shown above is reflected over the x-axis, the maxima will be intercepted by

(A) $x = 2$
(B) $y = 2$
(C) $y = -2$
(D) $x = -4$

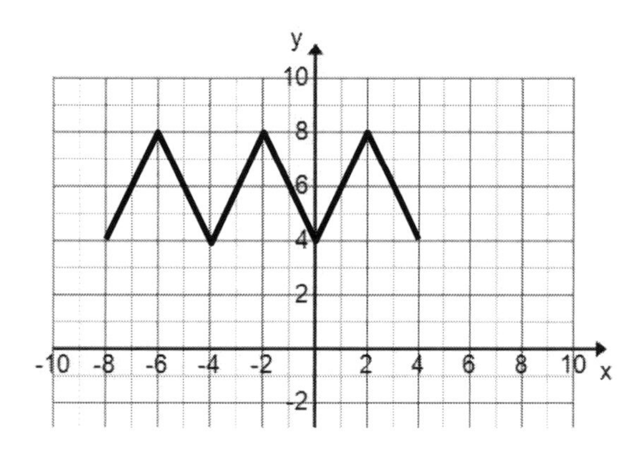

24. If the graph of $f(x)$ shown is transformed to $f(x-2)+2$, then which of the graphs below shows the transformation?

(A)

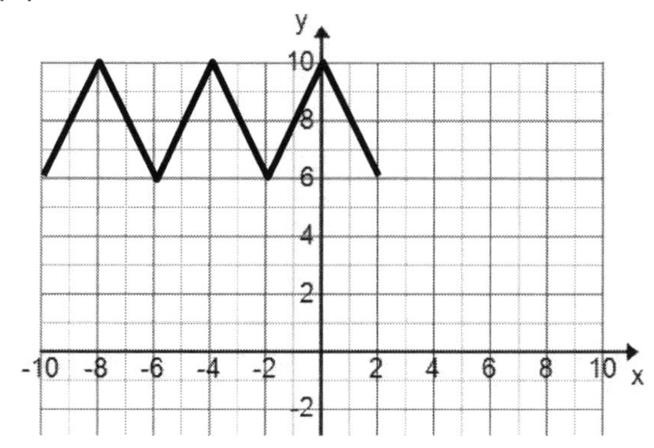

(B)

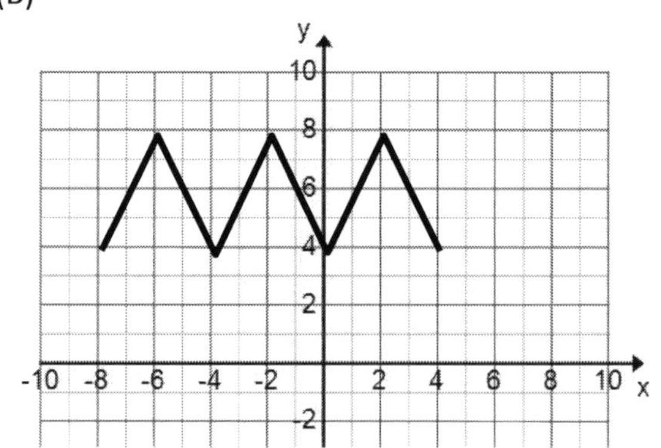

(C)

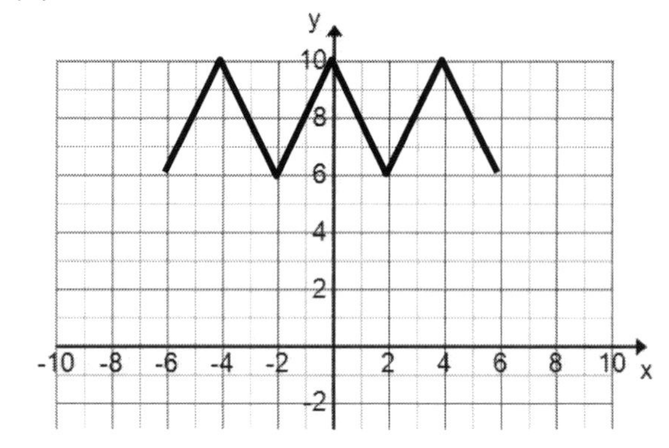

25. A manufactuing company makes wheels for automobiles. The monthly sales revenue of wheels can be modeled as $200\,t^2 + 50t$, where t is the month of the year (January=1, December=12). The monthly cost of manufacturing the wheels can be modeled as $125\,t^2 + 20t$. If the tax on the profits is 20%, which of the following functions can be used to model the tax paid each month?

(A) $75t^2 - 30t$
(B) $75t^2 + 30t$
(C) $15t^2 - 6t$
(D) $15t^2 + 6t$

26. The polynomial function that can be used to model the number of items sold at a store is $N(t) = 16t^3 - 2t^2 + 13$, where t is the month (Jan=1, Dec=12). The average price of the items each month and can be modeled as $P(t) = 2t + 4$. The function $R(t)$ that can be used to model the revenue from these items is

(A) $R(t) = 32t^3 + 60t^2 - 8t + 52$
(B) $R(t) = 32t^4 + 60t^3 - 8t^2 + 26t + 52$
(C) $R(t) = 32t^4 + 60t^3 - 8t^2 + 26t$
(D) $R(t) = 32t^4 + 8t^2 + 26t + 52$

CALCULATOR SECTION

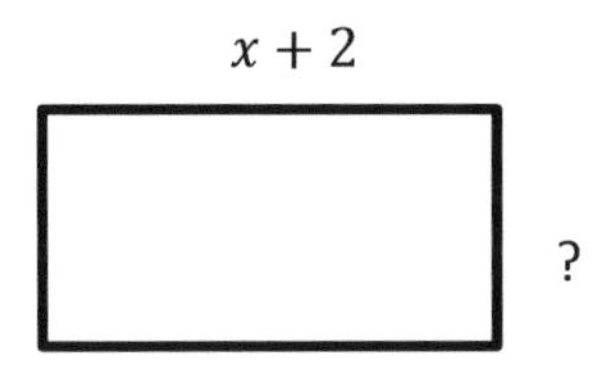

Questions 27 and 28 refer to the above figure.

27. The area of a rectangular carpet can be modeled as $x^2 - 2x - 8$, where x is a portion of one side that has a length of $x + 2$. What is the length of the other side?

(A) $x - 4$
(B) $x + 4$
(C) $x - 2$
(D) $x + 2$

28. If $x = 16$, what is the perimeter of the carpet?

(A) 30
(B) 38
(C) 56
(D) 60

#	Explanation	Comments
1 D	$f(2) = 3$ $f(g(2)) = f(4) = 7$ So $f(2) \cdot f(g(2)) = 3 \cdot 7 = 21$	Get the function values carefully from the table. For $f(g(2))$, get the value of the inner function $g(2)$ first and then $f(g(2))$.
2 C	It is clear from the table that $g(x)$ values are 3 times the values of $f(x)$. $So, g(x) = 3\,f(x)$.	Note that when $f(x)$ $becomes$ $3f(x)$, the graph of $f(x)$ is vertically compressed by a factor of 3.
3 B	$f(x) = x^2 - 2$ and $g(x) = 2x^2 + 5$ $(f - g)(x) = f(x) - g(x) = x^2 - 2 - (2x^2 + 5)$ $= -x^2 - 7$	Functions can be added, subtracted, multiplied, and divided. Be careful with the negative signs.
4 D	$f(x) = 1 + \frac{1}{x}$ and $g(x) = 1 - \frac{1}{x}$ $(fg)(2) = f(2) \cdot g(2) = \left(1 + \frac{1}{2}\right)\left(1 - \frac{1}{2}\right) = \frac{3}{2} \cdot \frac{1}{2} = \frac{3}{4}$	Note that the notation $(fg)(2)$ is not the same as $f(g(2))$.
5 B	$f(x) = x^2$ and $g(x) = x^4$ $\left(\frac{f}{g}\right)(3) = \frac{f(3)}{g(3)} = \frac{3^2}{3^4} = \frac{1}{3^2} = \frac{1}{9}$	
6 B	$f(x) = x^2$ and $g(x) = x + 5$ $g(f(x)) = g(x^2) = x^2 + 5$	Evaluate the inner function first.
7 C	$f(x) = x^2$ and $g(x) = \frac{1}{x^2}$ $g(f(x)) = g(x^2) = \frac{1}{(x^2)^2} = \frac{1}{x^4}$	Use the power formula $(a^m)^n = a^{mn}$.
8 B	$f(x) = 2^{x-5}$ and $f(b) = 8^3$ $f(b) = 2^{b-5} = 8^3 = (2^3)^3 = 2^9$ So, $b - 5 = 9, b = 14$	
9 B	$f(x) = \sqrt{2x}$ and $g(x) = \frac{1}{\sqrt{3x}}$ $f(x^2) = \sqrt{2x^2} = x\sqrt{2}$ $g(x^2) = \frac{1}{\sqrt{3x^2}} = \frac{1}{x\sqrt{3}}$ $f(x^2)g(x^2) = \sqrt{2}x \cdot \frac{1}{\sqrt{3}x} = \frac{\sqrt{2}}{\sqrt{3}} = \sqrt{\frac{2}{3}}$	
10 C	$g(-7) - g(2) =?$. Reading from the graph, $g(-7) = 8$ and $g(2)$=6. So, $8 - 6 = 2$.	
11 D	There are 4 turning points, where the graph turns at its vertices.	Turning point is where the slope is 0.
12 A	$g(x) = x - 3$ When this function is moved to the right by 4 units, the	When $f(x)$ is moved right by k units, the new function is $f(x - k)$.

	new function is $g(x-4)=x-4-3=x-7$. So, $h(x)=x-7$. $h(4)=4-7=-3$	Refer to the review section to learn about the translation of functions.
13 A	$g(x)=f(x-4)=3(x-4)+5=3x-7$ $g(6)=3\cdot 6-7=11$	
14 D	$f(x)=-2x-1$, move 2 units to the left $g(x)=f(x+2)=-2(x+2)-1=-2x-5$ $f(2)=-4-1=-5 \quad g(2)=-4-5=-9$ $f(2)g(2)=\ -5\cdot\ -9=45$	
15 C	$f(x)=2x^2-3$ shifting down $f(x)$ by 5 units gives $f(x)-5$ $g(x)=f(x)-5=2x^2-3-5=2x^2-8$	
16 A	$f(x)=\sqrt{3x+5}$ $g(x)=\sqrt{3(x-4)+5}=\ \sqrt{3x-12+5}$ $g(x)=\sqrt{3x-7}$ $g(6)$= $\sqrt{3\cdot 6-7}=\ \sqrt{11}$	
17 D	$f(x)=5x^2+12$ after shifting to right by 4 units, $f(x)$ *becomes* $f(x-4)=g(x)=5(x-4)^2+12$ After shifting 3 units down, $g(x)$ becomes $g(x)-3=$ $h(x)=\ 5(x-4)^2\ +12-3=5(x-4)^2+9$ $h(2)=\ 5(2-4)^2+9=29$	shift to the right by 4 and then shift down by 3; process these two transformation separately, one at a time.
18 D	Draw a line y=4 and count the number of intercepts of the line with the function. There are 6 intercepts.	
19 B	Pick 2 points on the line, (0,0) and (2,4) Calculate the slope = $\frac{(y2-y1)}{(x2-x1)}=\frac{4-0}{2-0}=2$ Equation of line is $y=2x+0$ since the y intercept is 0 Equation of reflected line is $y=f(-x)=\ -2x=mx+b$; So, the slope of the reflected line is -2.	Find the equation of the line using its slope and y-intercept. Then use the fact that if a function $f(x)$ is reflected over the y axis, it becomes $f(-x)$.
20 C	Observe the vertex of $f(x)$. If $f(x)$ is shifted to coincide with $h(x)$, then it has to be moved 4 units to the left and 2 units up. Consider these transformations one at a time. Shifting to the left by 4 units makes $f(x)=\ f(x+4)$. Shifting it up again makes it $f(x+4)+2$.	Focus on one point or the vertex and see what the transformation steps are. Then process each transformation one at a time.
21 C	Vertex now is at (4,1) Move left by 6 units takes the vertex to (4-6,1)=(-2,1) Moving it up by 4 units takes the vertex to (-2,1+4)=(-2,5)	Evaluate one move at a time to avoid mistakes.
22 D	$p(x)=8x^2+24$ Horizontal stretch by a factor of 2 $p(x)$ will become $p\left(\frac{1}{2}\ x\right)=\ 8\left(\frac{x}{2}\right)^2+24=\frac{8x^2}{4}+24$ $=2x^2+24$	Horizontal stretch formula $f(x)$ *becomes* $f(\frac{1}{b}\ x)$, $b>1$ is horizontal stretch.
23 C	The vertex is originally at (4,2). After reflection over the x axis, the vertex will be at $(4,-2)$. So, a line $y=-2$ will intercept the parabola at it new vertex.	

24 C	$f(x)$ is transformed to $f(x-2)+2$ This means the $f(x)$ was shifted right 2 units and then shifted up 2 units. Pick one point and trace its transformation. The leftmost tip is at $(-8,4)$. After shifting 2 units right and 2 units up, it should be at $(-8+2, 4+2) = (-6,6)$	
25 D	Sales revenue=$200\ t^2 + 50t$ Cost of manufacturing=$125\ t^2 + 20t$ Tax on profit =20% Profit=sales-cost=$200\ t^2 + 50t$-$(125\ t^2 + 20t)$ = $200\ t^2 - 125t^2 + 50t - 20t$ = $75\ t^2\ +\ 30\ t$ Tax = $\frac{20}{100} \cdot \text{profit} = 0.2(75\ t^2 + 30t) = 15t^2 + 6t$	Polynomial functions can be subtracted, and operated upon like numbers. This question tests your ability to apply the concept of polynomial operations to a real world problem.
26 B	Items sold each month= $\mathrm{N}(t) = 16t^3 - 2t^2 + 13$ Price of items each month= $P(t) = 2t + 4$. Revenue= N(t) · P(t)= $(16t^3 - 2t^2 + 13)\ \cdot (2t+4)$ $= 32\ t^4 + 64\ t^3 - 4t^3 - 8t^2 + 26\ t + 52$ $= 32\ t^4 + 60t^3 - 8t^2 + 26\ t + 52$	
27 A	Since $l \cdot w$=area, $(x+2)\ \cdot\ w = x^2 - 2x - 8$ You can find w by long division. $x - 4$ $x + 2 \mid x^2 - 2x - 8$ $-\ (x^2 + 2x)$ $0 - 4x - 8$ $-4x - 8$ 0 Another way is to factorize $x^2 - 2x - 8$ Find $p, q\ such\ that\ pq = -8, p + q = -2;$ try $p = -4\ \ q = 2$ $x^2 - 2x - 8$ $= x^2 - 4x + 2x - 8$ $= x(x-4) + 2(x-4)$ = $(x-4)(x+2)$	Long division is covered in the lesson on Polynomials and Quadratic Equations.
28 D	From the previous question, you know that $x - 4$ and $x + 2$ are the sides of the rectangle. So, the perimeter is $2(l + w) =\ 2(x - 4 + x - 2) =\ 2(2x - 2) =\ 4x - 4$. When $x = 16$, the perimeter= $4 \cdot 16 - 4 = 60$ units.	This problem extends your thinking from the previous problem.

PASSPORT TO ADVANCED MATH		
Lesson 23	Radicals and Fractional Exponents	Review

FOCUSPREP CHECKLIST

- What is a Radical?
- How do I solve a radical equation?
- What is an extraneous solution?
- How do I simplify an expression with fractional exponents?
- Workout practice problems in Radicals

Q1 What is a Radical? What is a Radical Expression?

A1 A radical is represented as $\sqrt[n]{x}$. x is the radicand, n is the index of the radical. $\sqrt[n]{x}$ is called the nth root of x. If n is not specified, it is assumed to be 2. A radical can be a square root, cube root, etc. Note that $\sqrt[n]{x} = x^{\frac{1}{n}}$.

A Radical expression is an expression with one or more terms inside the radical, including terms with variables. **Examples:** $\sqrt{x}$, $\sqrt[3]{x-5}, \sqrt{4-x}$, $\frac{1}{\sqrt{9-t}}$.

Q2 How do I simplify a radical expression?

A2 The table below shows the properties of radicals that can be used to simplify a radical expression. Radicals can be added and subtracted, multiplied and divided.

$\sqrt[n]{p} = p^{\frac{1}{n}}$ $\frac{1}{\sqrt[n]{p}} = \frac{1}{p^{\frac{1}{n}}} = p^{-\frac{1}{n}}$	$\sqrt[n]{p^n} = (p^n)^{\frac{1}{n}} = p$	$\sqrt[3]{-1} = -1$ because $-1 \cdot -1 \cdot -1 = -1$
$\sqrt[n]{pq} = \sqrt[n]{p} \cdot \sqrt[n]{q}$ $(pq)^{\frac{1}{n}} = p^{\frac{1}{n}} q^{\frac{1}{n}}$	$\sqrt[n]{\frac{p}{q}} = \frac{\sqrt[n]{p}}{\sqrt[n]{q}}$	$(3+\sqrt{7})(3-\sqrt{7}) = 3^2 - (\sqrt{7})^2$ $= 9 - 7 = 2.$

Q3 Is $\sqrt{x}$ the same as $x^{\frac{1}{2}}$? What is the formula for cube root and n-th root?

A3 The general formula to convert a radical sign to a fractional exponent is $\sqrt[n]{x} = x^{\frac{1}{n}}$. So, $\sqrt[2]{x} = x^{\frac{1}{2}}$, $\sqrt[5]{x} = x^{\frac{1}{5}}$, and so on. As a special case $\sqrt[2]{x}$ is written as $\sqrt{x}$ without the 2.

Examples: Simplify the following radicals.

$\sqrt[3]{27} = \sqrt[3]{3^3} = (3^3)^{\frac{1}{3}} = 3^{3 \cdot \frac{1}{3}} = 3^1 = 3$

$\sqrt[3]{27b^3c^6} = \sqrt[3]{3^3b^3\,c^6} = (3^3b^3c^6)^{\frac{1}{3}} = 3bc^2$

$\sqrt[3]{-8c^4} = \sqrt[3]{-2^3c^3c} = -2c\,\sqrt[3]{c}$; cube root of -1 is -1

$3\sqrt[3]{a} + 4\sqrt[3]{a} = 7\sqrt[3]{a}$; add like radicals

$3\sqrt[3]{a} + 4\sqrt[3]{b}$; cannot be added since the radicands are not identical

$3\sqrt[3]{a} + 4\sqrt[3]{ab}$; cannot be added since the radicands are not identical

$3\sqrt[3]{a} - \sqrt[3]{a} = 2\sqrt[3]{a}$; subtract like radicals

$3\sqrt[3]{a} \cdot 4\sqrt[3]{b} = 12\sqrt[3]{ab}$; multiplication property of radical

$3\sqrt[3]{a}(4\sqrt[3]{b} + 2\sqrt[3]{c}) = 12\sqrt[3]{ab} + 6 \cdot \sqrt[3]{ac}$; distributive property $a(b + c) = ab + ac$

$(3 + \sqrt{4})(3 - \sqrt{4}) = 3^2 - (\sqrt{4})^2 = 9 - 4 = 5$; difference of squares $(a + b)(a - b) = a^2 - b^2$

$(3 + \sqrt{5})(2 - \sqrt{7}) = 3 \cdot 2 - 3\sqrt{7} + 2\sqrt{5} - \sqrt{5} \cdot \sqrt{7} = 6 - 3\sqrt{7} + 2\sqrt{5} - \sqrt{35}$; use FOIL to simplify

$\frac{\sqrt{5}}{\sqrt{7}} = \frac{\sqrt{5}}{\sqrt{7}} \cdot \frac{\sqrt{7}}{\sqrt{7}} = \frac{\sqrt{35}}{7}$; multiply both numerator and denominator by the denominator and simplify

$\frac{(3+\sqrt{5})}{(2-\sqrt{7})} = \frac{(3+\sqrt{5})}{(2-\sqrt{7})} \cdot \frac{(2+\sqrt{7})}{(2+\sqrt{7})} = \frac{(6+3\sqrt{7}+2\sqrt{5}+\sqrt{35})}{(4-7)} = -\frac{1}{3} \cdot (6 + 3\sqrt{7} + 2\sqrt{5} + \sqrt{35})$; remove the radical from the denominator, use FOIL to expand the numerator, use difference of squares in the denominator.

Q4 What is a Radical Equation?

A4 When a radical expression is part of an equation, then it is called a radical equation.

Examples: $\sqrt{x} = 16$; $\sqrt[3]{x - 5} = 2$ are radical equations.

Q5 Is $\sqrt{x}$ positive or negative?

A5 While every positive number has two square roots, one positive and one negative, the square root symbol $\sqrt{\ }$ refers to the **positive** square root only. This is very important to remember while solving radical equations.

Examples

* $\sqrt{4} = +2$ only, it is not -2 ; $\sqrt{\ }$ by definition, refers to the positive square root only
* If $x^2 = 81$, then $x = \pm\sqrt{81} = \pm 9$ $(+9$ and $-9)$. Note the $\pm$ sign.
* $\sqrt{9 + 7} = \sqrt{16} = +4$ only; $\sqrt{16}$ is not -4.
* The equation, $\sqrt{x} = -8$, where x is positive does not have any solution, since the $\sqrt{\ }$ of a positive number cannot be negative. If you solve this equation by squaring both sides, you get $x = 64$, but when

you plug it back into the original equation, you get $\sqrt{64} = +8 <> -8$. Remember that the radical $\sqrt{\ }$ refers to the positive square root only.

* Note that the equation $x^2 = 9$ has two solutions. Applying the square root on both sides, you get $\sqrt{x^2} = x = \pm\sqrt{9} = +3 \text{ and } -3$.

* If you are applying the $\sqrt{\ }$ radical on a number, include the $\pm$ sign. If you are only evaluating the radical expression $\sqrt{\ }$, then remember that $\sqrt{\ }$ is defined for a positive number and the result of evaluating a $\sqrt{\ }$ is a positive number.

Q6 How do I solve a Radical Equation?

A6 If the radical is a square root, then square both sides of the equation to get rid of the radical and simplify. If it is a cube root, raise both sides to the power of 3 and simplify. Apply the rules of rational exponents as required and solve for the variable. Then, verify if the solution is valid by plugging it into the original equation. If the solution satisfies the original equation, only then it is a valid solution. If the solution does not satisfy the original equation, then it is NOT a valid solution. It is an extraneous solution.

Example: Solve for : $\sqrt{x} = 6;$

$\sqrt{x} = 6;$

$\left(\sqrt{x}\right)^2 = 6^2;$ square both sides

$x = 36;$ check: $\sqrt{36} = 6$ valid solution

Example: $\sqrt[3]{x-5} = 2$

$(x-5)^{\frac{1}{3}} = 2$; write the radical in exponential form

$(x-5)^{\frac{1}{3}\cdot 3} = 2^3$; cube both sides to remove the exponent

$(x-5) = 8$

$x = 13$

Check $\sqrt[3]{13-5} = \sqrt[3]{8} = 2\ ok$

Example: $\sqrt[5]{x} = 3$

$x^{\frac{1}{5}} = 3$

$\left(x^{\frac{1}{5}}\right)^5 = 3^5$; raise both sides to the fifth power

$x = 3^5$; check $\sqrt[5]{3^5} = 3$

Q7 How do I find if a solution is an **extraneous solution**?

A7 When solving a radical equation, you may end up with solutions that do not hold true when you plug them back into the original equation. These solutions are called **extraneous solutions** and must be discarded.

Not all radical equations have a valid solution. After you arrive at a solution, you must verify it by plugging it back into the radical equation. Only after the solution is verified, it is a valid solution. This is because of the fact that during the simplification process (by squaring or cubing both sides), you end up with a new equation, whose solution may or may not be valid for the original radical equation that you started with.

In summary, verify your result against the original radical equation to decide if it is a valid solution or an **extraneous** solution. A valid solution will yield equal values on both sides of the equation. An extraneous solution will not.

Example: Solve $\sqrt{x-3}+6=5$
$\sqrt{x-3}=5-6=-1$; isolate the radical to one side
$\left(\sqrt{x-3}\right)^2=(-1)^2$; square both sides
$x-3=1$
$x=3+1=4$
Check the solution: $\sqrt{4-3}+6=5; 1+6=7\neq 5$; Note that $\sqrt{4-3}$ = +1 only, not -1.
So, $x=4$ is not a solution to the radical equation. It is an **extraneous solution** that popped up during the solution finding process but it does not check out when plugged into the original radical equation.

Example: Solve $\sqrt{x+7}=x+5$
$(x+7)=\ (x+5)^2$; square both sides to remove the radical
$x+7=x^2+10x+25$
$x^2+9x+18=0$
$x^2+6x+3x+18=0$
$x(x+6)+3(x+6)=0$
$(x+6)(x+3)=0$
$x=-6$ and $x=-3$
Verify the solutions:
when $x=-6, \sqrt{x+7}=\sqrt{-6+7}=1$ and $x+5=\ -6+5=-1.$ So, $x=-6$ is not a solution.
when $x=-3, \sqrt{x+7}=\sqrt{-3+7}=2$ and $x+5=\ -3+5=2.$ So, $x=-3$ is a solution.
The **extraneous solution** is $x=-6$ and this is discarded. The **only solution** is $x=-3$.

Q8 What is a Rational exponent? How do I simplify rational exponents?

A8 A Rational exponent (fractional exponent) takes the form of $x^{\frac{m}{n}}$; $n\neq 0$. For example, $x^{\frac{1}{2}}, x^{\frac{5}{7}}$ are rational exponents. Rational exponents can also take the form of $a^{x/3}$ where the variable is in the exponent. Rational exponents follow the same rules as integer exponents.

Formula	Examples
$x^m x^n = x^{m+n}$	$2^{\frac{2}{3}}2^{\frac{1}{3}}=2^{\left(\frac{2}{3}+\frac{1}{3}\right)}=2^1=2$
$\dfrac{x^m}{x^n}=x^{m-n}$	$\dfrac{5^{\frac{2}{3}}}{5^{\frac{1}{3}}}=5^{(2/3-1/3)}=5^{\frac{1}{3}}$
$x^{\frac{m}{n}}=(x^m)^{1/n}=(x^{1/n})^m$	$8^{\frac{2}{3}}=(8^2)^{\frac{1}{3}}=\left(8^{\frac{1}{3}}\right)^2=2^2=4$ $8^{\frac{x}{3}}=(2^2)^{\frac{x}{3}}=2^{\frac{2x}{3}}=(2^x)^{\frac{2}{3}}$

$x^0 = 1$	$9 \cdot 15^0 = 9 \cdot 1 = 9$
$x^{-1} = \frac{1}{x}$	$(\frac{2}{3})^{-1} = \frac{1}{\frac{2}{3}} = \frac{3}{2}$
$x^{-m} = \frac{1}{x^m}$	$8^{-\frac{1}{3}} = (2^3)^{-\frac{1}{3}} = 2^{3 \cdot -\frac{1}{3}} = 2^{-1} = \frac{1}{2}$

Examples:

* $\sqrt[5]{2^5} = (2^5)^{\frac{1}{5}} = 2^{5 \cdot \frac{1}{5}} = 2^1 = 2$
* $27^{-\frac{2}{3}} = ((27)^{\frac{1}{3}})^{-2} = \left(3^{3 \cdot \frac{1}{3}}\right)^{-2} = 3^{-2} = \frac{1}{3^2} = \frac{1}{9}$
* If $8 = 2^{4x}$ find x. $8 = 2^3 = 2^{4x}$ So, since the base is eth same, exponents will be the same.

$3 = 4x => x = \frac{4}{3}$

Q9 How are radical equations used in real life?

A9 Radical equations appear frequently in Physics, Chemistry, and Biology. The following example shows how they may appear in a real life situation.

Example: A metallurgist found that the time T it takes in seconds to heat a circular metallic plate of radius R inches to a temperature of 120 degrees Fahrenheit is given by the following equation: $R = \frac{3\pi}{\sqrt{T}}$. How long does it take to heat a circular plate of radius 5 inches to 120 degrees Fahrenheit?

Solution: Notice that the equation is a radical equation. Rearrange to get T to the numerator.

$\sqrt{T} = \frac{3\pi}{R}$

$(\sqrt{T})^2 = \left(\frac{3\pi}{R}\right)^2$; square both sides

$T = \left(\frac{3\pi}{R}\right)^2 = \frac{9\pi^2}{R^2}$

So, $T = \frac{9\pi^2}{R^2}$

For a circular plate of radius=5 inches, the time to heat is= $\frac{9\pi^2}{5^2} = 3.55$ seconds.

PASSPORT TO ADVANCED MATH

Lesson 23	Radicals and Fractional Exponents	Practice

NO CALCULATOR SECTION

1. If $\sqrt{x+1} = \sqrt{2x-5}$ then $x =$
(A) 2
(B) 4
(C) 6
(D) 7

2. If $a = 1$, and $b = -1$, then
$\sqrt{a^2 + b^2 + 2ab} =$
(A) 0
(B) 1
(C) 2
(D) 4

3 If $8^2\ 8^3\ 8^x = 2^y$, what is x in terms of y?
(A) $y + 3$
(B) $\frac{y+15}{3}$
(C) $\frac{y-15}{3}$
(D) $y - 15$

4. If $\frac{1}{\sqrt{x-2}} = 5$, and $x > 2$, then $x =$

(A) $\frac{25}{50}$

(B) $\frac{25}{40}$

(C) $\frac{50}{25}$

(D) $\frac{51}{25}$

NO CALCULATOR SECTION

5. If $\sqrt{2^2 \cdot x} = 16$, then $x =$
(A) 4
(B) 16
(C) 32
(D) 64

6. What is the absolute value of the extraneous solution of x in the equation $x + 1 = \sqrt{5 - x}$.
GRID IN

7. If $\sqrt{2^{-3z}} = 8$, then $z =$
(A) -3
(B) -2
(C) 2
(D) 3

8. If $\sqrt{3}\,\sqrt{bc} = d$, what is b in terms of d and c?
(A) $\frac{d}{c}$

(B) $\frac{d^2}{3c}$

(C) $\frac{c^2}{3d}$

(D) $\frac{d}{2c}$

NO CALCULATOR SECTION

9. If $\sqrt{(k-1)a} = \sqrt{2a}$ then $k =$
(A) 0
(B) 1
(C) 2
(D) 3

10. If $\frac{1}{(a+\sqrt{5})(a-\sqrt{5})} = \frac{1}{20}$, then a could be
(A) -6
(B) -5
(C) 1
(D) 6

11. If $\frac{100^{-p}}{100^{-q}} = 10^2$, then $p - q$ is
(A) -3
(B) 0
(C) -1
(D) 1

12. If $p^2\, p^{-x} = p^4$ and $q^{-2}q^y = q^6$, then $x + y =$
(A) -2
(B) 4
(C) 6
(D) 10

NO CALCULATOR SECTION

13. If $2^{-1}\, 2^0\, 2^1 = 2^z$, then $z =$
(A) 0
(B) 1
(C) 2
(D) 3

14. If $\sqrt[3]{a^6 b^{15}} = b^3$, then $a^2b^2 =$
(A) $\frac{1}{2}$
(B) $\frac{1}{3}$
(C) $\frac{1}{4}$
(D) 1

15. If $a^{-\frac{5}{2}} = 2^5$, then $a =$
(A) $\frac{1}{8}$
(B) $\frac{1}{4}$
(C) $\frac{1}{2}$
(D) 1

CALCULATOR SECTION

16. In Physics, the motion of a falling object is given by the formula $s = ut + \frac{1}{2}gt^2$, where s is the distance traveled in time t, u is the initial velocity in m/s, and g is the gravitational constant of 9.8 m/s^2. If the initial velocity of an object is 0 m/s, how many seconds will it take for an object to fall a distance of 500 meters?

(A) 6.10
(B) 10.10
(C) 20.20
(D) 102.04

CALCULATOR SECTION

17. When an object is in motion, its velocity v is related to its kinetic energy E, and its mass m, by the formula $v = \sqrt{\frac{2E}{m}}$. If the velocity of an object of mass $m2$ is twice the velocity of an object of mass $m1$, and the kinetic energy of both objects are the same, then what is the ratio of $\frac{m1}{m2}$?

GRID IN

#	Explanation	Comments
1 C	$\sqrt{x+1} = \sqrt{2x-5}$ $x + 1 = 2x - 5$; square both sides $x - 2x = -5 - 1$ $-x = -6$ $x = 6$; verify the solution in the original equation $\sqrt{6+1} = \sqrt{7} = \sqrt{2 \cdot 6 - 5} = \sqrt{7}$	Be careful with negative signs.
2 A	$a = 1$, and $b = -1$ $\sqrt{a^2 + b^2 + 2ab} =$ $\sqrt{1 + (-1)^2 + 2 \cdot 1 \cdot (-1)}$ $\sqrt{1 + 1 - 2} = \sqrt{0}$=0	
3 C	$8^2\, 8^3\, 8^x = 2^y$ $2^{3^2}\, 2^{3^3}\, 2^{3^x} = 2^y$ $2^6\, 2^9\, 2^{3x} = 2^y$ $2^{15+3x} = 2^y$ $15 + 3x = y$ $x = \frac{y - 15}{3}$	Use the property of exponents $a^m a^n = a^{m+n}$.
4 D	$\frac{1}{\sqrt{x-2}} = 5$ $\frac{1}{x-2} = 5^2 = 25$; square both sides $x - 2 = \frac{1}{25}$ $x = 2 + \frac{1}{25} = \frac{51}{25}$	
5 D	$\sqrt{2^2.x} = 16$ $2^2 x = 16^2 = 256$ $4x = 256$; $x = \frac{256}{4} = 64$	
6 4	$x + 1 = \sqrt{5 - x}$ $(x+1)^2 = 5 - x$ $x^2 + 2x + 1 = 5 - x$ $x^2 + 3x - 4 = 0$ $x^2 + 4x - x - 4 = 0$ $x(x+4) - 1(x+4) = 0$ $(x+4)(x-1) = 0$	Note that the extraneous solution is $x = -4$, but the question asks for the absolute value of the extraneous solution. So $\lvert -4 \rvert = 4$.

	$x = -4$ and $x = 1$ Verify the solutions; If $x = -4, x + 1 = -4 + 1 = -3 = \sqrt{5 - (-4)} = \sqrt{9} = 3$ invalid – extraneous If $x = 1, x + 1 = 1 + 1 = 2 = \sqrt{5 - 1} = \sqrt{4} = 2$ valid	Remember that $\sqrt{9} = +3$, by definition. It is not -3. Review the lesson to understand this. If you assumed that $\sqrt{9} = -3$, then $x = -4$ would appear to be a valid solution, but that is incorrect.
7 B	$\sqrt{2^{-3z}} = 8$ $2^{-3z} = 8^2 = (2^3)^2 = 2^6$;squaring both sides $-3z = 6$ $z = -2$	
8 B	$\sqrt{3}\sqrt{bc} = d$ $\sqrt{3bc} = d$ $3bc = d^2$ $b = \frac{d^2}{3c}$	use $\sqrt{p}\sqrt{q} = \sqrt{pq}$ you can simplify directly as well by squaring the first step itself $\sqrt{3}\sqrt{bc} = d$; square each term $3bc = d^2$ $b = \frac{d^2}{3c}$
9 D	$\sqrt{(k-1)a} = \sqrt{2a}$; squaring both sides $(k-1)a = 2a$ $k - 1 = 2$ $k = 3$	
10 B	$\frac{1}{(a + \sqrt{5})(a - \sqrt{5})} = \frac{1}{20}$ $(a + \sqrt{5})(a - \sqrt{5}) = 20$ $a^2 - (\sqrt{5})^2 = 20$ $a^2 - 5 = 20$ $a^2 = 25$ $a = \pm\sqrt{25} = \pm 5$	Observe the equation for a few seconds; you can take the reciprocal of both sides; also use the difference of squares formula. Note that when $a^2 = 25$, then $a = \pm\sqrt{25}$. The $\pm$ sign is important, since the negative sign brings in $-\sqrt{25}$ as the solution in addition to $+\sqrt{25}$. If you wrote $a = \sqrt{25}$, that would include only $+5$ as the solution which is incorrect. Note that while a could be $+5$ or -5, only -5 is available in the answer choices.
11 C	$\frac{100^{-p}}{100^{-q}} = 10^2$ $\frac{(10^2)^{-p}}{(10^2)^{-q}} = 10^2$	

	$\frac{10^{-2p}}{10^{-2q}} = 10^{2q-2p} = 10^2$ $2q - 2p = 2(q - p) = 2$ $q - p = 1$ Multiply by -1 on both sides, you get $p - q = -1.$	
12 C	$p^2\, p^{-x} = p^4$ $p^{2-x} = p^4$ $2 - x = 4$ $x = 2 - 4 = -2$ $q^{-2} q^y = q^6$ $q^{y-2} = q^6$ $y - 2 = 6; y = 8$ $so, x + y = -2 + 8 = 6$	Pause and observe the equations; from one equation you can get x, and from the other equation you can get y; the question simply asks you the sum of x and y. Pausing and observing the problem for a few seconds is an effective time saving strategy to attack a problem.
13 A	$2^{-1}\, 2^0\, 2^1 = 2^z,$ $2^{-1+0+1} = 2^0 = 2^z$ $\text{so}, z = 0$	0 is a valid exponent.
14 D	$\sqrt[3]{a^6 b^{15}} = b^3,$ $(a^6 b^{15})^{\frac{1}{3}} = b^3$ $a^{\frac{6}{3}}\, b^{\frac{15}{3}} = b^3$ $a^2\, b^5 = b^3;$ $\frac{a^2 b^5}{b^3} = 1$ $a^2 b^2 = 1$	Use properties of exponents to simplify.
15 B	$a^{-\frac{5}{2}} = 2^5$ $\left(a^{-\frac{1}{2}}\right)^5 = 2^5$ $a^{-\frac{1}{2}} = 2\,;$ $a^{-\frac{1}{2}\cdot -2} = 2^{-2}$; make the exponent=1 by multiplying by -2 $a^1 = 2^{-2} = \frac{1}{2^2} = \frac{1}{4}$	Manipulate the exponents to get the required exponent; if you have $a^{-\frac{1}{2}}$ and want to get a^1, multiply the exponent by -2, $a^{-\frac{1}{2}\cdot -2} = a^1$.
16 B	The question asks for time it takes for an object to fall 500 meters, but the equation is for the distance. So, rearrange the equation to express t in terms of other variables. $s = ut + \frac{1}{2} g t^2$	Rearrange the equation and then use your calculator to get the results.

	$s = 0 \cdot t + \frac{1}{2}gt^2$ $t = \sqrt{\frac{2s}{g}}$ Plug in $s = 500$ and $g = 9.8$ to get $t = 10.10$.	
17 4	Though strange looking, this problem is easy to solve; there are 2 objects, of mass $m1$ and $m2$. Let $v1$ and $v2$ be their velocities. Their kinetic energies are the same. $v1 = \sqrt{\frac{2E}{m1}}$; $v2 = \sqrt{\frac{2E}{m2}}$ $v2 = 2v1$ - given fact So, $\sqrt{\frac{2E}{m2}} = 2\sqrt{\frac{2E}{m1}}$; square both sides $\frac{2E}{m2} = 4\frac{2E}{m1}$; don't forget to square the 2 Therefore, $\frac{m1}{m2} = 4$	Set up the equation and review the question to see what is asked. Then, isolate the variables and simplify to answer the question.

APPENDIX	
Lesson	**Title**
Lesson 24	Calculator

APPENDIX		
Lesson 24	Calculator	Review

FOCUSPREP CHECKLIST

- Which calculator models can I use?
- Can I use a calculator for any problem?
- Do I need to use a calculator?
- Workout practice problems using the Calculator

Q1 What calculator models are allowed on the new PSAT 8/9?

A1 Graphing and Scientific calculators are allowed. Visit https://sat.collegeboard.org/register/calculator-policy for a list of all approved calculators. The TI-84 Plus is the calculator that is most used. TI-83 calculators and Casio FX-9750 calculators are commonly used as well. Make sure you calculator has new batteries before you take the test.

Q2 Can I use a calculator for any problem?

A2 No. The PSAT and SAT exams have two sections that are clearly marked as CALCULATOR and NO CALCULATOR.

Q3 Do I need to use a calculator while solving problems in the CALCULATOR SECTION?

A3 Simple calculations in the CALCULATOR section can be made without a calculator. For example, if you have to find $2 \cdot 3 + 6$, you don't need to use a calculator. But, for more complex calculations, it may be advantageous to use a calculator to save time. For example, you can calculate $2.25 \cdot 15$ quickly and accurately using the calculator rather than multiplying it yourself and possibly making a mistake.

Q4 How do I practice using my calculator?

A4 Consider each row in the following table and use your calculator to find the result. Keystroke hints are provided for each problem along with a screenshot. In addition, use your calculator every day and get familiar with various functions. The keystrokes shown below are from a **TI-84 Plus** calculator. If you use a different calculator, it may have different keystrokes and screens. Get familiar with the keystrokes for your calculator.

APPENDIX		
Lesson 24	Calculator	Practice & Answers

Problem	Keystrokes	Screen/Answer
$\frac{(3-2)^2}{5+5}$	Use parentheses in the correct places using PEMDAS rules.	(3-2)²/(5+5) .1
Average of 10,13,45,57,92	Place numbers in parentheses before dividing.	(10+13+45+57+92) /5 43.4
Weighted average: $\frac{35\cdot 55+25\cdot 65+25\ \cdot 75}{85}$	Place numbers within parentheses before dividing.	(35*55+25*65+25* 75)/85 63.82352941
Standard Deviation of 6,5,4,7,6 Questions in SAT do not require you to calculate standard deviations, but it will be helpful to know how to use your calculator to find it.	STAT, 1, 6, enter, 5, enter, 4, enter, 7, enter, 6, enter, STAT, CALC, 1, enter	1-Var Stats x̄=5.6 Σx=28 Σx²=162 Sx=1.140175425 σx=1.019803903 ↓n=5 Note that σx refers to the population standard deviation (n=5) and Sx refers to the sample standard deviation (n=4).
$\sqrt{45}$ in decimals	2nd , x^2, 45)	√(45) 6.708203932
$\sqrt{4^2+3^2}$	2nd , x^2, 4, x^2,+, 3, x^2)	√(4²+3²) 5

$\sqrt{(4-6)^2+(5-2)^2}$ in decimals	2nd, x^2,(4-6),x^2,+, (5-2), x^2)	√((4-6)²+(5-2)²) 3.605551275
8% of 20	8%=0.08 $0.08 \cdot 20 = 1.6$	0.08*20 1.6
$\frac{7.05-3.02}{4}$	Remember to include parentheses.	(7.05-3.02)/4 1.0075
$\frac{60 \cdot 6+62 \cdot 9}{6+9}$	Remember to include parentheses.	(60*6+62*9)/(6+9) 61.2
Percentage increase from 200 to 300	Second number minus first number, divided by first number. Multiply result by 100 to get the percentage.	(300-200)/200 .5 Ans*100 50
Percentage decrease from 300 to 100	Second number minus first number, divided by first number. Multiply result by 100 to get the percentage. Answer will be negative since there is a decrease in percentage.	(100-300)/300 -.6666666667 Ans*100 -66.66666667

$\pi \cdot 4^2$	2nd , ^, x4, x^2	π*4² 50.26548246
$2\pi \cdot 4 \cdot 12$	2, 2nd ,^, x4, x12	2π*4*12 301.5928947
$180 - (32 + 47)$	Key parentheses.	180-(32+47) 101
$\frac{1}{2} \cdot 4 \cdot 12$	Key parentheses for fractions.	(1/2)*4*12 24
$3^2 \cdot 2^5$	3,x^2, x2, ^, 5	3²*2^5 288
$300 \cdot 1.05^{10}$	Use caret for exponents.	30*1.05^10 48.8668388
$400(1 - 0.02)^8$	Parentheses and exponent caret.	40(1-0.02)^8 34.0305209
$1200 \cdot 0.04 \cdot 12$		1200*0.04*12 576

Calculate x $\frac{x}{3}=\frac{20}{15}$	cross multiply. $15x=60$ $x=\frac{60}{15}$	60/15 4
$\frac{20}{3}\cdot\frac{6}{5}\cdot\frac{1}{4}$	Enter parentheses for all fractions.	(20/3)*(6/5)*(1/4) 2
$121\cdot\frac{\sqrt{3}}{4}$	Parentheses with square root.	121*(√(3)/4) 52.39453693
$200\cdot 24^{\frac{1}{3}}$	Place the exponent within parentheses	200*24^(1/3) 576.8998281
5!	5, MATH, PRB, 4	MATH NUM CPX PRB 1:rand 2:nPr 3:nCr 4:! 5:randInt(6:randNorm(7:randBin(5! 120
$5!\cdot 6!$	5, MATH, PRB, 4, x6, MATH, PRB, 4	5!*6! 86400
$(2+3)\cdot\frac{4}{5}\cdot(19-3)$	Three sets of parentheses.	(2+3)(4/5)(19-3) 64

$\frac{\frac{1}{3}}{\frac{4}{9}}$ in decimals	Parentheses for both fractions.	(1/3)/(4/9) .75
$\frac{\frac{1}{3}}{2}$ In decimals	Fraction in parenthesis.	(1/3)/2 .1666666667
$\frac{11827}{31134} \cdot 100$		(11827/31134)*100 37.98740926
$\frac{36}{96} \cdot 100$		(36/96)*100 37.5
Permutation 10P3	10, MATH, PRB, 2, 3	MATH NUM CPX PRB 1:rand 2:nPr 3:nCr 4:! 5:randInt(6:randNorm(7:randBin(10 nPr 3 720
Combination 10C2	10, MATH, PRB, 3, 2	10 nCr 2 45

NOTES

- Congratulations for completing the lessons and problems in this workbook. Hope you feel confident to take on the PSAT 8/9.
- Please visit the Downloads page in the website http://www.GiftOfLogic.com regularly for updates to lessons, additional practice problems, and other useful information.
- In the 10th grade you can take the PSAT 10, and in the 11th grade you can take the PSAT/NMSQT and SAT. These tests cover Algebra, Geometry, Trigonometry, Complex Numbers, and many more topics. FocusPrep's **PSAT 10 and SAT Math Workbook** contains additional lessons to help you score well in these tests.
- Good Luck!

Additional lessons in PSAT 10 and SAT Math Workbook

- Extended Thinking
- Lines and Angles
- Triangles
- Pythagorean theorem
- Circles
- Polygons
- Volume of Solids
- Complex Numbers
- Trigonometry
- Radians

Made in the USA
San Bernardino, CA
11 September 2016